MW00607433

Choreographing in Color

Choreographing in Color

Filipinos, Hip-Hop, and the Cultural Politics of Euphemism

J. LORENZO PERILLO

OXFORD
UNIVERSITY PRESS

OXFORD
UNIVERSITY PRESS

Oxford University Press is a department of the University of Oxford. It furthers the University's objective of excellence in research, scholarship, and education by publishing worldwide. Oxford is a registered trade mark of Oxford University Press in the UK and certain other countries.

Published in the United States of America by Oxford University Press
198 Madison Avenue, New York, NY 10016, United States of America.

© Oxford University Press 2020

All rights reserved. No part of this publication may be reproduced, stored in a retrieval system, or transmitted, in any form or by any means, without the prior permission in writing of Oxford University Press, or as expressly permitted by law, by license, or under terms agreed with the appropriate reproduction rights organization. Inquiries concerning reproduction outside the scope of the above should be sent to the Rights Department, Oxford University Press, at the address above.

You must not circulate this work in any other form and you must impose this same condition on any acquirer.

Library of Congress Cataloging-in-Publication Data
Names: Perillo, J. Lorenzo, author.
Title: Choreographing in color : Filipinos, hip-hop, and the cultural politics of euphemism / J. Lorenzo Perillo.
Description: New York, NY : Oxford University Press, [2020] |
Includes bibliographical references and index.
Identifiers: LCCN 2020001451 | ISBN 9780190054274 (hardback) |
ISBN 9780190054281 (paperback) | ISBN 9780190054298 (updf) |
ISBN 9780190054304 (epub) | 9780190054311 (online)
Subjects: LCSH: Hip-hop dance—Political aspects—Philippines. |
Hip-hop dance—Social aspects—United States. | Dance and race. |
Filipinos—Social life and customs. | Filipinos—Ethnic identity. |
Filipino Americans—Social life and customs. | Filipino
Americans—Ethnic identity. | Philippines—Relations—United States. |
United States—Relations—Philippines.
Classification: LCC GV1796.H57 P47 2020 | DDC 793.309599—dc23
LC record available at https://lccn.loc.gov/2020001451

3 5 7 9 8 6 4 2
Paperback printed by Marquis, Canada
Hardback printed by Bridgeport National Bindery, Inc., United States of America

*This book is dedicated to
my Inang, Oliva dela Rama Lorenzo
and Grandpa, Juan Pantua Perillo.*

Contents

Acknowledgments

In accord with hip-hop practices of giving credit where it is due, I have the honor of naming everyone who helped make this project possible. I would like to begin by reflection and respectfully acknowledging that much of this book has been written on traditional lands whose original people today are identified as Kanaka Maoli, Tongva peoples, Gayogo̱hó:nǫ' (Cayuga Nation), the Three Fires Confederacy—Potawatomi, Odawa and Ojibwe Nations, Menominee, Ho-Chunk, and the indigenous peoples of the Philippines. I recognize how this work owes its life to the assemblage of historical legacies including overlapping Native resistance against colonial violence and Native knowledge systems of generations that shaped these spaces. Maraming salamat (many thanks) to Norm Hirschy at Oxford for his first-rate advocacy and continued support of this work. You are a superstar editor and this project would not be what it is without you. Lauralee Yeary has been key to the manuscript's delivery. Thanks to Ayshwarya for keeping me on schedule. I must also recognize the multitudes of support from Jordan Beltran, Cathy Hannabach, Martha Murray, and Summer McDonald for ensuring my words are on point. Portions of this book appeared earlier and have since been altered and reworked anew. An earlier version of portions of the introduction have appeared in "Empire State of Mind: Hip-Hop Dance in the Philippines," *Hip-Hop(e): The Cultural Practice and Critical Pedagogy of International Hip-Hop*, edited by Michael Viola and Brad J. Porfilio (New York: Peter Lang Publishing, 2012), 42–64. A preliminary version of Chapter 1, "Zombies and Prisoner Rehabilitation," was presented at the 2008 Congress for Research in Dance Conference, included in its conference proceedings as "'Smooth Criminals': Mimicry, Choreography, and Discipline in Cebuano Dancing Inmates" in *Dance Studies and Global Feminisms: 41st Annual Congress for Research in Dance Conference*, November 14–16, 2008, Hollins University, Roanoke, VA, edited by Teresa Randall, Congress on Research in Dance, 2008; and as "'If I Was Not in Prison, I Would Not Be Famous': Discipline, Choreography, and Mimicry in the Philippines," *Theatre Journal* 63, no. 4 (December 2011): 607–621. Portions of an earlier version of

Chapter 3 appeared as "Doin' The Robot: Anxieties of the Racial Futures," *Extensions: Online Journal of Embodiment and Technology* 6.

This research is nothing without the energies and support of the individuals and groups of dancers and cultural workers that form a network across the globe. In Berkeley, thanks go to fellow Pilipino Culture Night (PCN) chairs, especially Rani de Leon, Sharlene Aquiler, Joey Bernal, Karen Merto, and Frank Lozier. PCN Choreographers—Garrick Macatangay, Sarah Escosa, Christine Gatchalian, Raynelle Gipson, and Trisha Mitra—generously shared with me their knowledge and expertise in dance. Frank generously introduced me to Culture Shock, where I shared many dance floors with Kim Sims-Battiste, Lee Lee Coleman, Dani Clement, Angie Bunch, and Morvarid Shahidi; each modeled for me a hip-hop dance way of life in their own ways. Thanks to David Montes De Oca of Urban Arts Academy. Pilipino American leaders including Allyson Tintiangco-Cubales, Tracy Buenavista, Hannah Masbad, Karmela Herrera, Tina Shauf, Stephanie Sampang, Tes Esparrago Lieu, Steph Carriaga, and Raissa Diamante guided my critical thinking about cultural politics. It was a privilege to collaborate with the 2010 PCN Producers Ading Brian Batugo, Eugene Pascual, and Joy Regullano and this work was rejuvenated by their creative community activism. I also thank Pedro Noguera for his mentorship.

Mahalos to my University of Hawai'i (UH) cohort—Johanna Almiron, Constancio Arnaldo, Daya Mortel, Kristy Ringor, Lani Teves, and Erin Falarca (in memoriam). My survival through this long academic journey is definitely owed to Jojoh Almiron, my academic galang-galang partner-in-crime. Ceej Arnaldo and Norma Marrun have been solid companions and academic interlocutors. Lani Teves has continued to share with me the secrets of success. Daya Mortel models for me a resilient activism I can only aspire to. I thank faculty and staff at the University of Hawai'i including David Stannard, Mari Yoshihara, Vernadette Gonzalez, Robert Perkinson, Rod Labrador, Jon Okamura, Theo Gonzalves, and Amy Agbayani. My gratitude to Clem Bautista and the Office of Multicultural Student Services. Thanks to Sheela Sharma for always being there for me. Ric Trimillos' influence was extremely formative and he is a paragon of mentoring excellence that I can only hope to live by.

Jerome Dimalanta warmly welcomed me into his dance circle. As one of the founders of street dance studies in the Philippines, his life and work always inspires me to organize, dance, and write better. Chelo Aestrid, my twinsie, has been one of the main reasons I can claim to know anything about Manila's hip-hop dance community. She is a triple threat in the performance world and I continue to learn from her hip-hop way of life. Jesse "Bboy Reflex" Gotangco and Phil "Adrum" Pamintuan are role models for dancers worldwide and I look forward to imparting the knowledge that they have shared with me. Deo Bantillo accompanied me to many research sites and shared many dance floors. I would not have been able to produce this study without the research assistance of Jared Luna, who was outstanding in his support. Von Asilo and Mycs Villoso welcomed me into their crew and schooled me about the world of dance. Lema Diaz deserves maraming salamat for always receiving my project and me with open arms. Mad props to Crisis Hyperion for bringin' the party to another level time after time.

In Manila, I spoke and danced with many people whose voices might not appear directly in this book, but who most definitely shaped its formation. Maraming salamat rin sa lahat ng mga dansers: Michelle Salazar, Sandy Hontiveros, Pinky Nelson, James Wong, Robie Punsalan, Japheth Reyes, Bgirl Eyevee (in memorium), Bgirl Beatch, Bgirl Phlo, Madelle Enriquez, Charm Esteban, Joshua Zamora, Angelica Arda, Niño Guerrero, JJ San Juan, Jason Cruz, Gino Ong, Nica Carlos, Joy Aggabao, Steffi Maala, Ace Lebumfacil, Vince Mendoza, Mycs Villoso, Kath Sison, Kel Pariña, Lovela Sabio, Coach Jungee Marcelo, Jim Libiran, Eauj Corpuz, and Hitmaster Fish. Big ups to the Crew—Aye Alba, JM De Jesus, Xernan Alfonso, Sam Abriza, Michael Arda, Jeremiah Carcellar, Vimi Rivera, Chinky Ramoso-Asilo, Hanna Sollano, Ron Pajela, Rosie Pajela-Marzan, Yang Gagelonia, Louie Canaria, Trizza Tolentino, Toki Sta. Maria, Erik Javier, Randell San Gregorio, Wincheska Young, Shayna Young. I am indebted to the Philippine AllStars, especially Naomi Tamayo, Heidi Riego, AC Lalata, and Krista Roma. Thanks also to Tha Project, Roz Manlangit, and Carlo Posadas. At UP-Diliman, I had the unexpected honor of sharing intellectual ground with Ruth Pison, Clod Yambao, Roland Tolentino, Elizabeth J. Aguilar, Neal Matherne, Sarah Raymundo, and Sir Steve Villaruz. I am grateful to the cultural workers at the Cultural Center of the Philippines including Josefina Guillen, Chinggay Bernardo, and Teresa Rances. I would like to extend much recognition to Jeng, Randy, and Zac Dizon for their wonderful hospitality. In Los Angeles, sunny smiles and thanks go out to Arnel Calvario, Anna "Lollipop" Sanchez, Anna Sarao, and Tiffany Bong for continuing to feed my thirst for dance histories. Thanks also to Stephen Grey, Del Mak, Paulina Pulido, Joel Gallarde, Ian Levia, Justin Sabino, Natsha Siri, Tiffany Lee, Michael Young, Tiffany Lee, Nesh Janiola, Mary Ann Bordallo, Iwa Clendon-Tau, Liz Rifino, Girese

Zimmer, Charity Nicholas, Yani Avelino, Leo Villar, Elden Christian Lao, Canter Alcantara, Mark Kevin Toy, Jose Dorado, Miss Joe Abuda, Tzielo Lopez, Xyza Ragunjan, Jeffrey Jimenez, and Don Campbell (in memoriam). I also give my gratitude to Ryan Ramirez, Clara Bajado, Duane Nasis, Reo Matugas, and Ricky Carranza for sharing their knowledge of Filipino popular dance in the United Kingdom, France, Norway, and Finland.

My humble and eternal thanks go out to Susan Foster for seeing me through this journey. My thanks for her unparalleled skills at teaching, cheering, nudging, believing, reality-checking, and keeping it real, in every step of my scholarly development. In Victor Bascara, I found a one-of-a-kind mentor whose counsel has shaped my academic and career trajectory in immeasurable ways. Timing can often be everything. I consider myself one of the privileged ones to have entered University of California Los Angeles (UCLA) World Arts and Cultures/Dance (WAC/D) in time to study with Lucy Burns and Janet O'Shea, and I am honored to have learned from their expertise.

This research benefits from the WAC/D Department's supplemental fieldwork fellowship, travel grant, Quality Graduate Education stipend, and Chair's discretionary scholarship. Also thanks to the support of Mr. Thomas Irwin and the Jean Irwin Scholarship. It is with honor that I recognize the UCLA Graduate Division's fellowship programs for continuing students including the Graduate Research Summer Mentorship, Graduate Research Mentorship, and Dissertation Year Fellowship. At the Graduate Division, Jessie Boutayeb has been exceptionally helpful and supportive. I also recognize the UCLA Asian American Studies Center's Tsugio and Miyoko Nakanishi Prize in Asian American Literature and Culture and the Office of Instructional Development's Collegium of University Teaching Fellowship, of which Cathie Gentile and Christopher Mott have been critical. I credit William Paul Taylor and Bernard Llanos, Veterans Coordinators at the Registrar.

My preliminary research in Manila was made possible through the Fulbright-Hays Group Projects Abroad, Advanced Overseas Intensive Language Program at the University of Hawai'i, Mānoa. Maraming salamat po to Tita Ruth Mabanglo, Teresita Ramos, Teresita Fortunato, Ate Vangie Alvarez, and the entirety of the Advanced Filipino Abroad Program 2009 crew. Special thanks to Randy Cortez for helping me when I was injured. My Manila fieldwork was aided by the Asian Cultural Council and the Humanities Program fellowship program, and I thank Jennifer Quiambao and Cecily D. Cook for their fantastic help. A heartfelt thanks to Teresa Rances for her guidance and caring generosity in my time living in Manila, especially when I was struck with dengue-like illness. I am thankful for the Fulbright-Hays Doctoral Dissertation Research Abroad Fellowship program of the US Department of Education and sponsored by both UCLA and the University of the Philippines–Diliman. I am in serious debt of gratitude for the patience and application support of Samantha Reyes, UCLA Fulbright Fellowships Coordinator. Maraming salamat goes to the Philippine-American Educational Foundation (PAEF) in Manila, particularly Dr. EC Cunanan, Con Valdecanas, Marge Tolentino, and Yolly Casas. My Fulbright year in Manila would not have been what it was without commuting, karaoke, and colloquia-hopping with fellow Fulbright scholars—aptly deemed "the lively bunch"—Andrew Plan, Nicole Oberfoell, Laurel Fantauzzo, Amber Ariate, and Jeff Sallaz. At the top of the list, a friendship with Fulbrighter Christina Durano kept my spirits up with our own brand of shenanigans even amidst the monsoon season. For the writing stages of this project, I am thankful for the Ford Foundation and the National Research Council of the National Academies. I have received unwavering support from the Ford staff, in particular, Pamela Tyler. I thank Ford fellows Vanessa Diaz, Maurice Magaña, Jonathan Rosa, Elliot Powell, Judy Kertesz, Angela Gonzalez, Koritha Mitchell, Yolanda Sealey-Ruiz, Rashawn Ray, Nicholas Reo, Steve McKay, Rhacel Parreñas, Denise Cruz, Faye Caronan, Isar Godreau Santiago, Katrina Roundfield, Chris O'Brien, Ebony Coletu, Kimberly Hoang, Laurence Ralph, and Joy Sales, they electrify me with their scholarship and activism, reflective of a community of scholars that I am lucky to call my own. A special thanks to Ellen Wu and Angelica Allen for reading earlier drafts.

At UCLA thanks to Tita Domingo and the Department of Asian Languages and Cultures, Barbara Gaerlan and the Center for Southeast Asian Studies, and Isamara Ramirez at the Graduate Division. At the Asian American Studies Department, credit goes to Stacey Hirose, Barret Korerat, Kenneth Kuo, Jessie Singh, Natalia Yamashiro-Chogyoji, Anne Bautista, Kyeyoung Park, Grace Hong, and Keith Camacho. Thanks to Melany de la Cruz, Meg Thornton, and David K. Yoo of the Asian American Studies Center. Thanks also to Wendy Brunt of the Office of the Human Research Protection Program. The production of knowledge about Filipino Americans lives on with the tireless work of Jade Alburo and Eloisa Gomez Borah, Librarian Emerita. In the department of World Arts and Cultures/ Dance, several people deserve more than these words. Silvily Thomas is owed a huge hug-size thanks for countless saves and Mimi Moorhead has always helped me put occasional crises into better perspective. Wendy Temple helped me get through academic hurdles big and small. Daniel Millner, Lillian Wu, Arsenio Apillanes, and Carl Patrick (in memoriam) all made my WAC/D experience better. In WAC/D I cannot thank our Student Affairs Officers enough: Nicole Fucich, Larry Blanco, Marissa Tinloy, Laurie Leyden, and Hayley Safonov. In particular, thanks to Eveline Chang for her guidance since my day zero at WAC (sans D). Thanks to Angelia Leung, David Shorter, Victoria Marks, Anurima Banerji, Lorena Alvarado, Samuel Anderson, Harmony Bench, Jenna Delgado, Doran George (in memoriam), Jelani Hamm, Mana Hayakawa, Leonard Melchor, Cristina Rosa, Michael Sakamoto, Carolina San Juan, Mathew Sandoval, Yehuda Sharim, Sara Stranovsky, Giavanni Washington, Alessandra Williams, and Sara Wolf. Many members of UCLA Asian American Studies and Graduate Students of Color communities have made unforgettable impact including Andrew Jung, Vangie Reyes, Erica Juhn, Mary Keovisai, Chun Mei Lam, Hugo Sarmiento, and Mzilikazi Koné. Thanks to Habi Arts and especially Melissa Roxas, Apollo Victoria, and Kuusela Hilo. Much recognition goes out to the LA Fil-Am community and Pilipino American Graduate Students Association (PAGaSA) at UCLA: Roland Remenyi, Cindy Sangalang, Anthony Ocampo, Anna Alves, Ellen Rae Cachola, Voltaire Sinigayan, and the exceptional Mike Viola. Thanks to Ana Paula Höfling for reading an earlier draft. A special thank you goes to Rosemary Candelario for lighting the path forward as an excellent role model in dance studies and friendship.

At Cornell, thanks to Sabine Haenni, Austin Bunn, Sara Warner, Nick Salvato, Amy Villarejo, Joyce Morgenroth, Ellen Gainor, Jumay Chu, and Byron Suber. Thanks to Asian American Studies and Derek Chang, Minh-Ha Pham, Viranjini Munasinghe, Shelley Wong, Chrissy Lau, and Vladimir Micic. Thanks to the Cornell Prison Education Program and Rob Scott. At the Mellon, I'm thankful for Judith Ann Peraino, Arnika Fuhrmann, Eric Cheyfitz, Deborah Starr, Lauren Alexandra Harmon, Margo Crawford, Maria Fernandez, Murad Idris, Nicole Giannella, Rafael Santana, Suman Seth, Michael Jones-Correa, Hirokazu Miyazaki, Anindita Banerjee, Travis Gosa, Yun Jung Choi, Mostafa Minawi, Danielle Terrazas Williams, and Kya Mangrum. Thanks to Katherine Reagan and Ben Ortiz at the Cornell Hip-Hop Collection. Thanks to Ryan Buyco, Theresa Buyco, Phuong Nguyen, Betty Chau Nguyen, and Vivian Chang for their support and community-building. Special thanks go out to Naminata Diabate and Christopher Pexa for their enduring friendship, feedback on drafts, and generous thinking.

At the University of Illinois at Chicago (UIC), a huge thanks to Anna Guevarra for her inspiration and unwavering support and guidance. Much thanks to Nadine Naber, Mark Chiang, Karen Su, Fredy Gonzalez, Roderick Labrador, Cynthia Blair, Gayatri Reddy, Xuehua Xiang, Catherine Becker, Diem-My Bui, Laura Hostetler, Mary Anne Mohanraj, Radha Modhi, and Corinne Kodama. I also thank Mark Martell, Jeff Alton, Elvin Chan, Alyson Kung, Amanda Lewis, Atef Said, Adam Goodman, Daniel Morales-Doyle, Elizabeth Todd-Breland, Jennifer Brier, Helen Jun, Nicole Nguyen, Lorena Garcia, Ivan Arenas, Faith Kares, Ryan Viloria, Hideaki Noguchi, Annie Pho, Kellee Warren, Alyne Connie, Stephen Wiberley, Nick Ardinger, Jordan Turner, Moises Villada, Antonio Santos, Mario LaMothe, and Anna Kozlowska. I'm grateful for the research assistantship of Bianca Gallarde and Kelly Hansen. Thanks also goes to the Chiya Café crew: Akemi Nishida, Patricia Macias, and Ronak Kapadia. Greg Calip deserves a special shout out for his collegiality and friendship. My work at UIC and life in Chicago has been sustained by the support of Michael Jin. I also thank my students, particularly Viet Phan, Ajibola Ayeni, Edwardjan Raya, Christina Khorn, Kevin Dimayuga, Tina Leong, Elizabeth Chang, Beth Skolba, Andre Castillo, and KatherynMarie Garrido.

This research is supported by the following: Faculty Fellowship, Institute for Research on Race and Public Policy (IRRPP), the Chancellor's Undergraduate Research Award, Office of Undergraduate Research in the Office of the Vice Provost for Undergraduate Affairs, and the Dean's Award for Faculty Research in the Humanities, College of Liberal Arts and Sciences, University of Illinois, Chicago; the Targeted Research Area Grant, American Society for Theatre Research; Mellon Summer Seminar on Dance Studies Fellowship; the Andrew W. Mellon Diversity Postdoctoral Fellowship, Department of Performing and Media Arts, Asian American Studies Program, American Studies Program, Cornell University; Ford Foundation Dissertation Fellowship, The National Research Council of the National Academies; Fulbright-Hays Doctoral Dissertation Research Abroad Fellowship, US Department of Education, UCLA, University of Philippines–Diliman; Humanities Program Fellowship, Asian Cultural Council, Philippines; Fulbright-Hays Group Projects Abroad, Advanced

Overseas Intensive Language Program, Philippines (Tagalog), US Department of Education, University of Hawai'i–Mānoa; Foreign Language and Area Studies Fellowship, Southeast Asia, Filipino, US Department of Education, UCLA.

In dance and performance studies, I would like to thank Thomas DeFrantz for his remarkable mentorship, uplifting exchanges, and feedback on drafts. I am grateful to SanSan Kwan for her comments on my introduction. I also thank Susan Manning, Sherril Dodds, Yutian Wong, Mary Fogarty, Mana Hayakawa, Thao Nguyen, Cynthia Lee, Melissa Blanco Borelli, Clare Croft, Carrie Noland, Janice Ross, Rebecca Schneider, Paul Scolieri, Heather Rastovac, Daniel Callahan, Dasha Chapman, Joanna Dee Das, Jessica Dellecave, Adrienne Edwards, Ninoska Escobar, Ashley S. Ferro-Murray, Amanda Graham, Laura Karreman, Michael Morris, Megan Nicely, Jade Power-Sotomayor, Hannah Schwadron, Noémie Bernier-Solomon Melissa Templeton, Lucille Toth, Christopher Wells, Hentyle Yapp, Natalia Zervou, Kareem Khubchandani, Meiver De la Cruz, Adanna Jones, Maya Berry, Harshita Kamath, and Seth Williams. Special thanks to Elizabeth Schwall for her superb writing partnership.

In Filipino Studies, I would like to thank Amanda Solomon-Amorao, Paul Michael Atienza, Christine Balance, Nerissa Balce, Joi Barrios, Jody Blanco, Rick Bonus, JP Catungal, Catherine Ceniza Choy, Genevieve Clutario, Roland Coloma, Emmanuel David, Josen Diaz, Robert Diaz, Irene Faye Duller, Bernard Ellorin, Augusto Espiritu, Kale Fajardo, Valerie Francisco-Menchavez, Armand Gutierrez, Florante Peter Ibanez, Allen Punzalan Isaac, Ryanson Ku, Dina Maramba, Joyce Mariano, Victor Mendoza, Roderick Labrador, Marissa Largo, Judy Patacsil, JoAnna Poblete, Joseph Ponce, Joseph Ruanto-Ramirez, Dylan Rodriguez, Jeffrey Santa Ana, Thomas Sarmiento, Theresa Suarez, Neferti Tadiar, Mary Talusan, Allyson Tintiangco-Cubales, Antonio Tiongson, Jr., Roland Tolentino, Heidi Tuason, Ethel Tungonan, Lilly Ann Villaraza, Steve Villaruz, Mark Villegas, and particularly Sarita See, Robyn Rodriguez, and Martin Manalansan. I would be remiss if I missed thanking Clod Yambao for his intellectual comraderie. I would like to thank the Association for Asian American Studies Junior Faculty Workshop and Nitasha Sharma, Priya Srinivasan, Min Hyoung Song, Tina Chen, James Kyung-Jin Lee, Richard Jean So, Crystal Baik, Melissa Borja, Jason Oliver Chang, Kevin Escudero, Quynh Nhu Le, Julian Lim, Kimberly McKee, William Nessly, Jan Padios, Terry Park, Christopher Patterson, Jeannie

Shinozuka, Anantha Sudhakar, Y-Dang Troeung, and James Zarsadiaz. In Asian Studies, I would like to thank Koichi Iwabuchi, Cristina Juan, Rosa Castillo, Ien Ang, Kim Soyoung, Yiu Fai Chow, Jeroen de Kloet, Chris Hearly, Jodi Kim, Chih-ming Wang, Chiara Formichi, Sze Wei Ang, Jiyu Zhang, Gladys Pak Lei Chong, Rossella Ferrari, and Stevie Susan. At the University of Hawai'i at Mānoa, I give thanks to Betsy Fisher, Jhalak Kara Miller, Amy Schiffner, Peiling Kao, Marcus Wessendorf, Vilsoni Hereniko, Lori Chun, and Peter Arnade.

Many people comprise the crew of my life. Auntie Charlene and Uncle Gene adopted me into their home and continue to shape me into the social actor I am today. Andrea Torres deserves all the goodness and light of life that continue to greet her. Much of my time living in Honolulu was filled with a youthful energy because of Kapuni Goes. Elsie Simpliciano exemplifies an effortless friendship that I continue to count my blessings for. Julie, Kawika, Akira, and Jolie Uyeno-Pidot and family welcomed me into their home during some of the loneliest stretches of the year. Jess and Keola Richardson and family continue to be my 'ohana since our days dancing kahiko at Cal. I would be remiss to neglect crediting Kenyon Tam, Brandon Kusakabe and family, Milo Smith, Tracy Higa, Jaren Adams, Nicole Fernandez, Katherine Martin, and Vincent Dora—they comprise my UH rainbow warrior and Intra-Mural Sports family. My time as a Bruin flew by with the help of friends Gabriel Nelson, Forrest Stuart, and Elena Shih. Hyeyoung Oh kept me grounded in LA and forged a friendship I will always treasure. Thanks to all that made my Berkeley-to-Bruin journey worthwhile including Erwin Ong, Usa Aroonlap, Lendy Le, and Emi Noguchi. In Chicago, my deepest gratitude goes to Forrest Stuart and Stephanie Hair for their boundless generosity and kinship. Forrest, thank you for exemplifying the balance of rigorous scholarship and everyday life. Thanks to Auntie Tessie, Uncle Ben, Tine, and Jo for always being there. Mahalos to Kalani, Kainoa, and Kris Cuaresma-Primm for all his support and brotherhood. I would like to extend worlds of love and respect to Dr. Jasmine Pedroso, who has been nothing less than a lifesaver throughout the dance of my life.

I am blessed with a large extended family to which I owe so much. Thanks to the Perillos: Aunties Manay, Flocer, Delia, Shirley, Mercy, Carolina, Clara, Marijo (in memoriam), and Uncles Nandy, Jason, Rommel, and Junior, and their families. Thanks to all the Lorenzos: Aunties Cora, Fely (in memoriam), and Lina, and Uncles Eddie (in memoriam), Ariel, Gani, and Cris (in memoriam), and their families. Thanks to all my cousins, especially Ate TinTin, Ate Cess, Ate Libay, Myleen, Noel, Raymund, and Rhea, for all they have given me. I never would have started dancing if I did not shadow my big sister, so to Ate Sherry I owe a lot. Thanks to Stacy and Stephanie for keeping me on track and well-fed. Thanks also to Gary, Jay, Nick, Benji, Sebastian, Mylo, Scout, and Kobe. My unending thanks to my Mom and Dad for teaching me the value of hard work and giving me strength and sustenance to survive.

About the Companion website

www.oup.com/us/choreographingincolor

The *Choreographing in Color* website complements your engagement of the book's words and still images and helps illustrate the arguments within. On the website, you will find two videos which are keyed to the text. The first video accompanies chapter 3 and features "Assembly Line" choreographed by Garrick Macatangay and Sarah Escosa and performed by students of the University of California Berkeley. To give viewers a sense of how the live performance was framed, this video includes a commercial that was projected onstage prior to the dance. Both are excerpted from the evening-length Home Pilipino Culture Night (2000), produced by Rani de Leon. The second video features "Pinays Rise" (2010), by artist Chelo Aestrid. This music video performance goes hand-in-hand with the conclusion.

Introduction

Being in the Philippines disorients me. In the late 1960s, my father dropped out of college and left the country. Forty years later, I found myself here. I was alone and doubting my decision to research the known birthplace of Asian hip-hop as I transferred to my second jeepney.[1] Stepping up and crouching down into the back, I squeezed my six-foot-two frame between two passengers, clutching my dripping umbrella away from their pleated trousers. I passed my fare forward, and we drove away from PhilCoA, the vernacular portmanteau for the gathering place of transportation options that line the road in front of the Philippine Coconut Authority.[2] Hand-to-hand, person-to-person, my grimy coins moved toward the front of the vehicle until they finally reached the driver, whose hand was cupped behind his right ear in anticipation. Once his palm closed, I looked in the rearview mirror and made eye contact with him to say, or mouth rather, "SM."[3] He nodded and scanned the streets. In a single year, Filipinos spend over sixteen days in the traffic of Manila, the world's most densely populated city.

Earlier that day, award-winning hip-hop performing artist Chelo A. had convinced me to endure the commute from PhilCoA to SM City North EDSA, a shopping mall in Quezon City, where Chelo and others in the hip-hop community were putting on a show.[4] In the way each of its five floors open like concentric donuts into a center courtyard, this mall makes a joke out of its name—"The Block"—and verges on the panoptic; each offers a 360-degree view into the central ground floor stage.[5] This is where the concert of the world-champion Philippine Allstars dance crew is to take place. Like many hip-hop artists, they started from the proverbial bottom—except their bottom was global. High above, skylights pop and hundreds of folks hang unceremoniously on the railings, leaning inward, with eyes on the stage. The dance floor is elevated, and its clear, backlit Plexiglas surface seems like it would be cruel to misplaced feet. The atmosphere is air-conditioned, clean, and shiny—a sharp and welcome contrast from the smoggy, muggy bustle

Choreographing in Color. J. Lorenzo Perillo, Oxford University Press (2020). © Oxford University Press.
DOI: 10.1093/oso/9780190054274.001.0001

just beyond the shopping center's doors. After all, malls do have meaning in Filipino society beyond mass consumerism.[6] Perhaps this is because malls are where folks go to escape the seemingly unavoidable moisture, whether summer sweat or unrelenting rain. The sweet and sour mix of mangoes and muddy water. Malls are the familiar words on a radiant jeepney's placard that tells you its route. Malls are where urban bakla cruise potential mates.[7] And as I learned first-hand one day, malls are also where multinational companies actively recruit labor for overseas employment. So today, in this mall, beside the Kultura native crafts store and below a cinema, the Manila dance community was taking center stage.

When I saw the royal blue booths designed to inform the Filipino public about visas, education abroad, and labor programs encircling the stage, I steeled myself. The hour-long concert turned out to be part of "America in 3D: Diplomacy, Development, and Defense," a series of U.S. Embassy events self-described as road shows that featured cultural performers like the Philippine Allstars.[8] The dancers, who also presented a subsequent choreography workshop, comprised a vibrant urban arts community including the Pinoy Funk 'n' Styles (poppers and lockers), Pinoy House Community, KrumPinoy, and Stellars, a women's dance collective. Before these groups took the stage, Harry K. Thomas Jr., the first African American U.S. ambassador to the Philippines, gave opening remarks and connected the events to his upbringing in New York, the recognized birthplace of American hip-hop culture.[9] The Quezon City event was just the first stop in a U.S. campaign that set up camp in five different areas across the archipelago including Ilocos Norte, Baguio, Cebu, and Iloilo.[10] The event prompted the question: What does it mean for Filipinos to engage and participate in forces of neocolonialism and state labor brokerage? And how did hip-hop and street dance come to be the vehicle for such cooptation? Moreover, and more broadly, is doing hip-hop in this way a cooptation of the culture itself?[11]

This book draws upon methods of multi-sited, bilingual ethnography and choreographic analysis to uncover how and why Filipino dancers have made such a tremendous impact on the global popularization of hip-hop and street dance since the late twentieth century.[12] By examining a varied archive of performance, from viral videos to migrant media, U.S. college culture nights to the "Olympics" of hip-hop, I argue that Filipinos engage hip-hop and street dancing in ways that work with and against empire, neoliberalism, and state-sanctioned violence, thus creating a space where their participation in hip-hop through dance can be regarded as something beyond cooptation, mimicry, or, even still, appropriation.[13] In so doing, moreover, we begin to unmask 1) the ways in which Filipinoness, particularly as it is understood by non-Filipinos, has been informed by Black cultural expression, and 2) also fully appreciate how Filipinos, and the forces that have driven their paradoxical visibility and illegitimacy, have been instrumental in making hip-hop a truly global entity.[14] As such, I argue for integration of these crucial aspects of hip-hop (dancing) and its broader multi-racial repertoire of cultural syncretism, whose significance has been heretofore virtually ignored, as necessary starting points to not only articulate against colonial and racial domination, but more importantly to express worlds much more just, inclusive, empathetic, and expansive than we know.[15] But to understand how we got here, we have to go further back.

Historical Context and Background

For over four centuries, from 1492 to 1896, the Philippines played a crucial role as the sole transpacific Hispanic colonial trade post, after which it declared independence. At the turn of the twentieth century, Filipinos survived the Philippine-American War (1899–1913+), only to find themselves formally subject to U.S. empire under "benevolent guises" until 1946. The history of Filipino peoples has been profoundly shaped by multiple colonialisms, foreign occupations (British in 1762–1764 and Japanese in 1942–1945), and continued struggles for independence. In the past twenty years, a growing body of scholarship has sustained a lively debate regarding how these historical formations shaped the folks of this archipelagic country and the postcolonial production of racial knowledge.[16] Modern racial knowledge, or the racial formation of Filipinoness, has been predicated upon colonial vocabulary rooted in contested ideas of indigeneity, Malayness, whiteness, Asianness, Latinoness, Blackness, and mixed race identity.[17] Even so, how Black cultural expression plays a role in Filipino life is often marginalized, erasing the complex processes of cultural formation along multiple axes of empire, gender, ethnicity, class, sexuality, and migration.

As the first chronicling of the development of Filipino popular dance and performance, this project addresses often overlooked processes of cultural formation and draws inspiration from the album by hip-hop pioneer Joe Bataan.[18] Bataan's songs like "Ordinary Guy (AfroFilipino)" (1967) and "Young, Gifted, and Brown" (1970) reflect his desire to fulfill a cultural need for Brown people; he ended up inspiring La Raza, Filipinos, and Third World folks.[19] Bataan emphasizes AfroFilipino masculinity to speak on his everyday struggles emerging from his experience as a Black and Filipino person growing up in a Spanish neighborhood and often being mistaken as an Afro-Latino person. In this book, I broaden the frame to explore the lived experiences of Filipinos that find articulation in Black cultural expression. I do not mean to suggest by this framework that Filipinoness and Blackness are seamless or commensurable. Rather, I draw from women of color feminism and queer of color critique to highlight how Afro-Asian formations are heterogeneous and complicated by particular histories, social trajectories, and aesthetic contexts in a way that, following Grace Kyungwon Hong and Roderick A. Ferguson, "refuses to maintain that objects of comparison are static, unchanging, and empirically observable, and refuses to render illegible the shifting configurations of power that define such objects in the first place."[20] By emphasizing U.S. empire and the structural dynamics of race and gendered labor as foundational to the particularities of AfroFilipino formations, I undermine the intersectional ways that hip-hop studies that neglect Filipino colonial corporeality, on the one hand, and Filipino studies that omit the politics of Blackness, on the other hand, work to marginalize particularly racialized and gendered subjects.[21] To be sure, I want to understand how anti-blackness and indigeneity are important and I recognize histories of extraction and honor efforts to contest them. But, I want to avoid reducing the experiences of my research participants and my analyses of those experiences to frames outside their worldview. Indeed, the systemic omission of colonial and racial histories and how their legacies shape the cultural engagements of formerly colonized and enslaved peoples complicates the criticism of Filipino appropriation and extraction of Black culture.

AfroFilipino formation nuances how Filipinos navigate and contest ordinary and extraordinary struggles on the dance floor.[22] At the same time, this book remains grounded in Asian American, Filipino American, and performance studies contexts, while addressing issues of Black dance and revealing how embodied encounters offer a crucial view of the messy contradictory processes of decolonial politics, gendered global labor migration, and transnationalism.[23] For example, for Filipinos, it is important to recognize how antiblackness has structured and continues to structure U.S. imperial expansion, the exclusion of and discrimination against Black Filipino Amerasians in Filipino society, and the putative fluidity of transnational migrations of hip-hop.[24] While this book offers crucial insights into Filipino identity and its performance, its more global contribution is linking cultural contexts across

U.S., Asian, Asian American, and African American contexts.[25] Advocating for an interpretation of the dancing body that centers Filipino performativity, I explore key roles through which individuals have engaged with hegemonic forces of both racial legacies of colonialism and gendered labor migration: the zombie (Chapter 1), the hero (Chapter 2), the robot (Chapter 3), and the judge (Chapter 4). To conceptualize how these formations both conjure and recode state violence, I reimagine the performative potential of "euphemism" as a mode of social criticism. The term "euphemism" has Greek origins, *eû* "well" and *phēmē* "speaking," and usually signals mitigation, censorship, or respectability politics. In performance, I recuperate the term and conceptualize the euphemism as an ambivalent expressive means for an individual or collective to give way to the exercise of power over it and at the same time resist, dampen, or divert that power. This book aims to interpret global hip-hop in terms of Filipino corporeality, which therefore necessitates recognition and critique of its colonial structural dynamics. Overall, the book asserts the importance in shifting attention away from the exceptionalist emphasis on Filipinos as superb mimics, heroic migrants, model minorities, natural dancers, and subservient wives, and toward a rethinking of movement and materiality.[26] It is about unlearning the exceptionalism around Filipino performance insomuch as that is a reconstitution of American exceptionalism, imperial expansion, and Philippine neoliberalization of global labor.

From local to international spaces, and increasingly over the last fifty years, Filipinos have emerged as an unlikely yet palpable force in the dance world. Understanding this phenomenon requires a reassessment of the ways Black culture and dance have long been deemed peripheral to the development of Filipino subjectivity. Dancers shape and are shaped by notions of Filipinoness and Blackness in ways that demystify and hinder their navigation of the crosshairs of colonialism and neoliberalism.[27] By reframing the ongoing, contested underdog relationship between Filipinos and U.S. global power in terms of performance, *Choreographing in Color* denaturalizes the Filipino dancing body as, paradoxically, globally recognizable and indiscernible.

The Colonial Corporeality of Dance and AfroFilipino Racialization

As a backdrop to my claim that appropriation and mimicry lack the explanatory power to understand Filipino participation in hip-hop dance, I turn to corporeality, or the issues of the naturalized body, its disciplining and meaning-making, and examine the multiple repertoires through which racialization informs the work of the Filipino dancer.[28] The "good" Filipino dancer, an individual with physical control and dexterity, rhythmic brilliance, and audience appeal, is a neocolonial construct used to maintain white supremacy and economic inequality under the guise of freedom and meritocracy. In this way, we must acknowledge the discourse around the good Filipino dancer as, just that, a good, both in terms of a supposedly inherent positive value and as a neoliberal commodity. Indeed, in the U.S. context, the stereotype of a naturalized Filipino dancing body exists alongside an ensemble of racial and racist caricatures: the rhythmic abilities of the Black body, the threat of the undocumented immigrant body, the passiveness of the East Asian body, the eccentricity and awkward movement of the white body, and terrorism and racial ambiguity of the Arab and Brown Asian body.[29] Challenging race-neutral analyses of dance and performance is an aperture through which to attend to the corporeality of Filipino dancers and its potential to expand upon current rubrics for the dancing body as a critical locus of power.

In U.S. dance history, for example, Ruth St. Denis's problematic relationship with Indian immigrant dancers in the early twentieth century produced the "Oriental Dancing Girl," doubly sexualized as Oriental (racial fantasy of sexual availability) and dancer (assumed sexual).[30] Asian American dance studies has performed the onerous work of clarifying the "genius" of American modern dance, with what dance scholar Yutian Wong calls "invisible Orientalism," or the exclusion of Asian bodies from the realms of making American culture.[31] This rubric of Asian American racialization counterposes Asian-ness and Blackness on a "disembodiment spectrum," such that one signifies "perpetual(ly) foreign" model minorities that "transcend" their racial bodies through naturalized intellectual power, and the latter reflects bodily excesses.[32] A spectrum-based configuration inadvertently reinforces problematic ways Asians and Asian Americans are often used as model minorities to denigrate Black and Latino groups or positioned as racial intermediaries between Blackness and whiteness.[33] Yet, unlike South Asians and Chinese, Filipino and Black people have a particular relationship rooted in American colonialism and similarly experience so-called positive stereotypes of naturalized dancing and rhythmic ability. As such, it is necessary to intervene in Asian American dance studies by foregrounding several historical touchstones of African, Filipino, and Asian interracial formations, and some of the processes by which *sayaw* became "dance," which in turn reveal the limits of oppositional and spectrum racial configurations.[34]

One of the foremost AfroFilipino crossings occurred 40,000 to 60,000 years ago when the first inhabitants of the archipelago now known as the Philippines are believed to have crossed a land bridge from Asia.[35] The object of Western anthropology, this group of indigenous hunter-gatherers shared linguistic, genetic, animist, and cultural elements and offered Western social scientists "a keyhole glimpse into how our human ancestors may have lived and died in prehistory."[36] In the white Western normative context, Spanish colonizers later called them "Negritos," as a diminutive marker of their perceived dark skin and small stature (see Figure I.1). Negritos now refer to thirty-three groups living across the archipelago (e.g., Agta, Aeta, Ati, and Ita) and continue to face anti-Black racism and anti-indigenous oppression.[37]

Figure I.1 "Negrito boy," Walter W. Marquardt Papers, Bentley Historical Library, University of Michigan. American occupiers used photography of Negritos alongside anti-Black notions to justify western expansion.

U.S. colonial state actors and cultural institutions deployed notions of Blackness as childish, queer, excessive, and inferior as lenses to view the broader Filipino population.[38] Application of U.S. racial logic to construct notions of Filipinoness helped justify a doctrine of manifest destiny during the Philippine-American War (1899–1913+) and signaled the Western imperial expansion of Jim Crow overseas. At the same time, indigenous people of the Philippines, alongside African Americans, Native Americans, and Pacific Islanders, were rendered within the common sense of white supremacy in the United States, popular print, visual media, and everyday vernacular expressions like the epithet of the n-word.[39]

For instance, in the *Boston Sunday Globe*, on March 5, 1899, a cartoon entitled "Expansion, Before and After" featured a panel with the inset image of a dark-skinned, big-lipped, and barefoot Filipino native with a spear, grass skirt, and shield (see Figure I.2).[40] This panel had another image in the foreground of that same figure dressed in a reddish three-piece suit, cane,

Figure I.2 "Expansion, Before and After," *Boston Sunday Globe*, March 5, 1899. White media naturalized post-emancipation Black dance as corporeal progress for Filipinos.

and top hat. A dark-skinned woman dressed in a red-white-and-blue gown is depicted marveling at the newly dressed Filipino and the caption reads, "From the war dance to the cake walk is but a step."[41] The caption and other "before and after" scenes depicting sports, transportation, and a beaming native primarily serve to caricature Filipinos as hostile and uncivilized, naturalize these traits as "well-suited" for colonization, and minimize the violence of war and subsequent "benevolent assimilation" to "but a step." In turn-of-the-century white media, the cakewalk was a buffoonish caricature of Black people. This particular cartoon draws a thread between indigenous dance practice, Western expansion, and post-emancipation Black dances. It is important to note that enslaved people had actually used the cakewalk to lampoon white enslavers.[42] Similarly, the Filipino-as-Black-dandy in political cartoons, as women's studies and literature scholar Victor Roman Mendoza astutely argues, was a remaking of the "butt of white U.S. culture's minstrel joke." Mendoza explains how the Filipino-as-Black-dandy consequently cast "Philippine emergence into racial recognition as socially ludicrous according to contemporary fashion norms and effeminate according to emergent gender conventions . . . style[d] after images found in post-Reconstruction cultural form that attempted to consolidate racial boundaries by mocking a stylish [b]lack bourgeoisie."[43] In these instances, Filipino corporeality was tied to American expansion in ways that were not simply about "whitening" natives, but also relied on the dichotomization of before and after, background and foreground, indigenous and Black, despair and joy, primitivity and dandyism.

All people of the Philippines, however, were not simply proxies for Black Americans during the U.S. colonial period (see Figure I.3). At the 1904 St. Louis World's Fair, as part of a 47-acre "human zoo," people of the Philippines were exhibited in four grand divisions within an explicit social hierarchy from "the most primitive" Negrito peoples to the "civilized" Christianized Visayans. To the fair's 4 million visitors, organizers framed Negritos with the following description: "small, shy, of distinct negro type, low in intellect, their food consisting of roots, grubs, snails, etc., these people are gradually becoming lesser and weaker and the day of their extinction is not far off."[44] "Barbarian" Igorot peoples from the Northern Philippine Cordilleras Mountains and "clannish" Samal Moro and Bagobo from Southern region of Mindanao were featured alongside natives from Central Africa. The World's Fair enabled U.S. audiences to witness, confirm, and qualify the

Figure I.3 "Ifugao dance 1918—Third Pose," Walter W. Marquardt Papers, Bentley Historical Library, University of Michigan. Indigenous dances were critical for U.S. audiences to witness, confirm, and qualify racial hierarchies.

racial hierarchies previously consumed in stereographs (see Conclusion) and cartoons like "Expansion, Before and After" that putatively justified the violence of expansion.

Moreover, the Philippines became a site for grappling with what H.T. Johnson called "The Black Man's Burden," or the notion that colonization led by elite African Americans was necessary and more benevolent than that led by white people.[45] Further evidence that the relationship between Blackness and Filipinoness is rife with complications, this burden reflected how African Americans were often ambivalent on the subject of U.S. imperialism and non-white peoples like Filipinos. The violence of U.S. empire further proved to be a vexed mechanism for Black masculinity. Some African American soldiers—like David Fagen in particular—recognized the injustice in the Philippine-American War, deserted the U.S. military, and fought alongside Filipinos, and some even remained in the islands after the war.[46] In contrast, four hundred African Americans followed journalist T. Thomas Fortune's expeditions, some finding relief from U.S. racial oppression through the masculinizing logic of U.S. settler colonialism in the Philippines.[47] Black American teachers rendered themselves simultaneously sympathetic to Filipinos' subjugation under white supremacy and also beneficiaries of their status as American, non-Filipino colonizers uplifting Filipinos.[48]

In this same period, developments in popular dance ushered in several formative changes that created new spaces for natives to remake social, professional, and educational forms of gender relations through Brown, Black, and white dances.[49] In the Philippines, Filipino vaudeville, or *bodabil*, was comprised of Filipinized content, ballet, modern dance, and African American dance forms.[50] Given the complicated dynamics between rural indigenous people, urban elites, and dance under U.S. empire, African American culture cannot merely be seen as a site for choreographing Filipino vernacular expression following a logic of extraction. Dance scholar Reynaldo G. Alejandro writes that these forms were "readily assimilated" and consisted of dances such as "incidental dancing in local *bodabil*," the Big Apple, Castle walk, foxtrot, Lindy Hop, swing, and tango that appeared in both social dance halls and theaters.[51] While much of the literature and historical perspective on Philippine dance in the American period is whitewashed, many social dances in this period had origins in Brown and Black communities from the Americas (United States, Brazil, Argentina, Dominican Republic, and Jamaica).[52] Importantly, some foreign and native women gained new authority and political capital under U.S. empire. For example, vaudeville entertainers rank among the first individuated in style and name in Philippine dance history—unlike the records of anonymous indigenous, folk, and Spanish dancers.[53] While African American settler dances circulated through *bodabil*, white settler dances from Scandinavia and Russian balletic techniques were institutionalized in the public colonial education system from 1919 and into the 1930s—omitting most indigenous forms of dance and further complicating the ways race, gender, modernity, and empire intersected with Filipino dance history.[54]

On the other side of the Pacific, Filipino men patronized U.S. taxi dancehalls in the 1920s and 1930s, with their "exceptional" dancing of Lindy Hop and the Charleston, dances that originated in African American communities. Filipino immigrants' relations with white working-class women led to visibility but also furthered hostility by those who regarded their relations as threats to white masculinity.[55] While Filipinos had liminal legal status as non-citizen nationals (compared to other Asians who were classified as "aliens") that afforded mobility to various opportunities in Los Angeles, Detroit, El Centro, and Watsonville, white men saw interracial intimacies in taxi-dance clubs as public challenges to their propertied claims on white women, and responded with violence in the form of anti-Filipino race riots.[56] For instance, in 1930, the riots in Watsonville included "Filipino hunting parties" of up to a hundred persons that terrorized known Filipino residences and workplaces with bullets and bricks—and messages that emphasized Filipinos as Black—and resulted in the murder of twenty-two-year-old Filipino Fermin Tobera.[57] These events, and how Filipinos were often blamed for the violence against them, were influential in arguments for anti-Filipino legislation that paradoxically led to the Philippine Independence Act, or Tydings-McDuffie Act (1934).[58]

In the latter half of the century, a much different dance landmark emerged on U.S. college campuses. "Culture nights" grew as a performance genre when post-1965 Filipino immigrants and their children sought to bring their local communities together in celebration of cultural heritage and ethnic identity (see Chapter 4). Produced and performed by mostly middle- and working-class Filipinos in the West Coast, culture nights represent the culmination of a year-long process distilled into a two- or three-hour theatrical production that incorporates dance, music, costume, and song from a standardized repertoire. In the 1980s, as flows of hip-hop artists, representations, and practices increased between the Philippines and the United States, student organizations like Filipinos in Alliance at the University of California–Berkeley, Samahang Pilipino at the University of California–Los Angeles, and Kababayan at the University of California–Irvine began to change culture nights, revamping theatrical elements to express immigrant experiences that facilitated transitions between the established dance suite format, and independently initiating changes in what eventually became the "Modern Suite."[59] Unlike the traditional suites that had derived from the Philippine's folk repertoire, Modern Suites displayed primarily Black forms, like hip-hop dance, and at times jazz, swing, and tap dance, that were essential fabric of American youth culture. The pre-modern, U.S. imperial, popular dance, and Modern Suite touchstones suggest that contemporary Filipino engagement with Blackness and dance is not particularly new or authentic.

Rather, Filipino hip-hop is imbricated within what notable cultural studies scholar Sarita See so vividly describes as a "scattered history, archipelagic sensibility" of corporeality and historical, social, and choreographic commingling.[60] See's *The Decolonized Eye: Filipino American Art and Performance* (2009) argues that Filipino American visual artists and writer-performers advance a political aesthetic that disarticulates empire within their cultural productions. By theorizing a subversive disarticulation of empire, See contends that Filipino American artists counter imperial disavowal and the lingual/textual degradation of vernacular and indigenous history, literature, and language. Similar to See's analysis of "archipelagic sensibilities" of performers, *Choreographing in Color* shines a light on a community connected through popular dance forms that serve as a source of joy, self-determination, original artistic creativity, identity formation, survival, and postcolonial repertoire. With each touchstone came a moment of translation, disarticulation, and contradiction and each moment of institutionalization brought a process of recoding the racial, gender, class, and national signs shaping Brown dancing bodies.[61]

Filipino Popular Dance in the Neoliberal Era

In order to accept my claim that Filipinos have played a key role in the global spread of hip-hop, one must recognize the contradictions between development, cooptation, and institutionalization that shape the multidirectional flows of Black dance in the Philippines and its diaspora. These contradictions also illustrate how dance, as an activity, is not naturally "freeing," but instead carries with it ethical and political memories. These memories, in turn, help us understand the deeper significances and mutual production of race, empire, and dance in the contemporary world. In the Philippines and its diaspora in the 1970s, the rise of Black dance forms amidst U.S.-backed dictator Ferdinand Marcos' martial law exemplified these intersections. During this period, Filipino dancers gained exposure to U.S. Black dance through increasing transnational mediascapes, folk dance tours to the United States, Filipino American returnees, and U.S. military forces stationed in the Philippines.[62] *Penthouse 7* was a weekly popular television variety show, where Filipino youth introduced and popularized Black social dances from 1974 to 1981.[63] According to Sandy Hontiveros, a *Penthouse 7* dancer, the idea behind the show was to feature dances in a party atmosphere by folks who were relatable to home viewers.[64] Videotaped in front of a live studio audience, *Penthouse 7* aired every Sunday in the Philippines and became a phenomenon for the generation of youth that grew up under the Marcos dictatorship. Its popularity is due, in part, because its instructional segments, modest staging, and lack of model physiques were deliberately designed to showcase dance as an accessible activity for the *masa* [social masses]. Recognized by scholars as a cultural descendant of *bodabil* [Filipino vaudeville], *Penthouse 7* dancers viewed their show as a significant vehicle for affording new gender roles and popularizing locking.[65]

Locking featured on *Penthouse 7* traces its history to a cafeteria at Los Angeles Trade Technical College in the early 1970s, when Donald "Campbellock" Campbell attempted to imitate the "funky chicken" and gave audiences the impression that the joints at his wrists, elbows, and hips were fixed, or locked.[66] Locking, along with another dance called popping, belongs to a group of hip-hop dances that developed out of the U.S. West Coast funk culture and movement (often referred to as funk styles).[67] In the Philippines in the early 1980s, popping came after locking and was first popularized by Filipinos and Filipino Americans in the television competition *Dance10*. The bold, colorful creativity of forms of street dance like locking and popping are grounded in the civil rights struggles of minoritarian communities for equality in voting, employment, housing, and education, and the shift toward increased visibility of racial minorities in television programming like Don Cornelius's *Soul Train*. Campbell and the group the Lockers appeared as guests for various white television shows such as *Saturday Night Live* and the shows of Johnny Carson, Dick Van Dyke, and Carol Burnett.[68]

Sandy Hontiveros' and other *Penthouse 7* dancers' experiences invite us to frame locking (and other hip-hop histories) in transnational dance terms.[69] With Fiesta Filipina folk dance company, Hontiveros toured for two years in cities like New York, Los Angeles, and San Diego, where the dancers would visit local nightclubs and learn contemporary popular dances.[70] The folk tours reflect cultural syncretism and hybridity between postcolony and former colonizer as dancers would export Filipino folk dances to U.S. audiences, often circulating conservative notions of Filipino femininity as coquettish and Filipino masculinity as dominant. They also imported Black social dances and thus helped introduce locking and dances like the "LA Walk" and "New York Hustle" to Philippine audiences.[71] In addition to this folk tour pathway of global hip-hop, diasporic Filipino relatives living abroad would circulate Betamax video recordings of shows like *Soul Train* and Jeff Kutash's *Soap Factory*; these would inspire dancers in the Philippines to imitate and remake the styles.[72] One of the *Penthouse* dancers also worked for an airline, which enabled him to import videos from diasporic relatives directly.[73]

The legislative gains that informed the colorful U.S. versions of locking find an ironic antithesis in the oppressive climate surrounding the same kind of dancing in Manila in the 1970s. In the Philippines, dictator Ferdinand Marcos made several institutional changes affecting dancers like Hontiveros in contradictory ways.[74] Briefly following the controversial "Plaza Mirada Massacre" that killed nine of the Liberal Party's senatorial ticket (opposition to Marcos establishment), Marcos issued Presidential Proclamation 889 (August 23, 1971), which suspended the writ of habeas corpus with constitutional justifications, under a provision in the 1935 Constitution about ensuring public safety.[75] The writ of habeas corpus ("you have the body") ensures the protection of arrested people against unjust (i.e., arbitrary, indefinite) detainment by requiring authorities to file charges and present the body before the court.[76] Marcos declared Martial Law (Proclamation No. 1081) on September 21, 1972. From then until EDSA I in 1986 the dictator eliminated Filipinos' civil rights.[77] The corrupt ruler and military-run government created a volatile climate that incarcerated opposition and innocents and made dissidents disappear in broad daylight.[78]

Marcos also drove the rapid urbanization of Manila through a series of increased neoliberal structural adjustments.[79] Third world feminism scholar Neferti Tadiar teaches us that martial law consolidated Manila as a "supralocal metropolitan government," formed the Metro Manila Commission, and drove a beautification and slum-cleaning movement, all essentially to seduce foreign capital.[80] As part of their objectives in elevating the Filipino national image to the world, Ferdinand and Imelda Marcos leveraged the local patron-client political system to make substantial institutional changes to the arts world via the Cultural Center of the Philippines, the National Museum, and the Philippine High School for the Arts (PHSA), inspired from Michigan's Interlochen Center for the Arts.[81] Between 1972 and 1986, Marcos also made several presidential decrees, proclamations, and executive orders that were ostensibly aimed at benefiting artists.[82] During this same period, Imelda Marcos often coerced Hontiveros and the *Penthouse* dancers to perform at parties at Malacañang Palace, thereby casting dancers, essentialized Filipina hospitality, and popular dance as state actors and practices of what Tadiar calls "fantasy-production."[83]

The Marcos dictatorship had contradictory consequences for Filipino dancers.[84] Even despite the volatility of the martial law era, the ways that some artists and dancers like Hontiveros benefited from Marcos's rule inform the surprisingly positive light with which they recall this period in their lives.[85] The martial law era changes in economics and infrastructure would contribute to the dramatic expansion of mass consumer culture and the urban middle class.[86] Given that Marcos controlled most media outlets and only allowed content that did not threaten his rule, it seems likely that

Penthouse 7's promotion of urban upper-middle-class culture through dance and its relatable delivery was contiguous with Marcos's aims of "decolonization" through the institutionalization or elevation of the global status of Filipinos through culture and the arts. Beyond systemic changes in arts and culture, Marcos also provided exemptions to many dancers from a widespread curfew that attempted to restrict people's mobility from midnight to four o'clock in the morning.[87] For *Penthouse* dancers, these exemptions gave the artists license to dance at a time when other youth were confined indoors.[88] The show also entitled *Penthouse* dancers with mobility—on Manila streets to get to and from the studio and also to travel to provinces like Bacolod or Iloilo upon Imelda Marcos's request.

Penthouse 7 aspired to educate the public about popular dance and music, while introducing their audiences to the latest Filipino trends, artists, and fashions. One of its striking features was its format, which categorized dancers in ways that indigenized the foreign forms they embodied by figuring them within existing bodily movement practices. The fact that the production entailed two groups—Latin and Modern—inadvertently spoke to the racial triangulation of Filipinos betwixt and between Brown and Black cultures.[89] The Robot, the Bump, the Jacksons, the LA Walk, and the New York Hustle give us a sense of the Black popular dances that inspired their programming.[90] As their show was upgraded from an hour to an hour and a half, additional dancers like Ray An Fuentes, Pipo Liboro, Poncy Quirino, and Gina Valenciano taught locking, swing, the Rock, and the Errol Flynn.[91]

By calling Black dances "Modern," the program destabilized gender norms and counter-posed what it conceived as "Latin" with relatively gender-fluid Black social forms. Both were necessary for the show to symbolically and un-ironically render the urban Filipino as a body with cultural fluency across a continuum from Spanish colonialism to American postcoloniality to Filipino cosmopolitanism. This point does not detract from the agency that dancers exercise in selecting particular American forms over others and introducing locking, or a variation of the form, in the Philippines years before it appeared in other parts of Asia. Echoing the turn to the mundane of Joe Bataan's "Ordinary Guy," *Penthouse 7* used what it saw as a relatable format to introduce Philippine audiences to Latin and Black social dances that offered alternatives to the typical patriarchal folk repertoire. Its dancers benefited from changing infrastructure, impacted the music industry as tastemakers, and inspired generations that would follow, including the Philippine Allstars, who headlined the U.S. embassy event I described at the outset of this chapter, while also demonstrating the unexpected ways that Black social dances were both inculcated in the martial law era and transmitted across the archipelago.[92]

Defining the Performative Euphemism

Filipinos are well-versed at euphemisms. I remember the first time that my older cousins in Bulacan gestured as if they were getting nosebleeds upon hearing my English.[93] They performed epistaxis, or nosebleeding, to express psycho-social discomfort with me, and in part, to subvert the authority of English as a particularly classed language rooted in U.S.-Philippine colonial education.[94] My cousins drew attention to my intra-ethnic, "stateside," masculine class privilege (though at the time, it went over my head).[95] Euphemisms typically allow users to employ one form of expression in order to avoid using another more direct one. Performative euphemisms like nosebleeds do more than that because they gain value by their capacity to articulate and carry meaning across racial, sexual, and class borders, like those between my cousins and myself. Their everyday performance riffs on the very lines of appropriateness, adjacency, and inequality they keep secure. Often seen as integral to the establishment of social conventions, scholars like J. L. Austin and Judith Butler have theorized performativity to denote the compulsory, reiterative regulatory patterns enacted by a verbal expression that naturalizes and exposes identity's constructedness.[96] While remarkably overlooked for their metaphorical, functional, and social properties, euphemisms summon performativity. The nosebleed gesture that my cousins performed reflects both a "doing" of identity and a repetition of the action's social impact. By the same token, performativity can take the form of euphemism, like enslaved and colonized peoples dancing the cakewalk, drawing upon the tension between expectation and reality, ineffability and legibility, and deviance and acceptability.

As such, in this context, euphemisms are ambivalent tools and slippery acts that participate in social formation and yet call attention to the disruption of social order. I use the performative euphemism as an analytical concept to center, interrogate, and distinguish the ways that individuals communicate indirect expression. While performativity might entail imitation, exaggeration, subversive identity, or liberatory utopia, it can also serve as a tactic in

Michel De Certeau's sense of the word, namely as a resistant instrument of world-making and moreover as a transitive mechanism for dealing with illegibility of the colonized, intergenerational state violence, institutional and everyday oppression, and ephemerality of performance media.[97] I unearth the ways performative euphemisms mitigate Filipino stereotypes and bodily rhetoric of the state, industry, and cultural authorities to reclaim power, albeit limited. Euphemisms serve as structural organizing points for an exploration of the ongoing political struggles around class, gender, race, and colonialism implicated with Brown bodies, dance, and hip-hop.

Most scholarship and popular media locate hip-hop culture's value as emanating from its ability to *speak* to power in direct political messages.[98] For example, in his critically acclaimed history, Jeff Chang centralizes the role of musicians, deejays, and rap artists, yet mentions dance only briefly.[99] For more than a decade, the Black Entertainment Television (BET) Hip Hop Awards showcased hip-hop musicians and dancers, only rewarding music producers and rap artists with the "I Am Hip Hop Award," and has yet to recognize dance as an annual award category. In their 2010 special issue of *American Behavioral Scientist*, authors Siobhan Brooks and Thomas Conroy analyze the interdisciplinary development of hip-hop from a neighborhood New York–based cultural practice to a global phenomenon, but also leave open a space for dancers, dance as political agency, and non-rap/music cultural practices.[100] I respond by theorizing how embodied practices confound the narrow boundaries of who is typically considered a "conscious" hip-hop artist. I encourage scholars and artists alike to see beyond the rap-as-social-commentary model of understanding hip-hop's emancipatory value and appreciate multiple modes of social criticism.[101]

While hip-hop studies scholars criticize the commodification of hip-hop and its capacity and possibility for resistance, my research found that hip-hop studies' dominant underground/commercial dichotomy could not accurately account for dancers' multi-modal realities—underground, commercial, educational, conceptual, competitive, and diplomatic. I remain hopeful in my stance that, in the area of dance, hip-hop still provides a relatively accessible, affordable, and empowering form of culture, especially compared to other forms of dance like ballet and modern, which remain largely elitist and inaccessible to everyday folks. Thus, I see value in the ways globalized forms of hip-hop dance, while tied to commodification processes oft criticized by scholars, sometimes still serve as an entry point for deeper appreciation and community engagement by practitioners.

My approach dovetails with academic conversations around hip-hop seeking to recuperate practitioner-based theories embedded in social practices and the internal discourse frequently overshadowed by literary studies on moral and artistic credibility.[102] While scholars, like ethnomusicologist Joseph Schloss, for example, have importantly recovered mind-body connections central to expressive cultural practice, much of hip-hop historiography has assumed either a descriptive or an a priori type of relationship between the mind-body and race, gender, and postcoloniality.[103] By deploying critical race studies and critical dance studies, I am able to extend this conversation and de-essentialize theories of embodied performance. Brenda Dixon Gottschild's scholarship offers a variety of ways to enter this conversation, particularly through political expression and Africanist presence.[104] For instance, Gottschild's work underscores the linkage between democratic principles and Black dancing bodies, stating, "Figuratively speaking, the social, cultural black dancing body had to be violated—deconstructed and dismembered—in order to conform to democracy's propaganda."[105] Black performance studies specialist and choreographer Thomas F. DeFrantz adds to Gottschild's theorization by persuasively describing corporeal orature as a system of communication that "aligns movement with speech to describe the ability of black social dance to incite action."[106] Corporeal orature is a way to address how dance practices do not merely reflect culture, but also produce meanings and effects of their own.[107] For example, dancers might simultaneously take pleasure in consuming music, interpret visual cues, physically carry another dancing body, and feel the intimacy of a stranger, all while producing a dance of their own flesh and bones. Given the violence and benevolence of manifest destiny in the Philippines, the questions of Black dancing bodies and corporeal orature carry particular weight in Filipino contexts.

Alongside this theoretical lineage of Black performance studies, I define performative euphemism as a type of corporeal orature to refer to the ways popular dance communicates political and aesthetic value. Performative euphemisms enable Filipinos a way to express their identities without having to resort purely on normative representational tropes. For instance, in *Home* (2000) Pilipino Culture Night, the emancipatory potential of hip-hop's overt political messages is conveyed through the replacement of the fluid sway-balance step of the Tinikling folk dance with a punctuated robotic dance (see Chapter 4).[108] In language, euphemism acquires its utility as a substitution practice through dual ineffability and fungibility, like when "fuck" is replaced with "f-bomb."[109] In music, the presence or lack of profanity and curse words in a song can be a simultaneous marker of youth market viability, respectability politics, sexual appropriateness, racial authenticity, and our ability to understand what is really being conveyed.

And in dance culture, euphemism takes on a different kind of labor. Dancers, in general, perform euphemisms by substituting elements like movement, comportment, and spatio-temporal configuration. Dancers also respond, affirm, and subvert governmental agencies' efforts to racialize, gender, and commodify their bodies. In Filipino dance, figures of euphemism are proxies for corporeality and necessarily recuperate the centrality of its racialized, gendered, and colonial dynamics. Examining how dancing bodies use performance to articulate ambivalent responses to bodily rhetoric ranging from mimicry to migrancy to minoritization, I demonstrate how euphemisms enable a fuller picture of dancers' experiences.

Unlike other forms of dance like ballet, modern, and folk, hip-hop and street dance have had a complicated history of class prejudice. In the Philippines in 2011, while hip-hop dance was featured in a couple of mainstream television programs, many of my interviewees recounted a general disdain that the broader society had for hip-hop and street dance, calling it *jologs* [pejorative for lower class] or *patapon* [trash-like] and dancers repeatedly relayed their treatment as second-class artists without labor rights.[110] While many universities have street dance organizations, dancers may face disapproval at home, for example, leading one collegiate dancer to resort to *takas* [sneaking out] in order to make rehearsal. Mindfulness about choreographic choices helps reveal how dancers respond to their simultaneous institutional inclusion and exclusion. Moreover, choreographic emphasis may also explain artistry that is often woefully derided as routines or predetermined sequences of physical gesture, a consequence of the prevalent notion that hip-hop's direct message is its only message. As such, my purpose in highlighting the performative euphemism is to problematize these misperceptions of hip-hop dance and the predominance of literary and textual analysis in hip-hop studies by emphasizing the relationship between performativity and contemporary modes of oppression and ***** out a space to imagine alternatives.

While euphemism might have a negative connotation, as in acts of censorship, it can be a generative concept regarding performance because it sheds new critical light on cultural expressions that play with bodily expectations in the hour of their cooptation. Similar to the way that precisely through kneeling rather than standing up, Colin Kaepernick, U.S. professional football athlete, challenged normative upright patriotism and protested against the institutional and everyday violence of anti-Black racism, the euphemism can work performatively within the oppressor's domain by drawing attention to a subject anew.[111] Euphemism in expressive culture is not merely a cultural borrowing; rather, euphemism responds to normative cultural expectations, like the replacement of traditional Filipina dancing with bgirling, krump, and swag dance, or male-dominated street dance forms in Chelo A's "Pinays Rise" (see Conclusion).[112] Albeit less direct than Kaepernick's actions, this type of euphemism responds to corporeal and thus biological determinism, and effectively produces legibility for marginalized subjects through racial adjacency.

In *Choreographing in Color*, I show how individuals cultivate figures of euphemism in the cultural imaginary as types of corporeal orature that similarly recode the violent and traumatic realities of anti-Filipino racism, sexism, and neocolonial inequity, but also fall short of moving outside the code. I trace the outlines of performative euphemisms that help individuals unlearn the normative expectations placed upon Filipinoness, as well as hold space to critique how Filipino and hip-hop nationalisms have been used to justify other modes of oppression. In this book, dancers perform as zombies, heroes, and robots as euphemisms for Filipino subjecthood in ways that both affirm and remake social worlds inscribed by colonial and neoliberal structural inequities. I find utility in the metaphorical power of euphemisms to articulate the copresence of Brown subjectivity with non-Brown Others. Unlike appropriation, which usually implies a ruling-class actor borrowing from minoritarian culture, euphemism enables an articulation of the theories generated by actors in which social relations are less clear, thereby spelling out the limitations and possibilities of hip-hop as a strategy for racial, gender, and sovereign recognition.[113]

Performance studies scholar E. Patrick Johnson brilliantly deconstructs discourses of Black authenticity when discussing a South Asian performance of Blackness: "Those two racial identity tropes collide in the moment of performance when self and Other call attention to the dissonance registered in their copresence as well as the communion exalted in the face of real difference."[114] While Johnson observes how his own Black body authorizes a "problematic 'authentic' reading and performance of blackness of texts," the performance of "black" texts by non-Black Filipino bodies gives rise to an ambivalent discursive space. Such space ranges from criticism of appropriation and extraction to complicity in U.S. imperial desire and fantasy that reproduces the Philippines and its people as "foreign in a domestic sense."[115]

The ambiguous language of Filipino corporeality finds one of its roots in the Insular Cases of 1901, a set of U.S. Supreme Court rulings that provided the legal infrastructure for the ways that the Constitution did not necessarily apply to indigenous peoples inhabiting newly "acquired" territories, like Hawai'i, Puerto Rico, Guam, and the Philippines.[116] In a dissenting opinion to *Downes v. Bidwell*, the most important of the Insular Cases, Justice Fuller characterized the majority ruling as such: ". . . Congress has the power to keep [a settled province of another sovereignty] like a disembodied shade, in an intermediate state of ambiguous existence for an indefinite period; and, more than that, that after it has been called from that limbo, commerce with it is absolutely to the will of Congress, irrespective of constitutional provisions."[117] Thus, to understand hip-hop in postcolonial contexts we must recognize how American empire, with roots in Insular Case doctrine, established a conceptual language of disavowal and deference, statelessness and incorporation, disembodiment and *shade*, each of which are underwritten by issues of managing a dual hunger for economic expansion and democracy. Further illustrating the entwined histories of Filipino and Black peoples is the ironic way that the Supreme Court majority in the Insular Cases deployed the 13th amendment to establish American colonial governance. Returning again to *Downes v. Bidwell*, the majority opinion used the amendment which had abolished slavery and involuntary servitude "within the United States, or in any place subject to their jurisdiction," to configure indigenous inhabitants as unequal, so-called alien races outside of civilization defined by Anglo-Saxon principles. This shaped a view of the territories inhabited by indigenous peoples as both outside the United States in terms of some constitutional provisions (like the prohibition of taxation of imports and exports between states) and inside the United States authority in others. Accordingly, the Insular Case doctrine, which has yet to be repealed, identified Congress with the power to determine whether such territories will be conferred statehood, relinquished, or otherwise.[118] Acknowledging the historical and contemporary contradictions within the constitutional rendering of indigenous peoples of U.S. territories and formerly enslaved peoples encourages a deeper conversation around the naturalization of Black social dance and "freedom."[119]

This conversation converges with those around José Esteban Muñoz's disidentification, or how minoritarian performers transform identity in relationship to mainstream culture in ways irreducible to assimilation or resistance. Similarly, subjects who perform hip-hop dance and street dance in this book reanimate the contradictions of the Insular Case doctrine and the multidirectional relations between Filipinoness and Blackness. Consequently, Brown dancers can lead to a deeper appreciation and intersectional understanding of the story of global hip-hop and street dance.[120]

Through multi-sited ethnography, I highlight the deep roots of performative euphemism to see anew the complicated and vexed cultural relations between Asian Americans and African Americans, variably described as Afro-Asian connections, Afro-Asian encounters, and Afro Orientalism.[121] Complementing influential works by Cathy Schlund-Vials, Sunaina Maira, and Nitasha Sharma on the experiences of Cambodian and South Asian Americans, this book centers a corporeal orature often absent from Afro-Asian cultural studies of hip-hop.[122] The book adopts a decolonial methodology of connecting by affirming continuities between folks, performances, and issues in the contexts of a community situated across Manila, Cebu, Tokyo, Los Angeles, Berkeley, Las Vegas, and the Filipino diaspora in the late twentieth and early twenty-first centuries. In so doing, my work expands upon existing studies by Oliver Wang, Anthony Kwame-Harrison, Antonio Tiongson, Mark R. Villegas, Kuttin Kandi, and Roderick N. Labrador and others who have shed light on the musical artistry of Filipino-Americans in U.S.-based hip-hop culture.[123] As a result of multiple acts of violence including colonial wars, foreign occupations, historical erasure, and contemporary dehumanization, the Philippines and its people are often rendered illegible, creating a condition for them to be read through more readily available, albeit foreign and potentially neocolonial, racial frameworks.

As evidenced by the 2018 controversy surrounding Issa Rae's *The Misadventures of Awkward Black Girl* (2015), Filipinos are substituted for and deployed as having metonymical, lateral cultural and social relationships to Black Americans, or "the Blacks of Asians."[124] In one sense, this reifies a critique of Black singularity and commensurability. In another sense, euphemism reveals how the dominant paradigm of white supremacy built upon U.S. exceptionalist racial logic reconstitutes itself. Ethnography allows me access to how these dancers navigate this logic in their artistry, what the dance means to them, and how it relates to their specific cultural, social, economic, and political contexts. As part of understanding what is meaningful in the form, I conducted over eighty open-ended and in-depth interviews with key dancers, choreographers, and judges. I observed live and recorded hip-hop performances and judged competitions. To highlight lived experiences of dancers in the Philippines and Filipino diaspora, I analyzed a varied archive including Philippine governmental records on labor migration, U.S. visa statistics and affirmative action policies, and hip-hop competition judging standards.

While I framed my excavation of performative euphemism with ethnography, a second component involved channeling energies toward choreographic analysis of dance. In Deirdre Sklar's "Five Premises for a Culturally Sensitive Approach to Dance," she writes, "Movement is always an immediate corporeal experience. Although one must resort to words to understand the symbolic meaning of movement, talking cannot reveal what is known through the media of movement. The cultural knowledge that is embodied in movement can only be known via movement."[125] This particular attention, which further explains the absence of dance from hip-hop studies, found resonance with the notion of taking dance seriously, or as one of my dance collaborators, Leo, described, "doing justice to the dance."[126] Thus, this book reflects my decision to continue training in the movement practices that I had performed since I competed nationally in high school street dance competitions in the late 1990s, but also my decision to attend to their corporeal oratures.[127] Inspired by Susan Leigh Foster's field-defining research, I lean on "reading dance" as method—visibilizing the role of the camera, discerning decisions by choreographers, analyzing movement sequences, and comparing judging criteria over time—partly because I seek to comprehend the ways hip-hop dances not only refer to the world but also reflect their own internal logic—an enlivening part of dance discourse.[128] Foster's work—and subsequent studies that employ choreography as a primary analytical method to investigate identity—have strengthened my decision to think about the ways Filipino and Black signifiers operate in these distinct "movement environments," to borrow a term from Cynthia Novack.[129] While much of hip-hop studies relies on literary and visual analysis to make moral and artistic legitimacy claims, much of Asian American dance studies' legitimacy has centered on particular modes of embodied knowledge—contemporary and folk forms in concert contexts. Thus, my attention to multimodal performance expands these fields by providing innovative vistas into the internal discourse, or means of production for racial knowledge and aesthetic theories practitioners generate.

The intellectual trajectory of this book stems in part from the movement environment of street dance competitions, when our crew of mostly Filipino dancers from Mira Mesa—a suburb of San Diego, California, often called "Manila Mesa" for its large Filipino presence—sustained a yearly rivalry with another team of mostly Filipino dancers from Oxnard. In graduate school, I had the opportunity to explore street dance competitions in the Philippines, but my accidental *balikbayan* [returnee] status often led me to question whether it was really my story to tell. On the one hand, one local popular artist who snidely quipped at me, "So what are you, like, searching for your roots?"[130] On the other hand, white academic colleagues were received by *kababayan* [fellow Filipinos] with red-carpet offers to chauffeur them to interviews and explain local social phenomena step-by-step. These divergent interactions reflected a frequently imposed suspicion around Filipino physical and social mobilities and tested my commitment to the dance community, as I sought to understand the ways the neocolonial, feminized labor of dance in the masculinist context of hip-hop articulates its story and values on the dance floor.

Dancing the Color Line

Choreographing in Color traces the Filipino dancer's ascent to global phenomenon status in the last fifty years. In order to understand the social and political conditions that gave rise to this ongoing event, I illuminate questions on the political efficacy of performance. The book's arc bends across the time period when both Blackness and Filipino expressivity became increasingly enfolded into neoliberal capitalism—prisoner rehabilitation via commodification, Philippine state-brokered migration, U.S. divestment in public education, and the naturalization of dancers of color as cheap, unskilled labor. Rather than focus on any single individual "great" artist or dance genre and risk treading the modernist and territorial waters of origin-making, I draw inspiration from Susan Foster's multi-vocality, Thomas DeFrantz's use of the break, and Randy Martin's "organizational force." Each allows dance to take the lead of their writing bodies, and then choreograph writing in ways that radically alter traditional academic research with formal aesthetic elements and internal logic of the dance.[131] Thus, I animate each chapter with a dance style or two—pop dance, bgirling, popping, competition choreography— each with its own flavor profile. For example, in Chapter 1, I deploy movement descriptions of the "Thriller" dance's main sections to provide entryways into the types of analyses each choreographic portion produces. Across these typically disconnected sites and styles, I trace the outlines of performative euphemisms—zombies, heroes, robots, and judges—that debunk the stereotypes of Filipinos as mimetic, exceptional, foreign, natural, and subservient. In the process, I offer a new language to critically understand the art and global labor of dancers of color.

In Chapter 1, "Zombies and Prisoner Rehabilitation," I address the contradictions involved when Filipinos shift from an invisible minority to a global dance phenomenon. In 2007, 1,500 inmates in the Cebu Provincial Detention and Rehabilitation Center (CPDRC) went viral with their online rendition of Michael Jackson's music video "Thriller." Representing an exercise program aimed at building teamwork and reducing gang activity through dance, the CPDRC version circulated as performance-based proof of prisoner rehabilitation. This chapter argues that central to the production's worldwide popularity are narratives of discipline, colonial choreography, and the queerness of Wenjiel Resane, the leading lady. By situating these components in relation to the African American original, the actions of the prison administrators, and ideologies of Filipino mimicry, this chapter examines how choreographic practices fundamentally influence the social construction of Otherness in the YouTube era.

The next three chapters suggest ways artists address the naturalization of the Filipino body, like that reflected in responses to the CPDRC "Thriller." In the summer of 2009, when I first began immersing myself in the hip-hop scene in the Philippines (and returning in 2011, 2015, and 2017), one of the most unexpected obstacles was the repeated emigration of key collaborators. In Chapter 2, "Heroes and Filipino Migrations," I address that predicament by challenging the existing conversations around global hip-hop that often assume a stable field site and reify an exceptionalist and clear divide between the United States and the rest.[132] By instead exploring the surprising gender and racial divisions of Filipino labor migration, I show how proximity to Blackness—in two figurations, Overseas Filipino Workers (OFW) and Petisyonados—connects economic, cultural, and personal rationales. OFW is a governmental grouping for labor migrants that usually includes musicians, singers, circus performers, and unspecified performing artists. Petisyonado is my term for a Filipino migrant who moves abroad through family sponsorship or petition.[133] These examples illustrate how working- and middle-class Filipinos occupied a space between the demands for "desirable" and "cheap labor" by Japan and emergent Asian economies, even as they faced the racial sexual exclusivity of the market for dance in the Global North. By revealing collaborators' ambivalent responses to these competing forces, the chapter complicates the Filipino migrant hero trope and Filipino "talent" exceptionalism.

At the University of California–Berkeley, I choreographed hip-hop in local student organizations and culture nights of the late 1990s and early 2000s. In Chapter 3, "Robots and Affirmative Choreographies," I dissect one of the dance theater productions I was a part of, *Home* (2000), as an entry point into the relationship between race-based admissions policies (affirmative action) and dance-based articulations of racial agency. Typically, these annual culture nights work to affirm a connection to the homeland through the performance of traditional folk forms. For *Home*, however, choreographers Garrick Macatangay and Sarah Escosa used hip-hop to construct a new narrative about identity and a critical relationship with the Philippines. While existing scholarship focuses on the "born again" mode of traditional folk dance within the culture night genre, my analysis centers on Filipinization of street dance styles (popping and robotic dancing); these elements exaggerate ideologies of multiculturalism and post-raciality in an innovative response to Filipino diasporic cultural aphasia, or the forgetting of the Philippine-American War and its aftermath. *Home* emphasizes the ambivalence of performative euphemisms. The substitution of Philippine folk dance with hip-hop resisted nostalgicizing the homeland, but reaffirmed the genre of culture nights and ultimately failed to sustain the departure from folk dance in post-*Home* Pilipino culture nights (PCNs).

If embodied critiques against liberal multiculturalism are within the realms of possibilities in the localized genre of PCNs, what criticism is achievable on the common grounds of international competitive dance? In Chapter 4, "Judges and International Competitions," I turn to judges and their increasing role in rejuvenating and circulating street dance globally. While some lament the death of American dance criticism, in this chapter I argue that dance criticism is far from "endangered" but rather thrives in adjudication. I draw from my experiences training in judging at the self-proclaimed "Olympics" of hip-hop from 2012 to 2014 to attend to the indirect ways that performance enables critical commentary, even though standardization euphemizes racial, gender, ethnic, and technical difference. The role of judging and standardization reflects a desire to elevate the global image of hip-hop dancers that echoes aforementioned Marcos-era neoliberal structural adjustments that endeavored to elevate Filipinos with the deployment of technical solutions to political problems. Even though judging communicates hip-hop dance and its values to new audiences and provides dancers with a platform for new forms of limited agency, it also elucidates the contradictions inherent in codifying multiple ethnic, indigenous, and gendered practices similarly amidst a vexed desire for hip-hop universalism.

In the Conclusion, "Hip-Hop Ambassadors and Conventions," I return to the diplomatic convention "America in 3D" (2011). I argue for more engagement between Black feminist theory and Filipina performances, like "Pinays Rise," a dance within the convention that challenged gender and class stereotypes of Filipinas as subservient wives. I also draw from stereoscopy, or the depth-enhancing imaging technique, to address the potential uses for performative euphemism in academic studies of culture and race.[134] Finally, I call for a holistic, intersectional approach to hip-hop that reckons with discourses of Filipino cultural politics and dance. As a person whose naturalization was, in part, a product of the U.S. Navy's neocolonial recruitment practices by which Filipinos like my father were limited to performing domestic work for white officers, this book is about how understanding postcolonial corporealities can speak to violent historical and contemporary asymmetries on the global dance floor.[135]

The limits of this book, which vary between those directly related to a lack of resources or access and the necessary borders drawn to maintain focus on the subject of my argument, point to future areas of study. Dance is not the only way Filipinos convey ideas about and produce culture, just as the sites of this study are not the only places where Filipinos dance. For example, there are hip-hop dance communities in Mindanao and Cebu that have varied histories of development and there is a story to be told about Filipino endeavors in hip-hop's other elements—like Filipino emcees like Francis Magalona and graffiti artists (writers) like Mike Dream.[136]

In 2016, I delivered a lecture at another convention in Manila, but of a different sort. This time it was not organized by the U.S. State Department, but by the extraordinarily funky dance community leader, Mary Chris "Mycs" Villoso, and LSDC Street, the official street dance company of De La Salle University, Manila. The Hip-Hop Dance Convention (HHDC), included dance workshops by the Kinjaz (U.S.-based Mike Fallorina, Ben Chung, and Vinh Nguyen), a film screening by Style Dance Industry's Ricky Carranza (Finland), an open forum by pioneers like Lema Diaz (Philippine Allstars) and Arnel Calvario (Kaba Modern–U.S.), a battle, and delegates from Filipino dance communities outside of Metro Manila like Bryan Grandeza (Groove Unlimited) from Mindanao, or the Philippine's southern region, and Step Bebe (God of Styles) from the Visayas, or the Philippine's central region.

This book bridges the experiences between both of these conventions—the "rubber-stamped" and the native-grown—by asserting the need for a critical examination of the colonial and neoliberal mechanisms framing Filipino engagement in Black dance. Similar to these two conventions, "America in 3D" and HHDC, *Choreographing in Color* immerses the reader in the political messages of cultural performance, between the ordinary, the exceptional, and the world-making practices of choreographers over the last fifty years.

1

Zombies and Prisoner Rehabilitation

On July 17, 2007, 1,500 inmates in the Cebu Provincial Detention and Rehabilitation Center (CPDRC) performed their rendition of Michael Jackson's "Thriller" music video.[1] The CPDRC's "Thriller" represents an exercise program initiated to build teamwork and reduce gang activity through dance. A local choreographer taught inmates American pop cultural works like those of Jackson, the Village People, and Souljah Boy, and the CPDRC used recorded performances to project an image of its program to YouTube audiences. Of all the performances, "Thriller" is the most well-known. First uploaded to the user-generated website by CPDRC administrators, "Thriller" has amassed a view count of more than 59 million, making it once the third-most favorite video of all time.[2] What precisely made the "Thriller" video so immensely appealing? What does it mean to choreograph discipline onto "deviant" Filipino bodies through Blackness and African American popular culture?

I respond to these questions by building from the history of complex racialization I laid out in the "Introduction," and examining the Filipino dancing bodies and figuration of the zombie in CPDRC's "Thriller" in order to grapple with the contradictory notion of Filipinos' simultaneous global recognition and indiscernibility. CPDRC's "Thriller" locates the global gaze on the incarcerated Filipino body, in relationship to Michael Jackson's "Thriller" music video, and euphemizes the colonial conditions that would otherwise overdetermine its ability to produce meaning. The CPDRC "Thriller" reflects the use of mainstream Black popular culture with aims at reducing gang violence and promoting discipline. This dance, however, discourages critical cultural engagement, configures the politics of sexuality and mimicry in new ways, and effectively extends racial and colonial inequalities.

This chapter introduces the dominant narrative of discipline surrounding the "Thriller" phenomenon through a consideration of the camera's role and the actions of prison administrators in relation to Michel Foucault's analysis of the modern prison, how "Thriller" intends to discipline prisoners, and how it convinces global audiences of its efficacy. Situating "Thriller" in

Choreographing in Color. J. Lorenzo Perillo, Oxford University Press (2020). © Oxford University Press.
DOI: 10.1093/oso/9780190054274.001.0001

a broader context of U.S.-Philippine neocolonial discourse enables an exploration of the dominant paradigm of dance in the Philippines and the cultural politics of Filipino mimicry, thus revealing how "Thriller's" popularity relies on misinterpretations of the Filipino dancing bodies in the video that betray its internal logic. Taking dance as an agentive strategy for individuals to rework power, opens up space to consider "Thriller" from the perspective of Wenjiel Resane, a gender fluid member of the dance, and examine how representations of sexuality complicate and even challenge viewers' reception of the performance.[3] By placing these interrelated media in tension with one another, the viral currency of the CPDRC's "Thriller"—and the Filipino dancing body as a global dance phenomenon more broadly—becomes clear. Central to "Thriller's" virality is a belief in the disciplinary powers of dance, the U.S.-Philippine neocolonial relationship, familiarity with and confirmation of stereotypes about Filipino mimicry, and pleasure in the consumption of modernist, sexual, penal bodily tropes and the potential that the inmates might subvert them. "Thriller" must be understood in relationship to its longer history of racialization, which reveals the colonial unconscious behind audiences' reactions and the roles that dance plays—as discipline, choreography, and mimicry—not in the valorization of a primordial precolonial identity but the cross-racial construction of postcolonial performance in the central Philippines. The zombies in CPDRC's "Thriller" euphemistically render the neocolonial and market-oriented structures enabling Black popular culture as a vehicle for communicating across the borders between the incarcerated and nonincarcerated.

Black Dance as Discipline

Backs facing the camera, Crisanto Nierre and Wenjiel Resane leisurely stroll until they are caught off-guard and surrounded by zombies in uniform orange jumpsuits. The mass of undead lurches toward them. Playing the role of Michael Jackson, Nierre wears an orange outfit while Resane is marked sartorially, choreographically, and spatially as the exception. As the zombies converge, Resane realizes their condition is contagious. Nierre has become a zombie as well, imitating their unsteady physicality and twitching his neck to the right as the beat progresses. Meanwhile, the camera figures this action within a vast prison courtyard bordered by a fenced "mezzanine" .

The opening scenes of the "Thriller" performance transport audiences into a story about the living interrupted by the undead, order threatened by disorder, all contained within the perimeters of the prison courtyard (see Figure 1.1). This narrative encourages the idea that the exercise program represented by "Thriller" is in control of the inmates, and thus, physical fitness is a euphemism for the carceral. CPDRC security consultant Byron Garcia confirmed his disciplinary intentions for the dance when he stated: "By music we can communicate more to the inmates, . . . penetrate their psyche, . . . using music. The end goal would be discipline. We have to achieve discipline. Three years ago these inmates were very unruly."[4] According to many of "Thriller's" over 85,000 online comments, audiences see the prisoners' dancing as an effective argument for discipline and consequently believe that the CPDRC's use of dance as "rehabilitative" labor works.[5] For instance, YouTube user tomaspinpin states that "it's true that they are all diciplined [sic], it's not easy to have a great performance like that!"[6] To understand just how the performance persuasively convinces viewers like tomaspinpin and to parse its immense global spotlight, we can juxtapose the narrative of discipline that emerges from Jackson's "Thriller" music video with Foucault's theory on discipline and the actions of the prison administrators.

Figure 1.1 CPDRC "Thriller," performed by Crisanto Nierre and Wenjiel Resane, screen still. The dance ties prisoner rehabilitation to public desire for the dancers' productivity as narratives of redemption and virtual commodities.

Jackson's "Thriller" (1983) was choreographed by the award-winning Michael Peters, also known as "the Balanchine of MTV."[7] Alongside Michael Jackson's prior music videos "Billie Jean" (1982) and "Beat It" (1982), his "Thriller" signaled a racial breakthrough.[8] These videos announced the shifting commercial viability of Blackness in an emerging media format and Jackson's global impact. The ambitious big-budget original winked at the classic American horror-film genre, featuring a heterosexual romantic courtship, alternation between fantasy and reality, and a damsel-in-distress plot. Modern mythic figures of Afro-Haitian religious zonbi origins were domesticated by synchronized dance and unspecified period dress, and Jackson portrayed a character who was part-hero, part-villain.[9] While Jackson did not save the "stock" female object of desire, he awakened her from the supposed zombie nightmare and, in an aside to the audience, revealed his were-cat nature. Jackson's character underwent continual transformations that, while correlating to his resistance to reduction to any single musical genre, also ultimately failed to challenge the stereotype that within every proper African American man was a sexual aggressor. These details about Jackson's "Thriller"—a racialized, ethnic, and gendered African American cultural work—reveal the irony of restaging that dance with an incarcerated cast for a global audience. In the CPDRC's version, as nameless inmates stagger toward the happy couple and Nierre betrays Resane, the dance maintains a subtext of amoral zombie behavior that it can both exploit and distance itself as a disciplinary tool.[10] Jackson's "Thriller" dance reworked the negative image of African American male heterosexuality into something more palatable and non-threatening to mainstream white MTV audiences, and the CPDRC's performance reworks that choreography to ostensibly reduce gang violence and persuade global viewers into believing that prisoners are disciplined by the power/knowledge of dance.

In line with Foucault's analysis of modern penology, rather than punishing the criminal's corporal body, the CPDRC replaces bodily pain with three- to four-hour daily performance rehearsals, and redistributes public responsibility online to discursively re-inscribe and bring offenders to justice.[11] The CPDRC dance rehabilitation program is a "technology" of power according to Foucaultian principles of visual spatialization (panoptic), temporal control (timetables), repetitive exercises, detailed hierarchies, and normalizing judgment. We can appreciate, for instance, how the panoptic, or the coercive inter-subject regulation aided by visual and architectural contexts, provides a way to unpack the CPDRC camera's role in the metaphorical and literal framing of the performance. Unlike Jackson's "Thriller," the camera for the CPDRC "Thriller" maintains a high angle position at the second floor of the prison courtyard and establishes a sense of objectification that reaffirms the viewer's superior position over the inmates. The CPDRC's lens uses mostly wide shots and establishes itself as the authoritative gaze, the social and political agent above and apart from the objectified inmates. While reifying this division and reinforcing it as the ontological border, the camera invites spectators, presumably law-abiding, nonimprisoned, conscious bodies, to assume this position of security and look down on the inmates as well. Garcia explains how looking down on the courtyard actually inspired him to initiate the exercise program: "One day, I saw these waves of orange people (in the exercise yard). I thought it looked very nice."[12] The fact that the inmates' moving image, rather than their health or social needs, instigated the dance rehabilitation program raises important questions. Was the notion of remedying gang violence, believed to result when opposing groups work together for a common goal in dance, at the heart of the program's origin? Or was it a rationale that was later added? How can the uniform prescription of dance adequately treat the needs of a variety of individuals with different charges ranging from theft to sexual assault to homicide?[13] These questions are left unanswered as the camera situates viewers closer to guards than prisoners, acting as an accomplice to the panoptic ways by which spectators view the inmates, to help "Thriller" appear like an effective disciplinary tool.

For some, the CPDRC "Thriller" did not convey prisoner reform, but, rather, inspired questions of abuse.[14] The human rights advocacy group Karapatan, for example, has condemned the prison for exploitation of prisoners. The inmates' worldwide fame and their precision movements have influenced administrators to host exhibitions and open the prison for bimonthly performances, in which donations are collected and deposited into individual inmate "prison passbook account[s]."[15] This popularity has also obfuscated more recent allegations regarding the mishandling of donations.[16] While the gaze might promote passive consumption, the prison's role in the commodification of its inmates—their dance performances—has been anything but passive. Beyond uploading videos online of convicted criminals without their consent, the mass of dancers reportedly includes many suspected criminals still awaiting trial, raising questions about the protection of inmates' rights and privacy. By building a business model around the dance rehabilitation program, the prison has incentivized participation beyond its original claims of promoting teamwork and reducing gang violence and elided the pressing issues that surround the politics of Filipino representation and the global prison industrial complex.[17]

At the same time, the prison has established itself as the arbitrary judge regarding the worth of the prisoners' labor, as is evident in comparing "Thriller" with subsequent performances. Administrators jumped at the chance to have prisoners perform for Sony Pictures Productions and Jackson's choreographer, Travis Payne.[18] Despite the brokerage of the prisoners' labor to promote the commercial release of the Jackson documentary "This Is It," Garcia has said that "[a]greeing to the project has no money consideration because it's priceless. I mean, no money can buy the prestige."[19] Inmates were reported to have practiced all day and received snacks and a T-shirt for their efforts.[20] Strangely, Cebu governor Gwendolyn Garcia refused a 250,000 Philippine peso (PHP) offer (over U.S. $5,700) by Procter & Gamble to make a Mr. Clean commercial at the prison, reportedly stating that she does not want the inmates commercialized.[21] Finally, transportation for audiences from city hall enables continued public-relations exposure and facilitates solicitation of donations, T-shirt sales, and photo opportunities. Marrying everyday performance (Black dance, popular culture, viral videos) with state-based propaganda, brings in questions of visual, material, and affective relations in a different yet related way.[22] With proceeds going to "defray prison costs," the government and prison have created a dance-based internal economy that tied prisoners' conditions of incarceration to the productivity of their fame.[23]

The narrative of discipline incorporates inmates and audiences into a productivity chain linking the amelioration of racialized sexual threat, surveillance, and reintegration. "Thriller" ensures that inmates re-enter society, at least as commodities, and connects their emancipation to the pleasure they derive from celebrity and the global public's desire to see them "live" in confinement. The actions of the CPDRC and the local government abstract the reality of prison in ways that legitimate the spectacle of Otherness. For "Thriller," as long as the inmates are seen as Others becoming less "Othered"—anonymous bodies gaining prestige, invisible Filipinos granted visibility, unruly masses achieving order—viewers and dancers can believe, invest in, and get pleasure from the narrative of discipline, whatever the costs.

Choreographing Colonialisms

Nierre proceeds to lead a group of thirty. He creates an inverted
pyramid spatial formation with himself at the focal point. The rest
of the masses form two blocks of columns flanking both the left

and right sides of the central pyramid group and a few rows lining
the back wall of the courtyard. The zombies move and form geometric shapes in uniform precision as if to send a message of order
and efficiency to their audiences, the camera, and Resane. 1,500
orange jumpsuits move in unison, with identical movements.
Same directions. Same phrasing. The undead army claps. And
steps widely left. Heads dis-align from torsos. Necks shifting left
and right. Zombies advance in alternation. Same bodily moves.
Opposing lines. A strict routine. Arms raise. Hands are
grasping, legs raised. Right,
two, three. Right, two, three, left. Nierre drops down to
crouch on the floor. Line after line does
the same. Building, building,
it's one body now. It's like
"the wave."

While the initial segment sets up the video's panoptic framing, "Thriller"
articulates its disciplinary power in the central body of the performance
(see Figure 1.2). The preceding vignette describes how the orderly mass of
synchronistic dancing inmates embodies modern norms of collective ob-
jectivity, rationality, obedience, and civility. According to Foucault, discipline produces subjected and practiced bodies through a micro-physics of
power, a correlation between the body and gestures, such that "a disciplined
body is the prerequisite of an efficient gesture."[24] But lest we conceive of "gesture" as universal, we must grapple with how values get specifically articulated in the inmates' precision dancing. To do so, we need to understand the
deep-seated colonial contexts of dance in the Philippines, a former Spanish
and U.S. colony—a necessity to situate "Thriller" and the Filipino dancing
body within a particular knowledge/power system. Afro-Caribbean religion
scholar, Elizabeth McAlister explains, "White Americans became fascinated
with zombie mythology and reproduced it in writings on Haiti during the
Marine Occupation between 1915 and 1934, usually overlooking its ob-
vious articulations with slavery, capitalism, and political control. Instead
the zombie myth authorized military intervention."[25] This system not only
influences the martial choreography, look, feel, function, and meaning
of "Thriller," but also directs the types of power that one engages with gesture as a material of intercultural performance.[26] Choreography, as both
a movement-based "text" and concept of an unspoken "tradition of codes

Figure 1.2 CPDRC "Thriller" central dance, screen still. The central dance section features the iconic claw sequence, inverted pyramid, and movement qualities as evidence of social discipline.

and conventions through which meaning is constructed in dance," produces and reproduces colonialism.[27] Following McAlister's work, two elements of "Thriller's" choreography in particular help shed light on the continuities between the U.S. occupation of Haiti and the Filipino neocolonial condition, beyond the throwback to the "human zoo" or Philippine Exhibition at the 1904 St. Louis World's Fair (see Introduction).[28] The dance's technical aspects and the stereotypes about mimicry surrounding "Thriller's" reception provide a window into how its choreography constitutes modernity, naturalizes empire, and reinforces limited cultural engagement.[29]

"Thriller's" movement quality, tactility, spatiality, and signification are vital for understanding the performance's bodily rhetoric as one that enacts modernity and the neocolonial body politic. In the post-U.S. colony of the Philippines, individuals have syncretized European, American, and Southeast Asian cultural practices with a multitude of indigenous cultures that hold contemporary postcolonial consequences for how individuals consciously and unconsciously understand dance performance. During the U.S. colonial period, Filipinos sought to preserve indigenous, pre-Hispanic,

and European cultural practices that proved the archipelago deserved recognition as a modern nation. Whereas natives were excluded from public
education during the Spanish colonial period, under U.S. rule, public schools
were accessible to most of the population and educators used them as a site
for dance preservation. The U.S. colonial origins of public education manifest contemporarily in the ways that Filipino folk dances, inclusive some
Spanish colonial and American social forms, are taught in the public school
physical education curriculum and contribute to the CPDRC program's design, choreography, and reception.

According to dance scholar Basilio Esteban Villaruz, physical education
reigns as the dominant paradigm of dance education in the Philippines,
heavily influencing dance's contemporary treatment, proscenium orientation, marginalization, and simplistic instruction.[30] The notion that dance
pedagogy rarely focuses on the sociopolitical and creative processes of dance
is a neocolonial bodily politic reflected in the technicality of "Thriller's" central dance segment. While Jackson's "Thriller" cast consisted of about thirty
dancers, the CPDRC's use of over a thousand dancers amplifies the original choreography into a type of calisthenic exercise.[31] The video frames the
dance as an act of reiteration, rather than a one-time flash mob, by supplying
the initial title "CPDRC inmates practice." The all-male group forms large
geometric shapes, almost never coming into physical contact with one another and thus asserting a type of desexualized masculinity that sharply
contrasts the narrative portions of the dance. Rarely facing any direction except forward, the cast seems entirely presentational and foregrounds their
arms, as in the iconic "claw" sequence, to demonstrate physical ability rather
than develop an artistic concept. The physical-fitness aura placed upon uniform zombie movement also removes the theatrical possibilities of horror,
irony, camp, and deadpan that are conventionally associated with zombies in
U.S. popular culture.

While the specifically linear, functional, and orderly traits of the dance
inscribe the prisoners' performance with modern rational qualities, these
traits seem to stand in opposition to the essentials of art-based criminal rehabilitation elsewhere in the world.[32] Michael Balfour, former director of
the Theatre in Prisons and Probation (TIPP) Centre in the United Kingdom,
writes that rehabilitation programs must "deal with an offender's belief systems and the interpretive frameworks by which they 'make sense' out of sen-
sory perception and direct their behaviour."[33] There is no evidence in the
existing discourse of ways in which the CPDRC helps inmates to "recognize

and change certain self-images, attitudes and beliefs."[34] In "Thriller," the top-down choreographer-dancer dynamic, regimented march, pyramid spatial formation, and homogenous orange jumpsuits place more value upon group conformity than individual development and growth. In this way, the performance misleads viewers by blurring distinctions between two types of discipline: the physical discipline developed from dance, a staple of modern physical education in the Philippines; and the social discipline developed out of grappling with individual criminal offenses.

Discipline through dance and mimicry are not the same thing, but interrelated. While, in one sense, the choreography of the Filipino neocolonial condition helps us understand the misinterpretation of the technical aspects of this individual dance, the second dimension of that choreography takes us in a completely different direction and helps us to see how many misunderstand Filipino mimetic practices. Whether deployed with a laudatory, derogatory, or matter-of-fact tone, observations on Filipino popular culture in the late twentieth and early twenty-first centuries have often asserted what I call the "Filipino mimicry" stereotype. Composed of two related notions, the stereotype holds that Filipinos are both virtuoso mimics—usually of U.S. culture—and that they are adept singers and dancers. Writing about popular culture during martial law in 1988, travel writer Pico Iyer described popular culture, music, and dance as the core of Filipino culture with the inaccurate presumption that Filipino modernity is only "Born in the U.S.A."[35] In his saccharine account of "smiles amidst squalor," Iyer proclaims that Filipinos produce good music because it is related to their natural hospitality, happy disposition, and friendliness. He states that "[m]aster of every American gesture, conversant with every Western song, polished and ebullient all at once, the Filipino plays minstrel to the entire continent."[36] Essentialist cultural accounts like this one persist in everyday discourse, promulgated by non-Filipinos and Filipinos alike, and unsurprisingly, such comments are congruent with responses to "Thriller." In the virtual comments on the YouTube video, diasporic viewers often invoke the Filipino mimicry stereotype to place themselves "inside" Filipino culture, expressing their belonging through self-identification, use of the Filipino language, and references to other Filipino popular-culture figures.[37]

The Filipino mimicry stereotype exemplifies how audiences situate "Thriller" in local cultural practices and provides a rationale, albeit unspecific, for the dancing that sounds something like "Filipinos dance in prison because they are Filipino." For example, in an article on the controversy over the inclusion of the inmates in Sinulog—a traditional Cebuano festival and performance competition—reporter Clifford Coonan writes: "The Philippines is one of the most musical countries in the world: people walk around the streets singing happily in the normal course of the day, and Filipino bands are famous for their skill in mimicking top tunes."[38] The logic that singing and dancing are norms for Filipinos helps create an elated sense of collective identity for a multicultural archipelago that has survived centuries of psychologically fragmenting and violent colonialism. Conversely, the mimicry stereotype also works to normalize the dancing inmates in "Thriller" as essentially Filipino. By reaffirming how commonplace American culture fits onto Filipino bodies, the mimicry stereotype breathes new life into colonialism by asserting the ordinariness of empire and constructing Filipinos as essentially criminal.

The ordinariness of empire encourages an uncritical engagement with popular culture in subtle yet powerful ways. In "Thriller," dance as a Filipino norm informs both administrators' and viewers' defensive posture about the prison's dance program as morally permissible. Melita Thomeczeck, the Philippine Deputy Consul General in New York, states that "[t]he Filipinos love music and they love to sing and dance. Whatever they are in a natural way, they can continue that habit in prison."[39] Chief administrator Patrick Rubio of the Directorate for Operations of the Bureau of Jail Management and Penology in the Philippines sees participation as wholly voluntary. He says that "[i]t would be different if they are being forced to dance. . . . I've never known any prisoners being forced to dance. It's normal to dance."[40] As Rubio suggests, to be "forced to dance" would be morally wrong. Because the responsibility lies on proof of force, rather than, say, a comparison to the UN Standard Minimum Rules for the Treatment of Prisoners, the dance program, as represented by the physically able and ebullient bodies it foregrounds, appears morally permissible.

The meanings attributed to the central dance segment, the disciplinary powers it blurs, and the hegemonic forces it mobilizes are glossed over by the Filipino mimicry stereotype. Observations like those made by Iyer, Rubio, and Thomeczeck often fail to represent the complex picture of Philippine-U.S. relations. Aphorisms like "Filipinos love to sing and dance" deny the prospects of seeing performance as a political act; Filipino mimicry elides the different meanings dance has come to acquire amid colonial contexts and thereby inhibits a deeper cultural engagement with anything except the viewer's own pleasure, guilt, or defense. For "Thriller," the stereotype of Filipino mimicry provides audiences with a rationale to normalize the CPDRC's unusual image of happy prisoners. This naturalization also obfuscates the possibility in viewers' minds of any prisoner mistreatment, for as long as the dance does not appear to be forced, then the activities within the CPDRC appear "normal." In fact, the naturalization of song, dance, and mimicry for Filipinos helps reassure non-Filipino world-gazers that any surprise or unease they might feel upon viewing the inmates on display can be dismissed and attributed to their status as outsiders regarding Filipino norms.

As children of the 1980s and '90s, my sisters and I grew up admiring the gestural and vocal styling of Filipino entertainers like Lea Salonga and Deedee Magno, and imitating the high kicks and crows of Ernie Reyes Jr. and Dante Basco (who was also a b-boy in San Francisco). While they often danced, fought, acted, and sang as non-Filipino characters, Salonga, Magno, Reyes Jr., and Basco were still figures that animated a sense of diasporic belonging in myself and my sisters. It was this thirst for seeing ourselves represented and familiarity of Filipino ambiguity that informed my own subject position upon first viewing "Thriller." On the one hand, I was proud to see representation of folks systematically marginalized or de-Filipinized in Hollywood. On the other hand, as a non-incarcerated person I felt uncomfortable in how viewing the dance furthered the commodification of the incarcerated and provided advertisement revenue to Garcia.

"Thriller's" "micro-physics" of power and "efficient" gestures are dialectically related to the existing forces that have constituted gesticulation as a local and global system of signification of Filipino culture. The dominant paradigm of dance—physical education for constructing modernity—and the mimicry stereotype are but two facets of this larger, constantly changing system. Choreographing colonialism for "Thriller" involves generating dual misunderstandings about dance, concerning discipline and mimicry, that thereby fail to situate the performance within its specific historical and neocolonial context. While I have sketched the dangers of inattention to choreography in "Thriller," it remains an open question whether inmates will engage in dance pedagogy and practices that genuinely "deal with an offender's belief systems and the[ir] interpretive frameworks."[41] Assumptions about the crossing of dance and Filipino identity exacerbate the unrelenting colonial desire to consume Otherness, or as bell hooks popularized, a sexual desire for "eating the Other."[42] These assumptions shape this intercultural performance's ability to mediate non-Filipino spectators' anxiety about that colonial desire and revitalize the postcolonial subject's desire to be recognized and recognize themselves as a culturally rich people that share common performative traits.

Filipinizing "Thriller"

> Wenjiel Resane is the first figure that appears on screen, as they sway their hips in heels and bare their back; their light salmon halter-top has all but faded to pink. Resane's left arm swings slightly off pace with a catwalk-worthy syncopation while their right arm links with Crisanto Nierre. Nierre walks arm-in-arm with Resane although it seems unclear which one actually leads. Resane's steady pace seems to counterbalance if not ground the lightly skipping Nierre, that is, of course until their stroll is cut short. When the couple realizes they have been surrounded, Resane begins to back away from Nierre, exits the stage, and does not return until after the central dance. Resane's return as the central object, a damsel in distress, seems to cue the zombies to break out of their precision routine and back into their tottering selves with ghastly hands grasping at them. Overwhelmed and left with no room to escape, Resane collapses to the floor. The image fades to black in time with the chilling laughter of Vincent Price.

The precision, certitude, and familiarity of "Thriller's" central dance as "text" form a counterpoint to audience anxiety generated by the performance's multiple differences: namely, dance in prison, the Filipino as subject, and Wenjiel Resane as "leading lady."[43] The above description helps to bring into focus Resane as a keystone of the CPDRC's "Thriller." Thus far I have argued that a narrative of discipline and colonial choreography constitute "Thriller" as a proponent, rather than self-aware parody, of its own spectacled Otherness. When viewers simplify the mimetic aspects of "Thriller" as mastery of American gesture, the performers' experiences are abstracted, and their actual political circumstances overlooked.[44] For example, few media note how Resane maintains their innocence against a wrongful conviction.[45] For an understanding of Filipino mimesis beyond minstrelsy, I consider Resane, doubly mimetic as a Filipino and part of a sexual minority. They shine as the most featured dancer of the CPDRC video and its striking focal point in a sequence of violated expectations. "Thriller's" viral success is predicated upon audiences' interpreting Resane as a multiple non-normative body, seen as unruly in terms of legality, sexuality, and gender. At the same time, Resane participates in an imaginative performance that undermines Filipino struggles for social justice by distracting the global public from the harsh realities of the Philippine's political climate.

Existing discourse on mimetic colonial performance of sexual minorities in the Philippines tends to focus on *bakla*, a Tagalog term conventionally used to describe effeminate and cross-dressed males.[46] Bakla are often stereotyped as talented singing/dancing mimic masters and arbiters of beauty.[47] During her ethnographic research in Bicol Province (my paternal homeland), social anthropologist Fenella Cannell found that "the bakla in fact often seem to assimilate their identity to a language of visibility and hyper-visibility, frequently talking about their charismatic power to seduce as 'exposing ourselves.'"[48] At the same time, a minoritizing discourse often oppresses bakla as inferior or different from "real" men, and as dangerous, deviant sexual and gendered selves.[49] Social anthropologist Mark Johnson conducted a study focusing on Muslim Samar and Tausug communities in the southern Philippines and found that sexual minorities are devalued because they are seen as "persons who have been overwhelmed by a potent cultural Other, an alter-identity defined in terms of American style and the penetration of the Christian Philippine State."[50] For Johnson, this "penetration" has also been characterized as "overexposure" to Western and American-identified beauty ideals mediated by Christian Filipino culture.[51] In these studies, terms like "exposing ourselves" (agentive) and "over-exposure" (disciplinary) suggest a correlation between exclusion and the beauty and mimicry practices of sexual minorities in the Philippines. The perceived excessive nature of alterity for sexual minorities has a corresponding performance trait—maarte (over-acting). The maarte element lies at the center of "Thriller's" narrative segments in the colonial, subjective, sexual, and gender difference performed by Resane.

Resane's character represents a choreographic and symbolic difference vis-à-vis the ensemble of zombies that helps generate an oppositional tension to drive the initial narrative of the CPDRC's "Thriller." While Resane plays the role—the object of desire—originally performed by Playboy centerfold Ola Ray as the leading lady of Jackson's "Thriller," Resane's performance differs in the ways that they constitute a sexualized and gendered Other (see Figure 1.3 and 1.4). For the first portions of "Thriller," their gender and sexuality are constituted through their coupled dancing. The video obscures their image until the forty-four seconds mark. By that time, Resane's flash

Figure 1.3 and 1.4 Wenjiel Resane in CPDRC's "Thriller" and Ola Ray in Michael Jackson's "Thriller," screen stills. Resane is a keystone in the video's virality and representations of legality, sexuality, and gender.

of jewelry—earrings, bracelet, and ring—and ponytail have left the spotlight, and the army has begun its routine. As their physicality and costume announce their body as an ostensible gender and sexual minority, Resane also distinguishes their self from Jackson's "Thriller" in the attitude and tone they bring to the character. While adhering to the original's scripted fearful retreat from the zombies, Resane's mobilizes maarte aesthetics through facial expressions and glaring eyes that resolve the extremes of pleasure and refusal. They seem figuratively to reject the zombies' collective choreography, which acts as a military Reserve Officer Training Corps drill team display seeking to recruit them. What historian Paul Kramer calls a "martial script of assimilation" acts out here as a call to action or invitation for Resane to enlist and join the ranks of the orderly, obedient, homogenous, and masculine.[52]

It is by Resane's genuine exaggeration of Jackson's "Thriller," or maarte mimicry, that colonial difference emerges as a political practice of transformative self-making. In response to the zombies' choreographed martial orders, rather than mimic their precision-styled hand gestures and metered march, Resane responds by affirming their individuality in ways that are much subtler and nuanced when compared to the zombies' movements. Their intense gaze moves from zombie to zombie and singles them out; their quickened pace conveys urgency. Resane embodies a powerful femininity by splaying their fully extended fingers. They slip in small, over-the-top details that the original damsel in distress did not, such as laterally fanning their temples— a move that symbolically frames their mindful, individual persona. With this combination of actions, Resane asserts their personality (pagkatao) and beauty (byuti).[53] Replacing "myself" with "my beauty" in everyday conversations, sexual minorities in the Philippines often figure beauty centrally in the ways they think about subjecthood.[54] For Cannell, mimicry refers to the bakla skill of mediating American ideals of beauty and glamour upon themselves (beauty contests) and others (parlors and dressmaking)— namely, their ability to transform appearances. Resane's localization of the dance and their subjectivity, which is governed by ideals of beautiful exaggeration rather than precise execution, are aspects of maarte mimicry that help constitute "Thriller's" Otherness. Crucial to maarte mimicry is the notion that the feminine-presenting moving image of Resane disrupts audiences' commonly held views of "Thriller" as a tale of heterosexual libido and the prison as a same-sex space.

Resane's exceptionality alters the conventionally negative image of prison life into a happy Hollywood music video—not just any video, but the quintessential Hollywood music video. While in many ways Resane appears as a prime example of sexual minorities in the Philippines, translating between local and global and personifying colonial paradoxes, their performance holds different stakes, because this act of transformation occurs against the prevailing perceptions of prison life as defined by invisibility, isolation, and deindividuation.[55] Taken in the context of prisons, Resane's position in re-historicizing the imperial dialogue is complicated, as they state: "If I was not in prison, I would not be famous."[56] Clearly, they knowingly gain legibility and fame from the state's logic. Beyond that, moreover, Resane's positive reception by individuals expressing Filipino pride subverts conventionally conservative ties between nationalism and sexuality. Circumscribed by the material and choreographic resources available to them, Resane re-scripts state-determined conditions of time, space, and symbolic order through rehearsal and training.[57] Their skills at imitation happen not by way or reason of some innate, natural, or internal truth affiliated to their identity as a Filipino or sexual minority, but as a recuperative maneuver amid varied and multiple conditions shaping subordination.

At the same time, Resane's assertion of individuality, byuti, emotion, and femininity come at the price of glamorizing everyday prison life and euphemistically misleading viewers about the political climate in the Philippines. Historian Michael Salman, after researching prisons in the Philippines under U.S. imperial rule, revealed how colonial officials treated prisons like laboratories for the larger society, as penal approaches and techniques generated a "colonial carcereal continuum" beyond the prison.[58] Salman asserts that "precisely to this extent the colonial regime classified Filipinos generally as subjects needing 'tutelage'—a supervisory, reformative kind of incarceration under colonial rule."[59] This logic of "benevolent" dominance worked to undermine ongoing Filipino struggles for self-determination and "bandolerismo" (a penal category created by the colonial state to criminalize and devalue resistance).[60] In light of Salman's study, the indirect costs of Resane's fetishized, red-carpet culture of imprisonment, which are perhaps those most difficult to measure, are the ways CPDRC undermines contemporary struggles for decolonization and social justice. Karapatan, the same human rights nongovernmental organization that filed a brief against the CPDRC, concluded that 2006 was the worst year for human rights violations in the Philippines since the toppling of the Marcos dictatorship in 1986.[61] Karapatan also noted that 2007—the year "Thriller" debuted—was a time when state terror, impunity in human rights violations, and general lawlessness gripped the nation under President Gloria Macapagal-Arroyo. Political killings, forced disappearances, and long-standing efforts to achieve independence from the U.S. military in the Philippines are not just a backdrop, but also the stakes of "Thriller." These stakes have only risen under a "war on drugs" that has resulted in more than 6,000 people killed by police under the direction of populist President Rodrigo Duterte, who some have called the "Donald Trump of Asia."[62] By its ability to generate an ordinariness of empire and colonial spectacle of choreographed "discipline" and physical fitness that euphemizes grim and unjust realities of the carceral, "Thriller" and the Filipino mimicry stereotype globally threaten contemporary Philippine-U.S. anti-imperialist, counter-hegemonic, and radical politics.

CPDRC's "Thriller's" narrative ending, unlike Jackson's, works to direct audience responses through its balance between fantasy (zombies) and reality (prisoners). The sense of realism is reinforced by the prison's confined performance space, which inhibits the damsel's ability to find refuge in a home or awaken from the nightmare, as in Jackson's "Thriller." Instead, the cross-dressed Resane writhes against the concrete and concretized fantasy of homonormativity and heteropatriarchy that threatens to gangbang them into civility. Subjected to the ghastly, grasping hands of the "undead," Resane's character is left with no room to move. Instead of retreating to a domestic, private, putatively safe house, as in Jackson's "Thriller," their "fugitive" body is literally Othered and grounded, leading one viewer to comment: "At the end, I was like 'is this rape or murder?'"[63] Rather than offer a moral lesson about "curing" the Filipino neocolonial prisoner of her conditions of nonassimilability, in its porno-colonial rapture, the CPDRC's "Thriller" sidesteps that ending; instead, we see the orange-garbed bodies engulfing Resane's body, and the visual images implode and fade to black.[64] The ending seems to continue in a time and space beyond the dance, sharply contrasting with the frozen Cheshire-cat grin in Jackson's "Thriller" denouement, but to what end? CPDRC's "Thriller" ending hails us, the spectators, as the putative damsel—the only scripted conscious, sentient character—and implores us to question our complicity and positionality as spectators.[65]

Dancing Inmates Resurface

LOLA
When I was a boy they told me that I was a little too girly
And as girl I always knew
I always knew I was a little too . . . boy
I always knew that had I come in my very own flavor.

It's only now that I'm allowed to share my story with you
That I'm a sensation

LOLA, OO OO and NANA
And we are sensational

LOLA
A viral sensation![66]

In March 2012, the narrative of CPDRC resurfaced (like any good zombie thriller) when *Prison Dancer* debuted its first episode on YouTube.[67] Marking one of the most notable artistic responses to CPDRC's "Thriller," the 12-episode web series and self-proclaimed "Glee meets Miss Saigon," enlisted notable Filipino diasporic, Broadway, and YouTube celebrities based in Toronto, Canada, to portray fictionalized accounts of the famed dancing inmates.[68] With a script written by Romeo Candido and Carmen De Jesus, *Prison Dancer* introduced audiences to a retelling of the CPDRC inmates' rise to viral sensation. While maintaining the same platform for distribution, this Filipino diasporic version emphasized a closer look at how the dance rehabilitation program transformed the lives of four main characters—Lola, Shakespeare, Hookaps, and Christian. Through the lens of Matt Wells, Memehunter/Western investigative reporter, and prison surveillance footage, *Prison Dancer* offers a mockumentary, multimodal glimpse of their experiences starting with day one (Episode 2) in the Manila-based maximum security MMDC. The series' message, "Dancing is more than choreography, it's a way of life," echoes a claim that many hip-hop practitioners espouse to distinguish their art in the shadow of neoliberal capitalism and amplifies the CPDRC's "Thriller" in persuasive, albeit, problematic ways.

One of the striking features of *Prison Dancer* is its status as an artifact of "transmedia storytelling," a world-building aesthetic practice of dispersing content, not simply cross-platform distribution, but with the function of developing an immersive story via overtly or peripherally connected representations and the active participation of consumers with different media and goods.[69] This practice traces back through anime, youth culture, and Japan's shifts in late-modern consumer practices and media technologies since the 1960s.[70] In most CPDRC videos, after the main performance video has completed, YouTube generates a set of related videos for suggested viewing. After the first episode of *Prison Dancer*, however, users are encouraged to select between the four main characters and experience the first day in MMDC from their respective viewpoints. By helping users to engage the content not just from different points of view but multi-modally—inviting participation in activities like remixing its songs, competing in karaoke, singing along with a co-star, and viewing behind-the-scenes interviews—*Prison Dancer* partly succeeds in decentering the passivity of digital consumption like CPDRC's "Thriller."

In addition to its transmedia features meant to provide users with multiple pathways of cultural engagement, *Prison Dancer* carves out an alternative space for minoritized sexualities in the popular imaginary, particularly in the character Lola, that subverts the dominant image of Filipino gays as comic relief (see Figure 1.5). Ruperto "Lola" Poblador (played by Jeigh Madjus) is the choreographer, who led the dance program. After the warden installed surveillance cameras, Lola's Single Ladies' choreography (backed by her minions "Oo Oo" and "Na Na") and its Black feminine gestures spread throughout the prison, and she was asked to lead the men to "put down their fists and step on the one" (Episode 1).[71] On Lola's first day, she deploys specifically Filipino tropes such as the "p vs. f" in language and the global phenomenon of Manny Pacquaio when she claims to put the "pf" in "pfierce" and to be the "pound for pound queen of the prison."[72] While Prison Dancer features four main characters, its main duo Lola and Shakespeare ("Shakes" as Lola enlightens) decenters normative heterosexual white-native couplings. By the time of her

Figure 1.5 Lola, performed by Jeigh Madjus in *Prison Dancer*. Photo by Billy Bustamante.

release, Lola's lover, the butch Jonard "Shakespeare" Cervantes (portrayed by Nicco Lorenzo Garcia) commits suicide (inverting the Madame Butterfly and Miss Saigon convention). This leads Lola to promise "I'll find my way somehow I'll/take you all with me," and emerge as the heroine of the story.[73]

One of the challenges of the "based on true events" nature of *Prison Dancer* is that performers have to make decisions about resolving contradictions in their rendition that remain unsettled offscreen. In *Prison Dancer* Episode 11: "Finally Free," for example, Lola provides her perspective to Matt Wells on her parole after serving four years (released on August 29, 2011).[74]

> You ask me what I have learned here. If I feel rehabilitated. For me sir, this is all a dance. Life is a dance. We start by moving on our own. Dancing our own steps. Needing no one else. But what I was looking for my whole life, I found here. I found that we are not alone. That there are others like me. Who want to move in the same direction. And when we move as one, we can change the world. We can change each other. We can change ourselves and our point of view. And I know it sounds ridiculous. But its only here that I found freedom.[75]

Echoing Resane's earlier claim, "If I was not in prison, I would not be famous," Lola's quote is significant because it similarly rationalizes her incarceration. When reflecting on the value of dance in prison, she highlights the educational and social benefits and expands the terms of dance to encompass life in totality. When we see "life is a dance," the rehabilitation program appears as a natural provider of happy endings (marked by Lola's ensuing ballad).

In comparing CPDRC's Resane and *Prison Dancer's* Lola, the most apparent difference is in their final scenes. Whereas the mass of zombies engulfs Resane, Lola exits MMDC in a white short sleeve button up shirt and khakis, and we cannot help but notice that she lacks her altered uniform/midriff (see Figure 1.6). Perhaps this fact—and also that Lola's "Finally Free" video lacks any post-content interactive features—echoes the sentiment that the interactivity of *Prison Dancer* has no clear effects on the actual inmates that inspired it. Moreover, with its focus on "how fears can hold us captive—and dreams can set us free to dance!" *Prison Dancer* echoes the critical dance offering specific to "Thriller" about Foucaultian discipline that I am interrogating: the problematic equivocation between social discipline (rehabilitation of deviant behavior) and technique/technical discipline (acquisition of learned skills in dance). My point is not that the stakes for performers in CPDRC and *Prison*

Figure 1.6 Lola in Khakis, performed by Jeigh Madjus in *Prison Dancer* (2012), screen still.

Dancer are the same, but that they both engender questions and assumptions around dance as a naturally liberating activity, and unlike other mediums such as writing, are somewhat dampened by the inability to suspend belief about the diasporic actors. In line with the CPDRC's ability to generate diasporic nationalism, one *Prison Dancer* cast member proclaims the musical "celebrates what is it to be a Filipino."[76] These factors suggest that while the *Prison Dancer* decenters the passivity of CPDRC, it maintains a surface consumption of CPDRC's "Thriller's" cultural politics. The series reproduces the perspective that dance naturally frees us and remains less concerned with how to help the inmates (and viewers) escape the dynamics of exploitation and mimicry that it brings back to life in the Filipino diaspora.

* * *

In its irresolvable culmination, the dance and story of "Thriller" leave us with more questions than answers. The program was suspended in 2017, but it is unclear why and for how long.[77] CPDRC "Thriller's" final image correlates with its ambiguous promise of discipline. Beneath this promise lies the narratives constructed by the African American original, the panoptic configuration, and the actions of the CPDRC and the local government. These narratives tie the inmates' conditions of imprisonment to the productivity of their fame and help audiences to believe that the dance is successful and unproblematic, thus stabilizing the caricatures of Otherness it presents.

Interestingly, Travis Payne, Jackson's "This Is It" tour choreographer, noted that the King of Pop watched CPDRC's "Thriller" during rehearsal and "he would get tremendous joy."[78] Moreover, to legitimate the spectacle of difference and appear as effective rehabilitation, the choreography of "Thriller"—its coding and specific meaning in neocolonial contexts—must be overlooked and abstracted by viewers in ways that do not interfere with "consumer confidence." The Filipino mimicry stereotype—a well-meaning, loosely descriptive perception of complicated historical processes—exacerbates misinterpretations of Filipino postcolonial performances like "Thriller." When the audience sees the "Thriller" performers as Others benefiting from the performance, their responses of anxiety, guilt, or disgust are alleviated. When the dance is oversimplified, audiences are distracted from the mutual construction of Otherness that is dependent not just on a white colonizer and colonized Other, but also on a subordinate Other—Resane. Their non-normative body enacts a transformative act of maarte mimicry that is individually recuperative and hypervisible, yet also participates in the ability of the "Thriller" phenomenon and its more interactive diasporic spin-off to undercut the obscene realities of the neoliberal privatization of prisons and Philippines' less visible human rights injustices. In light of these multiple contexts, the CPDRC's claim to demonstrate a model that can answer penology and terrorism problems internationally leaves this viewer, at least, less than thrilled.[79]

In its attempt to rescript the gang activities of inmates and its undermining of human rights injustices, this figuration of the zombie both succeeds and falls short of attending to the borders between viewers and incarcerated Filipinos. And over the next decade the global sensation of the once marginal Filipino dancing body only continued to proliferate on other user-generated and reality television platforms. Perhaps unsurprisingly, some sensations would even echo CPDRC and naturalize their own phenomenon as both Filipino and freeing.

2

Heroes and Filipino Migrations

After twenty years of uncertainty, Michelle and her family's petition to immigrate to the United States was finally approved. Her auntie, a nursing migrant who had immigrated to the United States from the Philippines in 1972, filed the petition in 1978.[1] In 1998, Michelle's family—her lolo and lola (grandparents), parents, and two younger sisters—left her behind and moved to Minneapolis, Minnesota, from a chain of over 7,000 islands to a land of 10,000 lakes. Why was Michelle not able to go with them? By then, she was over twenty-one years old, which lowered her preference category per United States immigration policy.

The Philippines' backlog for family-sponsored preference visas is often worse than every other country in the world (see Table 2.1).[2] Some Filipinos have waited over twenty-three years for their petitions to be processed.[3] For Michelle, it took an additional decade of waiting—and constantly checking the monthly Visa Bulletin—before she received the unexpected news that the United States had finally processed her own father's request.

When her father's petition for her "pushed through" in 2009, Michelle, or Bgirl Tzy (pronounced "chee"), had a successful professional dance career with her crew, the Philippine Allstars, who filled the void of her family's absence (see Figure 2.1).[4] "For months, my life was left hanging," she describes, "I was a bum, seemingly perpetually soul-searching, until I stumbled upon dance on April 3, 2000."[5] Tzy spent a decade dancing, cofounding the world-champion Philippine Allstars, cultivating the hip-hop dance community in Manila, and winning multiple world championship titles. As a pioneering Filipina bgirl, she found personal empowerment within a typically male-dominated dance culture, met the love of her life, and became a mother. She also made brief travels to the United States as an international competitor and as a cultural visitor of the U.S. State Department. In the Philippines, Bgirl Tzy was a hero, subverting hegemonic Filipina dance norms of modesty and self-effacement, and role-modeling provocative aggression to many young artists. So, when Tzy's case was suddenly approved in 2009, she faced the

Choreographing in Color. J. Lorenzo Perillo, Oxford University Press (2020). © Oxford University Press.
DOI: 10.1093/oso/9780190054274.001.0001

Table 2.1 U.S. Visa Bulletin (May 1998) chart with dates and preference categories. The U.S. Citizenship and Immigration Services (USCIS) determines the dates by which individuals from foreign states in which demand was "excessive" of numerical limits are given priority.

Family-Sponsored	All Change-ability Areas Except Those Listed	CHINA-mainland born	INDIA	MEXICO	PHILIPPINES
First (F1): *Unmarried sons and daughters of U.S. Citizens: 23,400 plus any numbers not required for fourth preference*	10/15/1996	10/15/1996	10/15/1996	08/01/1993	01/09/1987
Second (F2A): *Spouses and children of permanent residents: 114,200, plus the number (if any) by which the worldwide family preference level exceeds 226,000, plus any unused first preference numbers: 77% of the overall second preference limitation, of which 75% are exempt from the per-country limit;*	01/01/1994	01/01/1994	01/01/1994	02/15/1993	01/01/1994
Second (F2B): *Unmarried sons and daughters (21 years or older) of permanent residents: 23% of the overall second preference limitation*	10/15/1991	10/15/1991	10/15/1991	06/22/1991	10/15/1991
Third (F3): *Married sons and daughters of U.S. Citizens: 23,400, plus any numbers not required by first and second preferences.*	12/01/1994	12/01/1994	12/01/1994	08/01/1989	12/08/1986
Fourth (F4): *Brothers and sisters of adult U.S. Citizens: 65,000, plus any numbers not required by first three preferences.*	01/08/1988	01/08/1988	01/22/1986	03/22/1987	05/01/1078

Figure 2.1 Philippine Allstars' gold medal win at World Hip-Hop Championships (2006) in Los Angeles marked a turning point for hip-hop dance in Asia with increased popularity, employment opportunities, and respect. Featuring Bgirl Tzy, Deo Bantillo, Jhong Mesina, Maya Carandang, Kenjhons Serrano, Kyxz Mendiola, Laurence Chua, Lema Diaz, Madelle Paltu-Ob, Sheena Vera Cruz, and Reagan Cornelio.

decision of leaving everything in the Philippines to bring her child to the United States.

In the 1980s and 1990s, dancers like Tzy faced family- and employment-based emigration dilemmas that inadvertently reaffirmed Filipinos' global presence in hip-hop. In 1988, for example, nineteen-year-old Joshua started dancing with Octo Manoeuvres, an all-male group associated with Gary Valenciano, often called the "Michael Jackson of the Philippines."[6] Formed in 1987, the Manoeuvres toured with Valenciano to Hong Kong, the United States, and Europe, forging their status as one of the prominent street dance groups of their time. Like many dance groups today, the Manoeuvres worked to elevate dancers' second-class status in the entertainment industry vis-à-vis actors and singers (artistas).[7] In Filipino show business, "recording dancers" of all-male dance groups, like the Manoeuvres, the Streetboys, and Universal

Motion Dancers, promoted recording artists and their singles, and appeared regularly as house dancers on contemporary noontime television shows *ASAP, That's Entertainment*, and *SOP*, which were musical variety show descendants of *Penthouse 7*.[8] Yet, in 1991, Joshua migrated to Japan to work as an overseas Filipino worker (OFW).

Bgirl Tzy's and Joshua's stories underline two conditions of possibility that gave rise to global hip-hop and street dance. Through a discussion of OFW migration to Asian entertainment markets, this chapter explores how the surprising turns of Filipino migration impact both domestic developments and the transnational circulation of Black dance forms. Within the broader category of OFWs is a governmental grouping of overseas performing artists (OPAs), like Joshua, that usually includes migrant musicians, singers, circus performers, and generalist performing artists.[9] In contrast to OFWs are *Petisyonados*, or Filipinos like Tzy, who leave through family preference visas to reunite with relatives who have already emigrated through employment to the United States. A juxtaposition of the experiences of Filipino dancers who migrate as OFW dancers and Petisyonados conveys the similar racial sexual logic underlying the transnational circulation of Black dance and the uprooting of localized Filipino ideas, people, and culture through "dance drain."

In the previous chapter, the figure of the zombie largely failed to draw attention to the critical issues of incarceration and corporeality surrounding the global phenomenon of the Filipino dancing body. By turning to the 1990s and 2000s as a pivotal period in which the stereotypical rhythmic abilities of the Filipino body acquired newfound currency, this chapter examines another key configuration through which Filipinos have engaged the hegemonic forces of both racial histories of colonialism and gendered labor mechanisms. In its mundanity, OFW and Petisyonado discourse mobilizes the logic of performative euphemisms by recoding the "naturalized" heroic dynamics of neoliberal migration.

United States- and Philippine-based scholars have produced compelling accounts and criticisms of the Philippine government's neoliberal export migration allegory, "mga bagong pambansang bayani" (the new national heroes).[10] The migration of Filipino dancers similarly complicates this story. On the one hand, overseas entertainers like Joshua reveal a hidden history of state labor brokerage in which pre-departure testing works to destigmatize dance and sex work. On the other hand, Petisyonados like Bgirl Tzy downplay migration as ordinary and reveal multiple types of migrant relations—ambassador, competitor, and immigrant. Decisions around migration and

identity formation are not easily untangled. By understanding the complicated processes of how dancers circulate across Asia and the Global North,
I expand upon the current conversation across migration and dance studies
by sketching out sociocultural aspects of Filipino labor migration with an attention to dance.[11]

Here, dance provides alternative views into conventional contemporary
notions of migration *as movement*. And, conversely, migration shapes the
ways we have thought about dance as embedded in the global economy and
globalization of hip-hop. Media and narratives about dance emigrants lay
claim to a more direct, albeit complicated and uneventful, relationship between the simultaneous rise of the Philippine's as a global labor resource and
hip-hop's globalization in the 1970s.[12] OFWs and Petisyonados show how
state labor brokerage and movement of cultural forms co-create human capital flight, or "dance drain," whereby the Philippine's dance community is
constantly destabilizing and channeling both its working- and middle-class
dancers into the global elsewhere.[13]

Whereas OFWs faced Philippine regulations based on white feminine
aesthetics before popularizing forms of Black dance in Asia, Petisyonados
struggle against the Global North's entertainment industry that continues to
privilege white bodies and underrepresent Filipino Americans and tokenize
Asian Americans and Pacific Islanders.[14] These two figures—OFWs and
Petisyonados—place into relief the competing forces of the demand for
"desirable, cheap labor" in Asia. Filipino OFWs emigrate to serve the labor
demands of the emergent Asian economies like Singapore and Taiwan, as
well as the racial sexual exclusivity of the market for dance in the Global
North. Exploring these contexts provides further and clearer understanding
of why it has become common sense to associate Filipinos with "exceptional"
talent and gifted dancing ability, regardless of place, socioeconomic status,
or type of dance (see previous chapter on "Thriller").[15] These Filipinos show
how the global movements of people and individual movements of bodies
prove to be more complicated than previously thought.

"Dancers Wanted, With or Without Experience": Filipinos, Migration, and Dance

Unlike other labor-exporting economies like Indonesia and India, from
the 1980s to the early 2000s, the Philippine government, under Presidents

Corazon Aquino, Fidel Ramos, Joseph Estrada, and then Gloria Macapagal Arroyo, deployed a massive number of migrants under the occupational category "choreographers and dancers."[16] According to the Philippine Overseas Employment Administration (POEA), 435,824 Filipino dance emigrants were deployed from 1992 to 2010.[17] The number of dance emigrants over this 18-year span is roughly the same as the population of present-day Atlanta, Georgia. In 1994 alone, 47,686 "choreographers and dancers" emigrated.[18] One country served as the primary destination for an overwhelming majority of these migrants— up to 99.3 percent went to Japan.[19]

But Filipino dancers also moved across the globe to countries like Bahrain, Hong Kong, Saipan, United Arab Emirates, South Korea, Indonesia, Malaysia, Germany, Netherlands, Singapore, France, Palau, Croatia, Brunei, Qatar, and the Commonwealth of Northern Mariana Islands. This global diaspora suggests that Filipino choreographers and dancers also play a strategic role in serving historical circuits of empire and contemporary base sites of U.S. militarism.[20] The role that Filipinos play in sites of U.S. militarism continues their status in "rest and recreation" after the Vietnam War. Moreover, the Philippine state's manufacturing of Filipino migrant dancers helps us understand the promotion of the development of capitalism in Asia, as Filipino bodies become the racial other against which racial capitalist desires of Asian states and citizens are democratized and modernized. As performers in nightclubs, amusement parks, and professional folkdance troupes, Filipinos provide material, spiritual, and emotional labor for their employers, white businessmen, and "crazy rich Asian" audiences that endow them with markers of leisure and consumption through which emergent global racial capitalist economies are "developed."[21]

In the early 1970s, a few years before *Penthouse* dancers popularized Black social dances with Philippine television audiences (see "Introduction"), the large-scale international migration of "choreographers and dancers" and stereotype that Filipinos are born to move found one of its roots. Upon the directives of then-president Ferdinand Marcos, the Philippines began brokering labor in a neoliberal mode of governmentality. In migration studies, choreographer and dance migrants are usually enfolded into the category of OFWs. Moreover, some OFWs and "entertainers" are seen as sex workers, following the assumption that these individuals do not dance or sing primarily (and sometimes at all), but rather act as hostesses for Japanese and U.S. military in bars and gentlemen's clubs.[22] Their movement is part of a larger process of Filipino global labor export by which around 10 percent of the Filipino population have worked outside the Philippines, including 1 million Filipinos who are deployed annually by the government to work under temporary contracts.

Any understanding of Filipino hip-hop requires a consideration of the structural dynamics by which Filipinos circulate the globe. The institutional apparatus of Filipino labor brokerage—consisting of the Philippine Overseas Employment Administration (POEA), Technical Education and Skills Development Authority (TESDA), International Labor Affairs Service (ILAS), Department of Foreign Affairs (DFA)—works at mobilizing overseas Filipino workers (OFWs) globally.[23] Beyond institutions, labor brokerage occurs discursively in ways that construct common sense around emigration and new understandings of citizenship and patriotism that ultimately support brokerage.[24] The institutions, employment agencies, and discourse of labor brokerage authorizes, trains, and markets Filipino workers as well as negotiates between host countries and the Philippines. In order to capture foreign capital and alleviate underemployment, the state continues neoliberal reforms because they appear profitable today. For example, migrant remittances amounted to nearly $23 billion USD in 2013—proving to yield growth even despite the 2008 economic crisis.[25] Remitted monies secure more meaning given the fact that Filipino workers in the United States remit the most amount of money back to the Philippines—over $6 million USD in 2005 and 2006.[26]

Scholars of Filipino migration often deploy cases and metaphors reliant upon movement and performance while simultaneously overlooking the symbolic and materialist meanings of movement in these processes. In studies specifically about Filipina migrant entertainers, it is no small point that dancers are analyzed for their marginalization but marginalized for their dancing.[27] Dancers are typically lumped together with other professionals such as musicians, singers, and performing artists; one easily replaced for another. Dance should be differentiated as a category of migrant labor, however, because statistically, "choreographers and dancers" outnumber each and every other type of artist. Moreover, whether or not hostessing or actual dancing occupies most of their work schedule, dancers similarly shoulder much of the stigma attached to Filipina OFW discourse. Unlike the "caring" body of domestic workers, which is afforded respect through its association with normative gender roles, domesticity, and reproductivity, the dancing body of migrant entertainers is seen through a moral alterity that is sexualized and non-reproductive. Their degradation has led dance expert Steve Villaruz to advocate that the plight of Filipino dance migrants "should be a concern not only for those in the field of the 'cultural dancer,' but also for society at large."[28] Thereby, centering racialized and gendered dancers presents an opportunity to offer us a more precise and nuanced account of labor migration processes.

Anthropologist James A. Tyner provides an example of how dance is represented and under-theorized in Filipino migration discourse. He recounts the migration of "Lisa," a Filipina performing artist who worked as a migrant entertainer under a six-month contract in a nightclub in Okinawa, Japan, that catered to mostly U.S. Marines.[29] In the thick description designed to articulate globalization processes through Lisa's journey, dance appears in several forms. We are told, for example, dance is cast as a mere job, or a type of work that does not define the migrant. Dance appears in just about all the stages of Lisa's migration from pre-departure to post-contract. Yet even as dance is hypervisible, the actual substance of her dancing is exempted from analysis, interpretation, and evaluation. In pre-departure, many dance migrants travel from provincial regions to the urban setting of Manila to receive training by other Filipinos, often former migrant entertainers themselves. "Over the course of her training," Tyner writes,

> Lisa was taught three dance routines. In retrospect, she feels this training was pointless, in that she was never once asked to perform these routines in Japan. She says, "I asked that to myself—'Why did we learn those dances?' Yeah, it was stupid if you think about it." Rather, in Japan, Lisa and the other dancers were expected to perform "sexy" dances, those typical of strip clubs. For this type of training, which is not specified in official guidelines, the studio manager would take the trainees to nightclubs in Manila so they could watch other dancers perform.[30]

The account offers us clues as to how dance is similarly understood by both the researcher and subject throughout the OFW process. For Lisa, the research subject, training in a form of dance, regardless of its genre or sophistication of its choreography, is rendered "pointless" and irrational ("stupid") if not part of a repertoire to be used on the job. For Tyner, the researcher, whatever is sexy about the movement is rendered questionable and mute as signified by the scholar's scare quotes. In contrast, from a professional dance perspective, training with sequences of movement that are not actually used on the job is not unreasonable as they may be for purposes of conditioning or building skills like bodily awareness, showmanship, or flexibility.

After contract completion, upon reflecting on Lisa's post-migration experience and attitude toward her labor, Tyner wonders,

> What empowered Lisa to resist the negative discourses surrounding em-
> ployment as a performing artist? Consistent with work conducted by and
> about sex workers, Lisa readily acknowledges her previous employment,
> but she views erotic dancing simply as a job. It was not, and is not, her de-
> fining feature. Dancing, and more broadly sex work, to Lisa constituted
> an income-generating activity or form of labor, and not an identity. Lisa
> thus views her former occupation as do many other sex workers: Sex work
> becomes work, like any other, and this attitude removes stigmas associated
> with victimization.[31]

These responses by Filipina migrant entertainers and social scientific
depictions of them make evident the need for a cultural shift in the ways
that dance and performance are typically rendered in Filipino migration
discourse.[32] The argument here is less about the accuracy of the quoted
views than the interpretation of them. They overlook how training in "sex
work" is mutually linked to Lisa's dance education.[33] Because she is able to
disavow dancing as an identity, Lisa can destigmatize her labor. In order
to destigmatize OFW work as sex work, Lisa evacuates the dancing of any
creative, therapeutic, racial, spiritual, intellectual, proprietary, and cultural
features it might yield. At the same time, dancing is reduced to an "income-
generating activity," which is telling because while much of her account of
work is non-dancing, any dancing on the job is undervalued or assigned as a
punishment.[34]

Even as it is central to Lisa's narrative, dance is flattened and evacuated
from its aesthetic form, content, and history. Dance as discourse is denied
the same in-depth description Tyner provides for migration processes partly
because it can be distinguished as a "form of labor, and not an identity."[35]
In other words, this sociological understanding of Filipino migration is
based paradoxically upon the discrediting of movement and depreciation of
dancers.

What then happens if dancing is considered as an identity-generating as
well as an income-generating activity? As several key research collaborators
emigrated over the course of writing this book, I found this question to resonate even more. A consideration of dance discourse entails grappling with
the particular Filipino social and political contexts that act as conditions of

possibility for dance practice to come into being.[36] Asian American scholar and dramaturg Lucy Mae San Pablo Burns, for example, argues that the exceptionalism of the Filipino dancing body is dialectically linked to American empire's exceptionalism.[37] In part, Burns's book, *Puro Arte: Filipinos on the Stages of Empire*, looks at early studies of taxi-hall dancing in California and Detroit in the 1920s and 1930s to demonstrate the Filipino dancing body's corporeality as archival embodiment of the anti-Filipino movement in California.[38] Burns specifies how the subject of migrants dancing "splendid" simultaneously acculturated Filipinos, reproduced U.S. imperial grammar, and challenged white masculinity.[39]

An attention to the corporealities of OFWs and Petisyonados expands upon Burns's historical work to center the contemporary lived experiences that "fall out" of studies of Filipino global labor even as they seem to reside at their core. Similar to the taxi dancers in Burns's study, Filipino migrants develop "talent" in ways that show how the contemporary global dancing body is always constituted by racial, sexual, imperial hierarchies, but may also euphemistically respond to the naturalized heroism of its transnational mobility.

Toprockin': Dancers for Export

Some of the earliest dancing by b-boy pioneers was done upright, a form which became known as "toprockin'." The structure and form of toprockin' has infused dance forms and influences from Brooklyn uprocking, tap, lindi hop [*sic*], James Brown's "good foot," salsa, Afro-Cuban, and various African and Native American dances. Early influences on b-boying/girling also included martial arts films from the 1970s. Certain moves and styles developed from this inspiration.[40]

The critical and popular reception of Filipinos as natural entertainers situates Blackness and contemporary conditions of neoliberalism in unexpected ways. On a sweltering afternoon in June 2011, from a cafe on the University of the Philippines campus, Steve Villaruz relayed his firsthand knowledge of the ties between Filipino export migration and dance. Villaruz's expertise in ballet and dance criticism led to his position as a judge for prospective migrants applying for work visas through the Philippine labor brokerage apparatus, the Philippine Overseas Employment Agency (POEA). According to Villaruz, the POEA and later the Technical Education Skills Development Authority (TESDA), established in 1994 under the

Department of Labor and Employment, ensured that dance requirements were built into the processing of out-migrant labor.[41] In bgirling, toprocking is an important opening component that introduces one's character, style, and musicality through upright, improvisational dancing carefully measured to the music. Similar to the way that toprocking sets the tone for a bgirl's set, the Philippine government set the tone for migrant artists in the 2000s by requiring them to pass examinations of ballet and jazz dance (and later folk), regardless of whether they were booked for those dance forms (see Figure 2.2).[42] This process reaffirmed neocolonial, hierarchical norms that

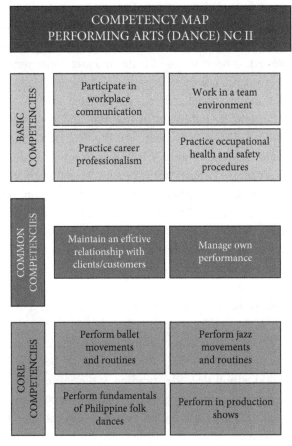

Figure 2.2 Technical Education and Skills Development Authority (TESDA) Performing Arts (DANCE) training regulations form (2017): moral purity, upper-class prestige, and whiteness attached to Western concert forms of dance counter "Japayuki" stigmatization.

subjugated Black popular forms in the Filipino dance world and reaffirmed whiteness as property.[43] In order to pass these exams, prospective migrants took ballet and jazz lessons in Manila for a few months, anchoring circuits of Filipino global labor to the moral purity, linear continuity, and aristocratic ideal of "technique" embodied within their dance forms.[44]

In the mid-1980s, "Japayuki" gained prominence as a pejorative term for Filipina migrant entertainers working in Japan.[45] In my fieldwork, several dancers and choreographers mentioned the stigma they faced from family members and other dancers when considering work in Japan. The stigma still exists and led dancers to encourage a distinction between dancers and hostesses in nightclubs.[46] "Japayuki," a term used in the Philippines that translates to Japan-bound, derives from the word *Karayuki*, for China-bound Japanese sex workers in Asia prior and during World War II.[47] Given this history, it's reasonable to surmise that the upper-class prestige and whiteness attached to Western concert forms of ballet and jazz dance were part of the Philippine government's efforts to compensate for the socially constructed sexualized and morally stigmatized body of the "Japayuki."

In an article originally published in the *Manila Times* on October 23, 1991, Steve Villaruz distinguished between the theatrical dance artist and the "cultural dancer."[48] According to Villaruz, working-class cultural dancers come from disadvantaged homes in the provinces, so they often have forces of business and life stacked against them. But protected from this fate by a controlled world of studio and theater, dance theater artists have resources of time and space to hone their art-making. Most studies of Filipino dance centralize practices of middle-class dance theater artists and folk dancers.[49] Dance migrants, in contrast, undergo culture shock in the Manila metropolis, only to be misled by recruiters, promotion companies, choreographers, and trainers. These handlers are unqualified to teach and create dances, and they withhold from dance migrants any knowledge of the art, choreography, and performance. Consequently, dance migrants 1) lack the legitimacy and apprenticeship of dance theater artists, 2) become shoved into the showbiz world with little understanding of their moral, economic, and human rights, and 3) have their wages exploited and cut by many promotions and agencies—a dynamic that resonates with the vulnerabilities of domestic worker labor migrants.

The reiterative enactment of the global social norm that Filipinos are culturally, if not racially, apt for export and import—as nurses, seafarers, domestic workers, and entertainers—reconfigures migrant experiences and types of labor performed by Filipinos.[50] In 1991, Joshua worked in Japan for six months as a migrant dancer and hotel waiter. In order to appreciate the labor that such a position entails, I quote Joshua at length here:

> I will serve the Japanese breakfast, breakfast buffet. I was a waiter then. So black vest and bow tie and white polo and black pants and black shoes. That's six o'clock in the morning until one in the afternoon and we would sleep from one to five then go to work at six o'clock at our club because that was a hotel. Breakfast then there's a club below, so I worked as a dancer also. But at that time, I was not a part of the Manoeuvers. I was working with, we were male and female, like we formed a group just for that club, just for that six months. . . . That experience, I learned a lot, eh, not only as a dancer but you work [at] something hard, you learn. Because that salary is in dollars but you earn much more. But that's where I learned to assign value to things.[51]

Joshua's personal dance history contradicts the assumptions exacerbated by sensationalist media portrayals that equate entertainers with sex workers.[52] In 2004, Japan increased immigration restrictions following the U.S. Trafficking in Persons Report, which identified Filipino migrant entertainers in Japan as trafficked into forced labor and sexual exploitation.[53] The social and moral stigma attached to Filipino overseas performing artists in the 1990s influenced the ways Filipinos perceived, valued, and made sense of their own dance-making.[54] As Joshua's personal accounts revealed, the process of assigning economic value to one's labor was founded upon the transitive properties of the Filipino body, a quality only highlighted by the incommensurability of dancing hip-hop (New Jack swing) and serving food.[55]

The system of state-brokered dance migrants, stigmatized OFWs, and Joshua's experiences mark the logic of euphemism as a root way that gendered racialized dancers are mobilized across borders. If this logic calls for a concealment between two objects, it also conjures what is being remade—that unregulated, unapologetic, and raw performance. This dynamic presents an opening to examine racialization through Filipino dance migration. Their stories largely stand in opposition to much of the extant scholarly and popular engagement with OFWs that typically begins with the assumption that exported dancers rarely perform their arts but rather hostess duties and place themselves, knowingly or not, at risk of sexual and physical abuse in exchange for higher wages.[56] Although out-migrants are commonly trained

in ballet and jazz as part of pre-migration preparation and testing, Black popular dances like New Jack Swing that are performed in nightclubs are also a
significant component of the OFW narrative. Moreover, Filipino bodies in
Japan engender a hypersexualized otherness that is both familiar and different
from white supremacist representations of American Blackness. Additionally,
their stories complement the normative portrait of migrant entertainers as a
phenomenon that consisted of entirely women and confines men to the limited positions of talent managers, club owners, and clientele. In fact, men are
also dance migrants, making up a statistical minority—about 3.7 percent
from 1992 to 2005.[57] Even though this percentage seems small, the total migrant choreographers and dancers that registered as men amounted to nearly
16,000. Albeit for different circumstances and types of work, Joshua and many
other Filipino dancers like Ricky Carranza left the Philippines in the 1990s
and some continue in the present day.[58] While their experiences may not be
generalizable to a broader range of migrant laborers or dancers, they nonetheless point to the links between human capital flight, or a Filipino "dance
drain," structural policies directed at globalizing the Filipino work force, and
the international spread and development of street dance styles.

Get Down: Dance Drain

Aforementioned restrictions in immigration to Japan, combined with global
capitalist developments in Hong Kong, Singapore, and Dubai, meant new
opportunities for individuals to transition from the Philippines dance world
into regional hospitality and care labor sectors. Attracted by tripled earning
potentials, a localized workplace, and access to international resources,
some members of the Allstars, The Crew, and other popular street dancers
in the Philippine mainstream entertainment industry took advantage of this
opportunity. This process of transitioning between different fields of labor
was often described by dancers as something that hip-hop, with its porous
borders, short-term work flow, and physical movements, prepared them for.
For instance, when legendary Bgirl Eyevee executes a get down (also known
as the go down or the drop) she rehearses more than simply a weight-shifting
transition from vertical to horizontal dancing.[59] With get downs like knee
drops and coin drops, she segues from high, upright to low and more prone
and supine positions. She enacts a creative shift in movement vocabulary
from toprockin' to downrocks, power moves, freezes, or floor moves. The

transitional qualities of the get down resemble the period of dance drain in Filipino hip-hop in the early 2000s, when the community witnessed an exodus of many of its most influential dancers and choreographers.

In Singapore in 2011, for example, Love Sabio, a street dancer and member of the Crew, no longer had to commute to teach, choreograph, and rehearse across half a dozen schools and studios in Metro Manila.[60] For her, Filipinos in Singapore are known for occupying the service jobs like baristas and personal trainers that Singaporeans feel "too superior" to perform. While Sabio was directly hired to work in a Singaporean fitness company for a two-year contract and did not go through the pre-migration testing, she still had to "fix her papers" with the POEA before visiting Manila mid-contract. While putting her dance career on hold, Sabio saw Singapore as a necessary migration to allow her body to heal from the injuries acquired by high-impact forms like hip-hop and gymnastics. For Sabio and many of the other interviewees, the opening of Hong Kong Disneyland in 2005 and Universal Singapore in 2010 were major factors contributing to recent Filipino migration of street dancers and the popular notion that Filipinos are known as "natural" dancers and singers. According to David Lightbody, the British entertainment and costuming director at Hong Kong Disneyland, "Filipino performers are globally respected because of their amazing qualities. Working with them Hong Kong Disneyland reconfirms those recognitions because Filipinos have that inner happy passion in what they do. Their great and amazing commitment is reflected in their smiles and their faces. They are exceptional."[61] While some Filipino artists found their way to dance in parades or the *Lion King* theatrical show in Hong Kong Disneyland, two of the leading street dance groups in the Philippine entertainment industry were cast in their own show as resident bboys, Rockafella Streetboys, in an area designed as a New York Broadway Street (read: urban American).[62] As dancers hired for these tourist locales, they present a racialized and gendered spectacle that aligns Black dance and American street busking culture with the subordinate role of Filipinos in the global care chain for the local Asian and international audiences that these emergent economies attract. Ironically, Filipino dancers in the tourist street scenes of Singapore and Hong Kong are compensated with salaries and even lodging unattainable in their homeland. At the same time, as Filipino hip-hop dancers, like Philippine national champion Bboy Reflex (Soulstice crew), increasingly compete in events in Korea, Singapore, and Taiwan, they develop understandings of style and form that decenter American iterations with a multi-Asian perspective.[63] These examples illustrate the complicated ties between the global circulation of hip-hop and street dance and the development of Filipino dancers.

For audiences who are members of the diaspora themselves, seeing Filipinos in foreign amusement parks and hospitality sites triggers a "Filipino radar" and mixed sense of pride and nostalgia that binds the diaspora.[64] But for many of the interviewees, this phenomenon reflects the costs of neoliberal restructuring and linkage between the circulation of Black dance and Filipino global labor in "dance drain." Hip-hop performing artist, Chelo A., says,

> It's definitely happening. Dancers are still not appreciated here. The amount of money that they would earn versus the amount of money they would earn elsewhere, even places as close as Hong Kong, here is sometimes only 10 percent of what they would earn there. And it's that bad. I think there's a drain in general of everything in this country because people are just not being supported and appreciated for their worth. I think, ultimately, Philippines has already stagnated; it's not going anywhere. Because they don't appreciate or they're not supporting the artistic pursuits of their people. For example, a few of the [Philippine] Allstars have migrated already, and a few of the dancers I know, most of them go to Japan or Hong Kong, or other nearby countries because straight up there's no work here. You can't provide for your family with [the] little TFs [talent fees] that you get."[65]

Chelo attributes the exodus of Filipino hip-hop dancers to the lack of respect and thus financial compensation they receive by the Philippine's entertainment industry. These structural dynamics shape the desires of Filipino dancers to emigrate and bring their expertise in hip-hop and street dance to other countries. As most of the Philippine-based dancers that I spoke with mentioned personal tales of working or considering dance work abroad, some of them described the 2000s, when many of the best dancers across several genres—spanning street dance to ballet—created a void in the Philippines.[66]

In 1991, Jerome "Sir J" Dimalanta began in street dance in Jungee Marcelo's classes at a privately owned gym called "The Sweatshop" on Katipunan Avenue in Quezon City, Philippines. Sir J then founded the University of the Philippines Streetdance Club (UPSDC) in 1997, the Crew, an elite dance company made of alumni and members of the UPSDC, and built a few cohorts, or "batches," of street dancers and choreographers that would become community leaders across the nation and region. Sir J was petitioned and immigrated to the U.S. leaving the Crew and UPSDC behind in 2010. He says,

> [B]rain drain has a specific effect on the local community, because they found that there's a lack of service in some of the areas because of a lack of nurses and a lack of doctors, and that impacts the community, that impacts society.... [W]hen it comes to dance and the dance industry, will it get affected as much. . . . [I]f key people and influential teachers and choreographers [are] leaving the country for better pastures, will it have a specific impact on the local community? Or will it somehow find a way to still exist?[67]

The problem of what Sir J calls the "cultural vacuum left behind" is particularly specific for hip-hop—a dance community that is more grassroots-based and less structured than Filipino folk dance, ballet, and modern dance institutions. If a dance group has an active recruitment and membership program, as some school-based crews like UPSDC do, they have the ability to mitigate the effects of dance drain. But as Sir J explains, these types of programs are not common for hip-hop dance; "It's not that structured."[68]

Freezes: Petisyonados

For Bgirl Tzy, her signature freeze involves supporting her entire body weight on one elbow planted on the floor, while stretching her opposing shoulder upward (see Figure 2.3). This movement requires technique, bodily awareness, and control as she flies her legs toward the sky. In bgirling, freezes like hollowbacks, baby freezes, L-kicks, and chair freezes isometrically build muscle strength and often conclude a set. As she describes her physical calling card, "It's easy when you get the form and technique even though it hurts," I am reminded of the ways her decisions around emigration are also apparently effortless.[69] Bgirl Tzy, like many other Petisyonados, ultimately decided to move abroad through family sponsorship or petition, also known as "chain migration."[70] Here I use Petisyonados as an analytical category. Akin to the way that freezes provide a kinesthetic foil to ebullient toprockin' and fast-moving floor work in bgirling, Petisyonados serve as a foil to the migratory rhythm of OFWs. Though migrants may not refer to themselves as such, "Petisyonados" resonates with the colonial history of government-sponsored

Figure 2.3 Michelle "Bgirl Tzy" Salazar and her signature elbow freeze: kinesthetic foil to toprocking and migratory rhythm of OFWs. Photo by Niccolo Cosme.

scholars, or Pensionados, sent to the United States in the early 1900s, and helps us understand the relationship between Black dance's transnational circulation and Filipino migration. While Petisyonados brush up against the "mga bagong pambansang bayani" (new national heroes) trope of OFWs manufactured by the state, their contribution to Filipino dance drain occurs not through employment preference visa but heteronormative family-sponsorship preference visa. Beyond reuniting with other family members that previously migrated to the United States, Canada, and Australia—to name a few destinations I commonly heard from interviewees—some Petisyonados also find ways to integrate into the host society by continuing social processes they practiced in the Philippines (i.e., joining ethnic associations, forming dance crews). Most Petisyonado dancers I interviewed expressed ambivalence about returning to the Philippines "down the road," but more than simply feeling split between the here and there, they experience a type of "gear shift" that serves as a conceptual coping mechanism to reinforce a sense of agency within a process that appears otherwise structurally overdetermined. Bgirl Tzy, for instance, anticipated a future life of monotony and routine in the United States that would take her away from the stresses of Manila, but force her to leave behind the dance community she helped cultivate and the career she developed.

Petisyonados differ from other immigrants and refugees not only because their decision to emigrate emerges from factors of reuniting with loved ones and pursuing economic opportunities and "passport power," but also because their liminal petition status has particular consequences for the transnational flow of hip-hop in that they receive more denials than non-Petisyonados when seeking visas to the United States for international competition and they are vulnerable to cooptation within U.S. neocolonial tropes of hip-hop "roots-finding."[71] Jerome Dimalanta, for example, was denied a visa to accompany his group, the Crew, when they competed in the 2005 World Hip Hop Dance Championship. The U.S. embassy officials cited his pending family-sponsored petition in his rejection letter and told him simply, and quite confoundingly, to wait two years for when he would likely be approved. According to my data, how officials interpret immigration policies and visa applicants varies and can depend on an applicant's demonstration of "close ties" to the Philippines (via certificates, employment, property ownership, and such), physical and sartorial appearance, class, and gender. The scenario that a coach or choreographer would be denied the ability to travel could be devastating to their competing crew, who have already spent resources, trained, and prepared for a year. In 2005, while two members of the Philippine Allstars were denied visas to travel to the United States to compete in Hip Hop International, Bgirl Tzy was approved to compete.[72] Prior to 2005, she was denied a visa three times because of her petition status. Evidently, those denied passage are those who have family in the United States and stigmatized as "flight" risks, seemingly predisposed to "overstay" their visa. It may seem like the easiest solution for Petisyonados is to simply refrain from dancing in competitions abroad. But two points are important here: First, international competitions in the Philippines (beyond qualifiers) are rare; Second, dance crews from the United States, Europe, or Asia do not join (or perhaps feel the need to participate) in Philippine-based competitions, beyond serving as judges or tour exhibition groups.[73]

Filipino crews generally enter international competitions for prestige, experiential knowledge, and cultural capital that increase their value in regional and national markets (see Chapter 5). Since most "international" competitions take place abroad in the United States, Australia, Japan, Korea, France, and Germany, visas and dancing abroad are issues that have led to annual fundraising dance concerts.[74] Thus, denied visas effectively exclude Filipinos who are, to use an immigration metaphor, "waiting in line," and reflect the reality that international competitive social capital—access to power—circulates unevenly, relative to the looming threat of undocumented immigrant bodies. It is important to note that, in early 2018, the Trump administration had recently cited terrorist attacks to advance intentions of ending family-sponsored immigration processes, mirroring the stigmatization some Petisyonados face at the U.S. embassy in Manila.[75]

Years before Bgirl Tzy's petition was approved, she traveled to Washington, D.C., Philadelphia, and New York as part of the U.S. State Department's Cultural Visitors Program. Tzy and six other hip-hop artists were sponsored for a two-week program designed to train professionals and help "cross-fertilize" American hip-hop culture with that of others.[76] Bgirl Tzy and the other artists from Argentina, Palestine, Vietnam, and Lebanon met with hip-hop pioneers, trained with U.S. artists, toured hip-hop landmarks, and performed at the Kennedy Center.[77] Tzy's visit was a tremendous dance opportunity, but it was also part of a longer history of U.S. diplomacy and cultural imperialism.

Six years before Bgirl Tzy's cultural visitor tour, the U.S. State Department, under the George W. Bush administration, had already begun administering a four-year dance residency exchange between Margaret Jenkins (San Francisco, California) and Tansuree Shankar (Kolkata, India), an echo of the American dance company tours that the State Department had sponsored from 1954 until the 1980s.[78] In 2005, the State Department also revived the 1950s Cold War era cultural diplomacy program, which strategically deployed ambassadors of Black culture (jazz, gospel, R&B, modern dance, and such) to respond to the newly independent developing nations in Africa, Asia, and Latin America. The U.S. State Department's new post-9/11 programs utilized hip-hop artists as ambassadors of African American culture while emphasizing Islam's importance to hip-hop's origins in order to offer proof of the successful integration of Muslims into American culture.[79] Aidi Hishaam reveals that as the United States deploys hip-hop as a diplomatic device to better their image to Muslim youth abroad, European nations also use hip-hop to manage perceived extreme Muslim groups.[80] These cooptations belie the ways hip-hop in the United States is still blamed for a range of social problems. Interestingly, the tragic death of Emmet Till in 1955 that stood as an emblem of civil rights during Jazz Diplomacy found a mirror in the tragic death of Trayvon Martin in 2012 as an index of civil rights for racialized bodies during contemporary hip-hop diplomacy efforts. The difference now lies in the fact that foreign diplomacy via Black culture is being pursued not just by U.S. State Departments, but also by anti-Muslim movements in countries like Tunisia, Cuba, and Venezuela.[81]

Bgirl Tzy's 2009 experience as a U.S. State Department visitor highlights another performative euphemism in the "roots-finding" metaphor within global hip-hop discourse. By portraying Tzy and other international artists from U.S.-occupied places as foreigners who were simply "finding their roots in the United States," mainstream media unknowingly highlighted the cultural visitor program's imperial amnesia even as it substituted the paternalist, hegemonic unseemliness with liberal multiculturalist rhetoric.[82] The substantial piece here is that Bgirl Tzy's autobiographical narrative—reflecting a Petisyonado in limbo and later "uprooted" Manila hip-hop community leader—contrasts sharply with the media narrative by which the United States serves as a place where hip-hop talents "find their roots."

Power Moves: From Hero to Zero

> If I was any other Filipina girl, I would be so very happy to leave the country and move [to] the U.S. . . . But that is not the case. In those eleven years, I have made a name, became a world champion (with Allstars), [been] given a venue to change things, and . . . traveled to different cities in different countries. And it will really be a huge, huge change of lifestyle if I move to the U.S. It would be like going back to zero. I know, I know, there are a lot of opportunities here. But thing is, I'm already in my early thirties! I'm old. Who would hire me?[83]

Petisyonados make sense of the racialized and gendered hierarchies impacting their mobilities, including racial exclusion in the U.S. entertainment industry, in ways that reveal migration-as-demotion or unheroic migrations. Rather than articulating the conventional rose-tinted American Dream-driven immigration story, Bgirl Tzy's decision to migrate to the

United States involved ambivalence, opposition, and anticipation of a loss articulated in her understanding of her migration as going "back to zero." But her loss is not only measured in terms of employment. In addition to Tzy being an independent dancer in Manila, many in the community depended upon her. In 2009, for example, she was in charge of establishing and directing the Allstars Dance School (ADS), which holds an annual summer workshop, produces a theatrical recital, and hosts foreign choreographers and artists. For Bgirl Tzy, dance not only mitigated the experience of being left behind by her parents and sisters, it saved her life, gave her new purpose, and empowered her to bring social change to Manila and the Philippines more broadly. Related to Tzy's anxiety of migration-as-demotion was the way that moving from a Filipino-majority hip-hop environment to a multi-racial hip-hop environment led to shifts in her understanding of gender, race, and hip-hop authenticity. Bgirl Tzy had preconceived notions of dancing hip-hop in the United States as "dancing Black." As she saw it, the U.S. entertainment industry had a standing demand for Black dancers in music videos and she, as a short Pinay body who could not "pass," would likely only book Filipino and Vietnamese productions. In bgirling, power moves like windmills, headspins, swipes, and flares are essential components of a dance that demonstrate endurance, flexibility, skill at building and sustaining momentum, and reclaiming hypermasculine spaces. Similarly, Bgirl Tzy's narrative reclaims migrant discourse with a nuanced understanding of Filipino dance and subversion of the heroic migrant trope.

Bgirl Tzy's thinking isn't unusual. Consider for example, the American ABC network sitcom, Black-ish (2014), in which Anthony Anderson portrays Andre "Dre" Johnson Sr., who laments the trade-offs between upward mobility and loss of Black culture.[84] He imagines a tourist van passing his wealthy family in front of their large house, the tourists gawk at them as "The Mythical and Majestic Black Family—White Neighborhood (Circa 2014)," described as living out of their "natural habitat, and yet still thriving."[85] The next scene shows Dre at the kitchen table scrolling through his tablet at announcements of music awards, a celebrity gossip site, and a user-generated video titled "Kick Ass Asian Dance Moves," with a tally of over 54 million online views. Dre narrates, "Sometimes I worry that, in an effort to make it, Black folks have dropped a little bit of their culture and the rest of the world has picked it up. Justin Timberlake and Robin Thicke are R&B gods, Kim Kardashian's the symbol for big butts, and Asian guys are just unholdable on the dance floor. Come on! Big Butts/R&B and dancing?

Those were the Black man's go-tos!"[86] In this pilot episode of the series, Dre acknowledges the common sense that dance was and is racialized and gendered as Black masculinity in American contexts, yet problematically locates the visible success of Asian men as supplanters. In this context, Bgirl Tzy's anxieties around racial expectations in the U.S. commercial entertainment market align with particularly classed and gendered configurations around whom is constructed as a legible authority on dance.[87] Her assessment of the desire for the U.S. dance industry to hire Black dancers, shaped by her own ideas of "dancing Black," would be refuted later by her L.A.-based crewmates who asserted the exceptionalism of Filipino dancers.

Related to this question of racial expectations is one of the main questions that emerged in my interviews around whether there were aspects of colonial mentality in Filipino hip-hop, and if so, what did it look like? Bboy Reflex links colonial mentality to conyo mentality in hip-hop, wherein conyo refers to the language, conspicuous consumerism, and mannerisms of upper-class youth that believe being from outside the Philippines is inherently better. He sees it in the way some audience members tell him he does "New York style" bboying, a dance with well-known roots in New York. Bgirl Eyevee also frowns at the colonial mentality she sees when breakers immediately adopt the styles, moves, and skills learned from visiting Canadian and American breakers as their own, unwilling to develop their own style. Moreover, she sees a gendered dimension to colonial mentality in that more bgirls allegedly lack the self-confidence to create of and for themselves as Filipinos without relying on external influences from outside of the Philippines. Moreover, as Vince "Crazy Beans" Mendoza suggested to me, colonial mentality emerges from a lack of self-esteem and insecurity in one's self that obstructs them from investing in themselves, attending classes by visiting hip-hop authorities, and ultimately inhibits progress within the Filipino hip-hop community. In order to counter colonial mentality, dancers develop their own fresh strategies. For instance, Crazy Bean's freestyle pedagogy around bilog, or circle in Filipino language, emphasizes relaxation, and honing in on one's pagkatao (personality) without set choreography or technique. He stresses exercises for fluidity and musical interpretation (that can include T'boli music) around four principles: yamak (freehand), apa (feet), tulay (pas de deux), and pangya (pangyari or situation).

Given the discourse around state-sponsored labor migration, the practices of Filipino hip-hop dancers and Bgirl Tzy's reading of her migrant experience undermine the corporeal limits on Filipinoness I discussed earlier. This is the essential point of Bgirl Tzy's story: her anxieties around "aging out" and U.S. racial hiring preferences in entertainment—inverses of the overseas Filipino migrant's supposed natural hiring ability—informed Bgirl Tzy's "talent" and a self-narrative of migration as a downfall "from hero to zero."

Floorwork

> If I could conquer the floor, the guys would have to wait 'til I was finished or risk getting hurt. They would think twice before tryin' it. And so began my quest for floor moves.[88]

Floorwork has a strategic role in enabling bgirls to evade bboy attempts to grab, bump, or hump them, as pioneering Spanish Harlem-born hip-hop dancer Ana "Rokafella" Garcia illustrates. Similarly, by self-narrating the complicated processes of leaving "home" in terms of dance, OFWs and Petisyonados illuminate how gendered, classed, and racialized difference plays a vital yet overlooked role in emigration. The overseas Filipino dancer and Petisyonado euphemize the Black and Brown racial, class, and sexual material that constitutes, in part, the transnational circulation of dance forms in the age of neoliberalism. Overseas Filipino dancers deepen cultural globalization discourse with methodological and dance-based vistas into uprooting and returning. Overseas Filipino migrants underscore how middle-class dancers passed pre-migration exams that reaffirmed neocolonial, hierarchical norms that subjugated Black popular forms and reaffirmed whiteness. Their migration emphasizes the social dynamics shaping the state-brokerage of dancers, and how said mobilities often depended on particular meanings of racialized movement held by government officials, club managers, and migrants. Similarly, fraught with contradictions, Petisyonado migration inverts both the Philippine state's heroic migrant worker branding campaign and the "roots-finding" narrative co-opted by U.S. state-sponsored hip-hop. Interestingly, OFWs, mostly from working-class backgrounds, lack control over their work hours in a market that naturalizes the value of Filipino talents, while middle-class Petisyonados endure the insecurities of petition-processing limbo, only to enter a market that underrepresents Filipinos.

Filipino migrations reveal the connection between race and dance, with particular attention to movement in dance across Japan, emergent Asian economies, Dubai, the United States, and the Philippines. These migrations implicate the ways Black expressivity and labor forces circulate in other parts of the globe to co-construct aesthetics of desire, "freedom," and containment. The euphemistic figuration of the heroic migrant is contested—dancing between limbo and lottery, loss and gain, despedida and reunion, demotion and promotion, hero and zero—such that a Filipino's movements index their very own uprooting. But this perspective fails to go so far as to articulate the "how" of Filipino bodily movement.

3

Robots and Affirmative Choreographies

Bass booms. Arms bend. Eyes gaze outward. A group of robotic dancers dressed in shiny black aprons pushes large cardboard shipping boxes onstage in their theatrical rendition of a factory production line.[1] Collectively, steel-faced robot-dancers move about seemingly detached from their actions. Each of them holds a uniform, almost generic expression devoid of emotion. This detail highlights the miming nature of their dance and packing process. Each of their balikbayan *boxes, or remittance parcels, contains an automaton—an animatronic interpretation of Philippine folk dance. While the robots resist emoting, the automata perform signature personalities differentiated by costume, affect, and movement vocabulary that derive from Philippine tradition. Both the robot and automata execute a bodily movement intent on distinguishing "natural" human movement from artifice. As the two groups dance, we hear Nine Inch Nails' "Closer" echo across the 2,000 seats of Zellerbach Auditorium at the University of California–Berkeley.*

In the 1970s and 1980s, Pilipino culture nights (PCNs) grew as a performance genre that played a critical role in building Filipino diasporic community, resisting marginalization in U.S. universities, and celebrating cultural heritage.[2] Performed by middle-class and working-class Filipino Americans, PCN is an annual three-hour-long theatrical "culture-in-a-box," or a "Pilipino American experience" play with Philippine folk dance, music, costume, and language, and Philippine and American national anthems.[3] In the 1990s, increasingly costly PCNs that reached thousands of audience members came under attack by academics and community veterans for a wide variety of reasons not limited to content, format, and productivity.[4] Scholars addressed PCN issues of essentialism, authenticity, Orientalism, and the adverse effects on participants' academic success.[5] In 1986–1996, as California began removing race-based policies including university admissions and as part of

Choreographing in Color. J. Lorenzo Perillo, Oxford University Press (2020). © Oxford University Press.
DOI: 10.1093/oso/9780190054274.001.0001

intensifying neoliberal divestment from state obligation, Filipinos turned to the stage and radically played with the PCN genre's form and content.[6]

"Assembly Line," ⊙ the dance performance in the epigraph, reflects these histories and forms an integral part of a more extensive theater production, *Home*, the Pilipino American Alliance's 24th Annual PCN in April 2000. The show departed from standard conventions by removing traditional dances.[7] More specifically, it queried the centrality of Philippine folk dances, folk music, and linear narrative. Instead of reconstructing the usual repertoire, *Home* created new works built around Filipino American history, removing opening national anthems, while maintaining familiar material of Philippine culture (bamboo sticks, costumes, and immigration narratives). In addition to a series of varied, original pieces (spoken word, vignettes, dialogues, monologues, and skits) engaging with Filipino American themes, *Home* utilized innovative choreography, the Africanist aesthetic of call and response, and digital technology in constructing narratives of Filipino American experiences. *Home* participants turned to anti-essentialist critique, revision, and choreographic strategies of abstraction. While the show's production went against the wishes of some community members, Rani de Leon, the trailblazing coordinator of *Home* and a professional DJ, envisioned PCN as a space to revise history, and did this in part by incorporating movements from hip-hop dance.[8]

An analysis of "Assembly Line," a central dance of *Home*, choreographed by Garrick Macatangay and Sarah Escosa, demonstrates that when read in terms of both Filipino and African American relations, we see more clearly how its euphemistic integration of popping and roboting generate a social critique of the mechanical reproduction of culture.[9] Racial essentialism and authenticity form the core of any defense or critique of PCN. Those who defend the genre argue that it provides young Filipinos with space to define themselves within an educational system in which they remain largely invisible, whereas those who critique it counter that the form is stiff, mechanistic, and a poor substitute for "real" political action.[10] As a response to the culture-in-a-box formula of multiculturalist PCNs developed in the 1970s and 1980s, *Home* was also a byproduct of changes unfolding within the broader political culture. These changes included the addition of Black forms of dance in a section entitled "Modern." How individuals valued modern dancing bodies chronicle racial strategies of multiculturalism and post-raciality that help us better understand often overlooked dynamics of educational segregation.

A discussion of "Assembly Line" that underlines its embodiment of earlier PCN criticisms put forth by Filipino scholars and veterans helps unpack these shifts in bodily rhetoric of racial performance. For practical matters, the portions of "Assembly Line" proceed in this chapter out of chronological order, and rather, in terms of its three components: automata, robots, and balikbayan boxes (remittance parcels). As described in the epigraph, automata situate the restricted artistic freedoms afforded by folk dance within a broader system of multiculturalism. Asian American literature expert Victor Bascara teaches us of the resonances between multiculturalism and globalization as they relate to the failures of U.S. imperialism and manifest as tools for managing American difference.[11] In "Assembly Line," this difference is signaled and ironically subverted by automata performing animatronic movement vocabularies and upset by their smooth movements and musical accompaniment. Like the automata, the robots similarly contest the naturalized medley of Filipino culture that PCNs usually display albeit in very different ways. The uniform robot dancers assign a negative value to racial difference and symbolize post-racial ideology.[12]

The previous chapters contextualized the global recognition of exceptional Filipino dancing in the prison industrial complex and out-migrant discourse. In this chapter, a reconfiguring of Black dance, Filipino folk tradition, and post–Civil Rights structural inequalities in the euphemistic emblem of the robot demonstrates how performers remake Filipino American affinities. Conservative public policies laid the groundwork for what I call the affirmative body, a robust and full-bodied subject and subjecthood that remains in step with statist racial codes and a particular corporeality engaged by Filipino Americans on PCN stages. This chapter provides the book's third of four examples which denaturalizes Filipinoness. Much like the zombie and hero in previous chapters, the robot offers an opportunity to read the performative euphemism as a mode by which dancers of color criticize the estranging conditions shaped by anti– and post–affirmative action racial politics. *Home* presents a sophisticated layering of colonial legacies, globalization, and racial formation in the United States. In the late 1980s and 1990s, PCNs functioned as laboratories for hip-hop with the potential to argue for a race-conscious agency, centralize Black dance in a Filipino coming-of-age process, and challenge cultures of imperialism.[13]

Affirmative Choreographies

To understand "Assembly Line," we must consider the context within which Filipino undergraduates in California stepped onstage. In the U.S. context, critical race scholars have made strides in exploring different Filipino racial formations by looking at ways legislation has inhibited immigration, citizenship, employment, language, and educational attainment based on race.[14] Attention to these dimensions of race enriches the image of the Filipino dancers in migrant discourse in the previous chapter by offering a more specific understanding of how discrimination operates unevenly. At the same time, the ways Filipinos have experienced racism differently from other minorities also reaffirms the utility of disambiguating conversations about race and hip-hop.[15]

The 1990s witnessed the passage of constitutional amendments ending California's affirmative action policies in public sector employment, education, and contracting. In the United States, affirmative action is a set of federal and state government policies that considers race, color, religion, national origin, gender, and sexual orientation.[16] As a sequence of executive orders and legislative shifts, affirmative action began in 1961 with President John F. Kennedy's Executive Order 10925 that ensured "minority" inclusion and redressed historical and existing injustices. These policies comprise the codes of institutional racial legibility that provide certain bodies with entitlements, reparations, or adequate services. For Filipino racialization, these policies are compounded with multiple notions of liminality.[17] The Filipinos' historical positioning as foreigners, subjects of the American colonial racist project, and immigration status as "nationals" in relationship to racialized labor practices constitutes its figure as liminal (between two ambiguous states).[18] This status may be seen as the antithesis of the affirmative body. The dancing in PCN should thus be seen as a vehicle for sustained efforts at resolving the tensions between the affirmative body, or the coherent subjecthood that remains in step with statist racial codes, and Filipino body, the liminal subjecthood that slips between states of colonial and national racial and sexual normativity.[19]

To help outline some of the concrete events that inform such conditions of uncertainty, we can look at various sides of the affirmative action debate. In the 1990s, the University of California Regents, the governing board of the university to which California Governor Pete Wilson served as president, and U.C. Regent Wardell "Ward" Connerly led a movement to pass Proposition 209. Their actions led to the elimination of all affirmative action programs "based on race and gender preference in admissions, hiring, and contracting in the U.C. system beginning in the Fall of 1997."[20] Proposition 209's passage was part of a larger attack on affirmative action that created a dynamic that sent contradictory messages about race. While legal cases—for example, *Regents of the University of California v. Bakke* (1978) and *Grutter v. Bollinger* (2003)—upheld the rights of academic institutions to consider race and ethnicity in policies with the reasoning that diversity benefited people from all races and ethnicities, affirmative action policies have receded in particular states.[21] Proposition 209 emphasized "merit" in a way that offered post-raciality as the alternative to race-conscious affirmative action. While purported to serve institutions that valued diversity, the new policies in effect disavowed difference and removed programs that worked to redress racial and gender injustices and proved historically beneficial to underrepresented minorities, including Filipinos, at academic institutions. While the post–Civil Rights era augured the affirmative subject, the following (re)emergence of "meritocracy" would generate ambivalence—attributed to mixed attitudes of institutions toward different racial groups. In justifying the racial order and status quo of white supremacy through an obscured, abstracted, and ahistoricized term like "merit," the institutionalized ambivalence converged with the liminal racial formation of Filipinos.[22]

Promoted by conservative politicians and lobbyists, Proposition 209 was part of a series of anti-diversity referenda that had terrible consequences for California's racial minorities. According to the decade retrospective study by Equal Rights Advocates (ERA), a nonprofit legal women's rights organization, Proposition 209 led to an increase in alienation and racism for students of color and proved to be effective tools for mobilizing the state's white voters against a majority non-white demographic.[23] While affirmative action admission policies ended for most minorities in 1996, Asian Americans were actually removed from affirmative action and educational opportunity programs in 1986.[24] At that time, the U.C. Regents had passed a referendum in part resulting from the perception that, unlike African Americans, Latinos, and Native Americans, Asian Americans were "overrepresented" in universities.[25] This action can also be traced to the Asian American model minority myth, or the naturalized academic success of people of Asian descent.[26] Tracing back to multiple origins before the mid-twentieth century, the model minority myth ignores and thus reinforces class hierarchies within the Asian American category.[27] Anti–affirmative action groups relied on the model minority myth to explain Asian American educational achievement.[28] In this strange twist, while the referendum privileged merit as a post-racial metric, anti–affirmative action groups used essentialist notions of race to help attract support. Others reaffirmed anti-Black racism and white supremacy by inferring that dismantling affirmative action would ultimately benefit Asian Americans most at the cost of African American and Latino groups.[29]

The affirmative action discourse around Asian Americans illustrates the discriminatory effects of treating groups within racial categories similarly.[30] Unlike (North)east Asian American groups, Filipinos display lower statistical admission, occupation, and educational attainment rates.[31] According to legal scholar Citadelle Priagula, while Asian Americans as a group increased in representation (33 percent of U.C. Berkeley in 1991), Filipino American admission and enrollment rates for U.C. Berkeley declined.[32] According to Asian American studies scholar Tracy Buenavista's analysis of Filipino higher education, positive changes to a small Filipino admit population makes any change seem significant and obscures the reality of underrepresentation of Filipinos.[33] Although scholars predicted that the removal of affirmative action would result in an increase of Asian American students, such a rise has not been the case for Filipino Americans.[34] Given the similar numerical populations of Chinese and Filipinos in California, their contrasting student enrollment is indicative of the drastic differences in access to selective institutions between U.S. Asian American communities.[35] Also unlike Chinese Americans and Japanese Americans, Filipino Americans see less faculty and staff role models, as well as Filipino American courses, curriculum, and research—all factors that can exacerbate alienation and increase attrition rates.[36] At the same time, Jonathan Okamura observes that post–affirmative action admissions of Filipino American students in the broader U.C. system have been much more positive than those of African Americans and Latinos, who remain underrepresented compared to California public high school demographics.[37]

Despite these differences and efforts by many to disaggregate Asian American difference in public policy, Filipinos remain institutionally circumscribed within Asian American studies, departments, and courses.[38] Affirmative action discourse has been framed in dichotomous terms of Asian American versus Black and Latino to ultimately benefit white supremacy.[39] Proposition 209 proponents argued that higher educational success rates of Asian Americans proved that affirmative action was no longer necessary, and some even argued that admission chances for Asian Americans were negatively impacted by affirmative action.[40] Others have countered how these views neglect to see how affirmative action has historically benefited specific Asian American groups like Filipinos, thus problematizing the framing of competition between racial minorities—the "overachieving" model minorities and the "lazy" or "unqualified" other minorities.[41] Anti–affirmative action arguments often relied on the false parallelism between an existing racial order and an abstracted, ahistoricized meritocracy.

These brief glances into the affirmative action debates reveal regional particularities for Filipinos, differences between Filipinos and African Americans, and Filipino Americans and Asian Americans that give texture and weight to the post–Proposition 209 atmosphere that brought "Assembly Line" dancers together and which they then recreated on the stage. These intersections call for a more nuanced attention to multiple dimensions of race—one that does not dichotomize Asian-Black relations and treats anti-Filipino discrimination as uniquely different from anti-Asian discrimination.[42] This call is distinct from particular forms of multiracial and post-racial politics. African American studies scholar Jared Sexton criticizes multiracialism for reinforcing normative sexual racisms even as they deviate from racialization.[43] In this context, we should understand PCN practitioners' actions as a strategy for building a fluency in the grammar of racial structures that attempt to regulate their freedom to express the widest ranges of humanity.[44] Their dancing addressed the shifting rhetoric of the body. The former rhetoric entitled minoritized groups to state provisions as a means of addressing historically rooted injustice in the Civil Rights movement. The new language centered on abstractions—underrepresentation and merit— by which the students, instead of the state, were burdened to prove their value. As part of the latter, people were to disregard their physical phenotype (race) but regard their physical capabilities (merit), to be appropriately legible to the state. The liminal body of Filipino racialization forms a counterpoint to the affirmative body of U.S. racial politics, law, and education, that provide critical context into the indiscernibility of the Filipino dancing body and PCN in the late twentieth century.

Rehearsing the Repertoire

The PCN process begins when the student community elects the coordinator in the spring. The coordinator role is demanding, stressful, and overwhelming. Despite these hindrances, I was so impacted by the contradictions between affirmative choreographies and Filipino racialization, that in the spring 2001, I gave a public presentation on my vision for PCN 2002 in front of the community and other candidates. After a question-and-answer period, the community then voted and elected me. During the summer retreat, other organization officers and I worked on team-building and planning for the upcoming academic year. During the year, I (1) formed a committee, (2) organized the various aspects of PCN, (3) facilitated monthly workshops, and (4) held auditions, casting, rehearsals, and an elective class through the DeCal program, a democratic education program by which participants learn Filipino American studies typically excluded from the general education curriculum. The demand for regular mandatory meetings can be both a burden and strength of PCN.[45] While weekly practices mark out space and time to develop social bonds that go well beyond PCN season, some students opt out of PCN during their junior or senior year because of the sheer commitment expected of them.

Affirmative choreographies inform the history of PCN, its critical reception, and adaptations, as one of the dominant modes of formal cultural production by Filipinos in the U.S.[46] San Francisco State University produced the first in 1970, and I counted at least twenty-nine PCNs on California college campuses from March to May 2017 alone.[47] These student-initiated cultural programs began at different points in California's public education history with inaugural PCNs including Berkeley, Irvine, and Los Angeles in the late 1970s, then a decade later at Davis, Riverside, San Diego, Santa Barbara, and Santa Cruz in the late 1980s and early 1990s, and at Merced in 2007.[48] PCNs belong to a broader culture and network of Filipino American-based collegiate organization events in which thousands of Filipino young adults reconnect with former high school classmates to collaborate and compete. This network at times includes Filipino groups from other West Coast states and includes events such as California State University at Fullerton's Friendship Games, California State Polytechnic University Pomona's Sports Fest, and fraternity-hosted dance competitions.

For audience members, PCN can perform the work of building community between Filipinos, defining "Filipino" against a white majority, and distinguishing Filipinos from other Asians and racial minorities.[49] With such a high level of significance, it should come as no surprise that scholars have undergone extensive analyses of the PCN genre, establishing foundational understandings for the types of ideological and practical work such productions can accomplish.[50] American Studies scholar Theodore Gonzalves recounts the main criticism shared by veterans in the community over what he described as the "culture-in-a-box" PCN formula—Philippine and U.S. national anthems, Tagalog language, Philippine costumes and folk dances, and "Pilipino American experience" theatrical drama.[51] The formula provides a useful and familiar format within which audiences could learn, celebrate, and produce something by Filipinos and for Filipinos. It served as a template for the yearly event and space where folks from different disciplines could converge and collaborate. This space was one in which Filipinos could expect to re-enact Philippine traditions of dance while acting out contemporary Filipino American narratives. These expectations make more sense when considering how specific Philippine dances became standardized as part of a PCN canon of dances arranged into four distinct suites. The PCN canon refers to the format in which organizers divide PCN content in terms of suites, or ethnic, linguistic, regional cultural groupings. In the 1996 PCN at Berkeley, for example, the show's program included categories of dance, or suites: Muslim, Spanish, Regional, Barrio.[52]

These PCN suites sought to draw their authority as authentic sources of Filipino performance through their source material, the repertoire of the Bayanihan Philippine Dance Company.[53] In 1958, Bayanihan won first place at the Brussels World's Fair against thirteen other national dance groups, and subsequently began touring the globe promoting and popularizing Philippine dance customs.[54] Indeed, these dance customs were the product of the pioneering work of Francisca Reyes Aquino, researchers, educators, and cultural nationalists in the 1930s, who collectively documented sacred rituals, games, and ceremonies from mostly rural provinces for preservation and education.[55] During the American colonial period (1898–1946), the Filipino national folk dance repertoire emerged amidst generational anxieties over increasing American cultural consumption, concern over the effects of industrialism on women and children's bodies, and the disciplinary technologies of public institutional physical education.[56] The dances were employed in public schools and reflect the tensions between benevolent assimilation and sovereignty.[57] In today's U.S. universities, derivations of these folk dances are reconstructed to produce counter-narratives to a hegemonic curriculum that often omits, deletes, or suppresses Filipino-specific knowledge.

In the 1980s and 1990s, dancing in PCNs became faster-paced, heavily produced, and more concerned with virtuosity and movement skills.[58] This popularity led to scholars across Asian American studies, Southeast Asian studies, and ethnomusicology to express concerns about a range of PCN issues including their mechanistic spectacularity, detachment from contemporary Philippine politics, Orientalism, and adverse effects on the academic success of its participants.[59] One might add to this list of criticisms that PCNs rarely deal with dances as dynamic products of historical and social contestation. Even though these cultural politics usually remain absent from multiculturalist PCNs, they still accomplish a particular type of cultural work for both performers and audiences as year-long processes of community building.

PCN as identity practice can incite conflicts over value, authenticity, and legitimacy at multiple levels. The Philippine folk authenticity paradigm holds PCN bodies to the culture-in-a-box essentialism rooted in a specific Philippine nation-building history. How graceful and lithe one can perform Spanish dances, or how fast one can perform the Tinikling—these were the informal standards of dancing in a PCN, and they were the hallmarks of its worth and success. Rather than strictly following the templates of folk dance preserved by Francesca Reyes Aquino, Filipino Americans often unknowingly respond to such expectations by producing hyper-staged folk dance.[60] With each decade, the canonical dances seemed to go through a game of "telephone" that altered their forms with faster tempos, increasingly difficult spatial formations and transitions, and arbitrary costume substitutions. These changes codify "authentic" Filipino subjecthood while creating ideological, cultural, and dance hierarchies within which less than authentic Filipinos/dance could have a place.[61]

In this context, Filipino dancing bodies in the PCN genre did not construct authenticity as an either/or quality, whereupon one is or is not authentically Filipino. Instead, PCNs became the contested sites of authenticity as a question of gradation, with levels of authenticity correlating to the presence of select dances (e.g., Singkil and Tinikling) and achievement of spectacle and exoticism approaching Bayanihan's performances. The frequency with which multiculturalist PCNs have operated in confluence with a white supremacist discursive apparatus, which I read in the affirmative body, has perhaps hindered even the most successful scholars from an accurate assessment of the multiple architectures of Filipino cultural activism. As elements of virtuosity and authenticity were also measures by which audiences with little access to Filipino racial histories "read" dance in PCNs, they compounded notions of meritocracy and anti–affirmative action groups' use of Asians as a racial wedge between Asian, Black, and Latino groups.

The Rise of the Modern Suite and *Home*

U.C. Berkeley campus has a rich history in student protest, from one of the earliest ethnic studies departments emerging from the student strike by Third World Liberation Front (twLF) in 1969 to a series of actions in 1999 including ethnic studies demonstrations, occupations, and hunger strikes. This history connects the demands for community-engaged Filipino-centered education to the broader struggles of Native American, African American, Chicano, and Asian American students, even as it foregrounds the differences between these struggles. For instance, in the late 1990s, Black students engaged in silent protests, occupying Sather Gate or walking into large lectures with linked arms. Their shirts read "less than 4%, represent" and compelled witnesses to reckon with the mix of privilege, oppression, and resilience that characterized Black struggles on campus. In the Pilipino student community, these shared struggles for educational equity manifested in adaptations and rethinking of the Philippine folk repertoire.

Contrary to what their name suggests, PCNs are not only concerned with culture and dances rooted in the Philippines. In addition to producing counter-narratives to hegemonic curricula out of Philippine folk dance, with this formula PCN organizers often strived to express the cultural interests of Filipino Americans in the United States. As such, they address the double bind of modern minority performance. On the one hand, this bind asks subjects to return to tradition, or undergo a process of "restoration of a cultural heritage to a social identity."[62] On the other hand, subjects are expected to distance themselves from that very tradition as proof of their modernity in a way that counters the stereotypes of backwardness historically placed upon Filipinos.[63] In the 1990s, these subtexts manifested in changes made to the PCN canon with the inclusion of Filipino cultural forms from outside of the folk repertoire in what is termed the Modern Suite (see Introduction). Unlike the traditional dance suites, Modern Suites feature Black dance forms—usually hip-hop dance, but sometimes jazz, lyrical, Lindy Hop, or tap—as fundamental to one's membership to contemporary youth culture in the United States.[64] PCN programs or playbills from late-1990s U.C. Berkeley PCNs, those preceding *Home* (1999–2000), situate the role of the Modern Suite, and provide a better understanding of how the cast and audience made sense of Filipino diasporic and Black dances.

Four years before *Home*, choreographers of the PCN *Pakinggan Mo Ako* (Listen to Me) (1995–1996) looked to the 1920s, and configured Modern

Suite as proof of the growing need to connect to the U.S.-based histories of Filipinos and perhaps a classical sociological view of immigrant adaptation that assumed innate links between assimilation and social success. The *Pakinggan Mo Ako* program reads:

> Modern Suite reflects the dual nature of Pilipino American culture. It is as much a symbol of our adaptation and assimilation into the American cultures as it is a continuance of our strong Pilipino tradition of expression through music and dance. Just like our *manongs* and *manangs* who danced Swing in the 20s taxi-dancehalls, we, as Pilipinos in America, have been carving out our own niches within American culture. This year's Modern Suite incorporates some of the many flavors of Pilipino American dance, which include Hip-Hop, R&B, House, Jazz, Techno, and Pop.[65]

It is important to note that *Pakinggan Mo Ako* fit the PCN formula in some ways as it began with both the Philippine national anthem "Lupang Hinirang" and "Star Spangled Banner." Like many multiculturalist PCNs, the Modern Suite was sequenced just before the intermission at the end of Act One. The strategic ordering of dances accomplishes at least two things. It encouraged those that attend PCN only to see the Modern Suite a chance to leave without disturbing the show. It also ensures these folks will stay for the entire first half of the program. The multiculturalist program lists the choreography by name and choreographer. Dances such as "Smack It Up, Flip It . . ." and "Like It Raw" by Frank Lozier, "Deep XTC" by Elwyn Cabebe, and "Mellow Cats Dig" by Julie Munsayac and Pat Taba, offered a dramatic tonal contrast to the conventional Philippine folkloric components in PCN (see Figure 3.1).[66]

By 1997, choreographers renamed the Modern Suite as "American Suite," a move that un-ironically echoed the modernist, "benevolent assimilation" propaganda during the American colonial occupation of the Philippines in the early 1900s.[67] In so doing, choreographers of *Tagasalaysay/Storyteller: A Story of Culture* (1997–1998) redefined the suite as space not simply for racial crossing, or mobilizing notions of Filipinoness through African American practices, but also for asserting American citizenship (see Figures 3.2 and 3.3).[68] Choreographers sought to link dancing with a scripted play that attempted to keep in mind its multi-generational audience: It framed hip-hop dance as a part of a daughter's cotillion, a traditional coming-of-age event for Filipinas; it included the mother as she recalled her memory of her own cotillion; it featured swing dance (Lindy Hop) that was written as the "hip-hop dance"

Gayle Bernabe, Elwyn Cabebe, Cynthia Casasola, Liz Casasola, Marites Cristobal, Cielo de la Paz, Jess Delegencia, Warren Fu, Joanne Hwang, Marco Jastillana, Frank Lozier, Sal Macasieb, Alexis Miranda, Julie Munsayac, May Rafanan, Angie Realce, Marianne Santos, Rick Sarmiento, Eric Set, Pat Taba, Alvin Teodoro, Paul Villareal

Modern suite reflects the dual nature of Pilipino American culture. It is as much a symbol of our adaptation and assimilation into the American cultures as it is a continuance of our strong Pilipino tradition of expression through music and dance. Just like our *manongs* and *manangs* who danced Swing in the 20's taxi-dancehalls, we, as Pilipinos in America have been carving out our own niches within American culture. This year's Modern Suite incorporates some of the many flavors of Pilipino American dance, which include Hip-Hop, R&B, House, Jazz, Techno, and Pop.

Choreography
Hit Squad — Warren Fu*
Mellow Cats Dig — Julie
        Munsayac & Pat Taba
Like It Raw — Frank Lozier*
Deep XTC — Elwyn Cabebe
Dangerous — Warren Fu
Smack It Up, Flip It... —
        Frank Lozier
Moments of Madness — Alvin
        Teodoro
Miami Style — Frank Lozier
Final Mix by David Maduli

* Head Choreographers

Figure 3.1 *Pakinggan Mo Ako* (Listen to Me), Pilipino Culture Night program (1996)—Modern Suite.

of her grandfather's time, when in the 1920s and 1930s Filipino men would frequent taxi-dance halls.[69] *Tagasalaysay/ Storyteller*'s sepia-colored program evidences a combination of retention and revision in the description used by PCNs to communicate the rationale behind the Modern Suite dances.[70] In some instances, complete sentences are recycled (or plagiarized) to convey the ideas behind Filipino American culture. The common themes in *Pakinggan Mo Ako* (1995–1996) of duality, adaptation and assimilation, permeability, and niche-carving were traded in for more specific attention to issues of contemporary racial politics in *Tagasalaysay/Storyteller* (1997–1998). Changes such as these only intensified for the next years. For instance, organizers designed the program for *Re: Collections* (1998–1999) like a photo album, featuring various rapid-print photos, handwritten and typewriter fonts, and irregularly spaced text.[71] The Regional Suite was divided into the Mountain and Tribal Suites. Instead of the frequent theme of assimilation of the previous years, the program highlighted themes of "resistance to the mainstream" and culture as a response to "modern oppressive forces." In many ways, these changes represented modestly shifting ideas around race and performance.

In contrast to these PCNs that confined Black dance forms to the Modern Suite, *Home* (1999–2000) integrated hip-hop and contemporary movement practices into most of the components of the production. Instead of suites and the multicultural hybridity paradigm they displayed, *Home* made novel use of "Water," "Earth," "Air," "Fire," and "Love" as elemental tropes around which performances of immigration, agricultural labor, communication, activism, and family relations could be organized. Each element began with a reading of spoken word poetry. There was a pre-show element in which dancers dressed from the traditional suite dances, Pandanggo Sa Ilaw, Lumagen, and two museum docents posed in the foyer of Zellerbach Hall. Audience members posed with these living artifacts of Filipino culture in ways that intimated what Filipino studies scholar, Benito Vergara, succinctly described as the Kodak Zone.[72] To the bewilderment of many in the audience, the show opened with the sounds of a woman in labor, rather than the Philippine and American national anthems, and curtains raised to the cries of what symbolized the birth of a new kind of show. As coordinator Rani deLeon's acknowledged the United States as a settler colonial space.

Several other elements demonstrate *Home* as a departure from PCN conventions (see Figure 3.4). The first act of the program, Water, featured a "lyrical" dance section that mimicked a popular creation myth accompanied by percussive wooden instruments and flutes. As a musician played the kulintang, or indigenous percussion instrument, a colorguard/flag-waving performance, entitled "Tides," began with a cast of twenty-four women forming the waves with their fingers, arms, and scarves. As the waves cleared, a Spanish galleon named "Señora de Buena Esperanza" emerged, made up

Figure 3.2 *Tagaalaysay/Storyteller: A Story of Culture*, American Suite, Pilipino Culture Night program (1996).

Hip Hop

encompasses a variety of dance styles characterized by innovation and improvisation

dance hall days

For P/F/Philip(p)ino-Americans, a passion for dancing doesn't stop at traditional choreography. At a cotillion this past winter, part of the court celebrated their friend's coming of age by performing a Hip-Hop routine. At the end of the night, the girl's parents thanked the group for participating in this momentous occasion. The girl's mother, remembering her own cotillion, shared with the group a story that her father had shared with her. During the late 1920s and early 1930s, her father worked the agricultural circuit on which so many other young Pilipinos worked. They earned little money, and worked long hours.

Alicia Jeu, Tina Huynh, Cielo de la Paz, Sarah Escosa, Kelly Dumlao, Christine Gatchalian

Cielo de la Paz
Maricel Diwa
Kelly Dumlao
Sarah Escosa
Warren Fu
Christine Gatchalian
Philip Huang
Tina Huynh
Marco Jastillana
Alicia Jeu
Fernando Lavin
Frank Lozier
Garrick Macatangay
Alvin Teodoro

Alvin Teodoro, Fernando Lavin, Marco Jastillana, Frank Lozier, Philip Huang, Garrick Macatangay, Warren Fu

Figure 3.3 PCN performers connected Filipino agricultural labor, Lindy Hop in taxi-dance halls in the 1920s and 1930s, and hip-hop in the 1990s.

of eighteen bare-chested men lunging forward and through the stage as if it were the Pacific Ocean. As a drum sequence began, the "Indios" used each lunge to "row" with bamboo sticks as oars and scraped the stage with large circular motions. Resembling the Vinta dance in the Philippine folk dance Muslim Suite, two parallel sticks formed the ship's deck as one Spanish

Figure 3.4 *Home,* Pilipino Culture Night (2000) program cover marks a radical shift toward integrating Black cultural expression within the embodied histories of Filipino America.

conquistador stood and perched five feet above the stage. After the conquistador descended and exited the stage, the "Indios" remained and proceeded to move about in a series of formations. This dance culminated in the construction of the skeletal form of a stilted fishing house, representing the first Filipino American settlement in St. Malό, Lousiana in the early 1800s.

The second act, Earth, featured "Toil," a performance that creatively imagined the migrant laborer struggles of Filipinos in the United States. In this act, dance resonates with the previous chapters' accounts of OPAs and Petisyonados, whereby it mitigated the monotony and everyday struggles of contract labor and emigration. Using rakes, shovels, spades, and buckets, dancers orchestrated the percussive musical accompaniment to their original rhythmic choreography. They performed similarly to stepping, a dance with origins in collegiate Black Greek Letter Organizations, and formed duets, quartets, and large circles, passing their tools to each other and clapping against each other's bodies. As the program booklet reminded audiences, the farmworkers' toil was amplified by the 20-to-1 ratio of men to women and anti-miscegenation laws, in "Toil," the stooping, sweeping, and stepping Filipinas seemed to reclaim a place in history alongside Filipinos. One charismatic choreographer, Sarah Escosa, an engineering major, led a call-and-response segment, part of what dance scholars Thomas F. DeFrantz and Halifu Osumare identify as Africanist aesthetic associated with American hip-hop dance, and elicited audience participation in creating the rhythm for the dance's final section.[73] In these ways, the dancers merged Africanist aesthetics with the agricultural migrant labor histories in which "[t]housands of Pilipinos became farm workers in the fields of Hawai'i, Alaska, and California in conditions that can only be seen as criminal."[74]

"Assembly line" was sequenced in the third act, Air, after a central video section, which had two parts—Travel and Commercialism. Commercialism featured parody video advertisements for cultural commodities—a T-shirt company called "So So Brown," fish sauce (patis), and a Tinikling and Tae Bo-inspired fitness program, "Tinkling Bo with Tito Boy Banks." The latter promised consumers the ability to get in shape and feel the Filipino pride in their abs and in their buttocks, all for five easy payments of $49.95. A mock CNN, PCN 4 (Pilipino Communication Network), informed audiences with statistics about the Filipino population according to the U.S. Census. The last commercial ⓥ was for "Those Darn Filipinos," Balikbayan Box Set, a five-piece product distributed by the Consumer Culture Network (a spoof of the

Figure 3.5 *Home,* Pilipino Culture Night (2000)—"Those Darn Filipinos" commercial, screen still.

QVC) (see Figure 3.5). The product advertised, "We got all kinds of Filipinos from all walks of life," and listed its selling price as twenty installments of one million dollars, the price by which the U.S. bought the Philippines from Spain in 1898. For those in the audience familiar with the Philippines' colonial history, they might notice that the advertisement made explicit reference to the temporal and psychological dimensions of colonialism with its unit label #400yrs ofLife5 and the caveat "consciousness sold separately." This advertisement for the heterogeneity of Filipinos tells the audience to "Buy culture. Buy Filipinos. In a Box," and helps set the critical tone for the dance which followed. In the context of the introduction and development of the Modern Suite in Philippine folk dance, these performances do more than reflect the desires of diasporic Filipinos to articulate multiple cultural citizenships. These performers indirectly drew attention to the indigenous worldviews, labor struggles, commodification, and affirmative choreographies circumscribing racial minorities in the late twentieth century.

Automata and Multiculturalism

Picture this: Several bodies push balikbayan boxes (remittance packages) onstage, placing them in varying formations. No sooner have they situated the boxes, started miming the act of packaging their parcels, when another set of dancers emerges from within the cardboard containers (see Figure 3.6). These are the automata. They represent the traditional Philippine dance repertoire. There is an automaton from the Spanish Suite in a lavish gown. There is also a Tinikling dancer from the Rural Suite. Each automaton proceeds to strike poses from their respective dance while remaining inside their box. Each one also maintains the appropriate facial mannerism. If we go to PCNs looking for authentic Philippine dance, this is probably the closest thing to it we will see in *Home*. As performative euphemisms, the automata render and critique the immigrant Filipino, middle-class politics of multiculturalist PCNs.

While the "Assembly Line" dance begins with Robots on stage alone, I start with a discussion of the automata because these dancers signal the Filipino-specific multicultural racial politics which *Home* problematizes. Philippine folk dances are the main referent for the ironic register that automata choreography aims to achieve. The automata dance teaches us that these folk dances are not givens, but rather, contested sources of Filipino meaning.[75] Also, the automata have a particular time signature, in that they don't simply

Figure 3.6 *Home,* Pilipino Culture Night (2000)—Automatons in "Assembly Line," screen still. Dancers employ animation as a critique of romanticized folk dance and Filipino exhibition.

map the cadence of music onto the body. The automata direct the dance's trajectory between bodily endpoints, or dime stops, and smooth out the path in-between. The dancers imitate automata that in turn render Philippine choreography and individual personalities—derived from culture-in-a-box essentialism. They parody the proud mountain warrior, regal Muslim court subject, graceful señorita, and enthusiastic rural peasant that have become PCN standards for distinguishing one ethnic minority from another. This ironic version of "searching for one's roots" calls attention to a blanket past and compels us to wear the mask of our possible future—auto-exotification.[76]

The automata do not just address PCN culture but also indirectly express a message about how the givens of Filipino culture relate to the broader system of U.S. multiculturalism, an alternative to assimilation. For Filipinos, the limited space for multicultural representation exists in the culture-in-a-box formula, a diverse pluralism of ethnolinguistic groups that is handy for refusing a singular, monolithic definition of Filipino culture. The automata, however, inject a sense of artifice and detachment and suggest that it may not be as functional as previously thought. Appearing like music box figurines, automata alternate posture and perform the variety of traditional dancing bodies not as a menagerie but as a simulacrum. The mechanized types of folk-lore dancing bodies appear like equals, in what seems to reflect how dances in multiculturalist PCNs are plucked from their respective local time-space for a common purpose—be it through graceful, joyous, or savage presence—to look "traditional." Dancers usually take the wide array of movement qualities and collapse them into the automata's flat, uniform quality. The flatness of their gestures renders critiques of the evenness of presentation in multicul-turalist PCN. In so doing, automata generate a brand of multiculturalism that might be described as tolerance-but-not-acceptance. These representatives move like propertied Disneyland animatronics to bow to their ethnographic origins and blankly smile at their facsimile. The Tinikling dancer takes what would previously be the dynamic, sweeping, curved arm, and breaks the se-quence into fragmented segments, each with its own tickin' endpoints.

In the context of hip-hop, this choreography is not a pure deconstruction of "folk" but rather draws from the popular dance roboting, as it exhibits "traditional" dance infused with dynamics of isolations and dime stops. As Thomas DeFrantz writes, "Power in hip-hop is most apparent in the aggres-sively layered, dynamic array of shapes assumed by the dancing body. Hip-hop dances contain an assertive angularity of body posture and an insistent virtuosic rhythmicity."[77] In the context of postcolonialism, these postures and fragmentation bring to mind Sarita See's theory of colonial melancholia, in which the frequency in fragmented bodies offers an aesthetic useful for understanding the counter-normative will to abstract.[78] See's *Decolonized Eye* locates "disenfranchised grief" and two components of melancholia—unconscious nature and lowered self-esteem—that also confront the psycho-logical functions of multiculturalist PCN.[79]

Like commas of dance, the popping style forces the majority Filipino audience to break from naturalized linear expectations of folk dance and ethnic criteria in the post–affirmative action era.[80] The bodily rhythms of the automata apportion the folkloric gestures into discrete measures of time and space to convey a message about multiculturalism and its artificial re-duction of individual, different cultures—uneven inter-regional histories of slavery, colonialism, and genocide—into discrete time-space. It suggests that multiculturalist PCNs flatten uneven histories and trade on grappling with intra-group hierarchies in exchange for celebrating diversity. The contained, managed life of their own, and lack of contact with other dancers on stage, adds to the frozen, plastic personalities of the ethnic regions, and detached affect projected by individual automaton to generate an air of estrangement around the performance. This subtlety implies to the audience that the dancers are compelled to embody an "It's a small world" mechanics of multiculturalism, because, while multiculturalist dance often fails to comment directly on something more tangible (i.e., racial exclusion), it exists as one of the few spaces for "cultural" representation. This also works to question the multiculturalist PCN ideal of egalitarianism beyond the realities of contemporary Philippine political culture. When rendered by automata, the usually dynamic, at times participatory folk dances appear merely for display. While the U.S. State Department's dance diplomacy programs in the previous chapter, portrayed artists from Argentina, Palestine, Vietnam, Lebanon, and the Philippines, within "hip-hop roots-finding" narratives that mitigated neocolonialism, this dance points at the white flag of multiculturalism—its surrender of multi-dimensional engagement with difference.

By representing an estranging, artificial process of PCN in "Assembly Line," dancers take what have usually been the ready-made tools for celebrating the importance of Filipino culture for those coming-of-age in the U.S. during the rise of multiculturalism, and retool them to reveal the faulty wirings of that same repertoire. Their message is not about multiculturalism's tolerance or diversity, but about the estranging cloud of difference as the result. In sum, their choreography informs practitioners and viewers about how minorities in the United States are now triply bound. PCN dancers must be "authentic" but constantly new. They must be modern, but not ahistorical. They must be Filipino, but locally situated.

Robots and Post-Raciality

The historical and technical components of the robot dance in *Home* provide another critical component of its euphemistic performance. Historically, the robot dance emerges from the decentralized history of West Coast, American popular forms like popping and locking. The "pop" in popping refers to a sudden muscle contraction usually executed with one's triceps, forearms, neck, chest, and backs of knees. According to Jorge Pabon aka Popmaster Fabel, popping gained popularity in Northern California in the 1970s by folks like the Electric Boogaloo Lockers (later to drop the "Lockers") who were inspired by Chubby Checker's "Twist," James Brown's "The Popcorn," "The Jerk," and cartoon animation.[81] African American dancers turned to everyday movement and developed different local forms of popping.[82] Various cities in Northern California—San Jose, San Francisco, Oakland, East Palo Alto, Richmond, and Sacramento—had their own specific dance culture/ styles, perhaps informed by the fact that back then imitating another's style (biting) was prohibitive and met with physical violence.[83] While Pabon documents roboting as a style that came from, if not at least associated with, Richmond, we are left wondering what exactly roboting involves.

What does it mean to dance the robot? How does it look, feel, and move? For Hitmaster Fish, "Poppin' is the dancing robot."[84] Fish, a self-proclaimed 1.5 generation O.G. (aka hip-hop dance veteran) grew up in the Bay Area and is one of only a few African American expats living and teaching popping in Asia. He rarely shies away from defining dances and the moves that make them up. Fish operates from the premise that the classical robot dance is stationary, without music, and without rhythm. In contrast, popping ("dancing robot") moves follow the rhythm, pacing, and temporality of music. In this definition, the "Assembly Line" dancers perform popping choreography that is based on the basic vocabulary and energy of the robot. While studying popping under Terry "Hitmaster Fish" Williams in Manila, I learned what makes it a unique form of dance when compared to bboying, locking, or general hip-hop. The difference lies in how popping works as an individual versus group dance. When performed as an individual, as in an urban street performance, one can highlight original thoughts, musicality, and creative style. In contrast, when performed as a group, as in "Assembly Line," popping more easily displays uniformity than both bboying and locking. It allows the dancers to look similar to each other, to be perceived as sharp and synchronized. To fully interpret the robot popular dance in PCN, we must attend to its function amidst the post-racial politics framing Black-Brown relations in the late twentieth century.

In "Assembly Line," the main scene features robots assembling automata in cardboard balikbayan boxes. Performing the robot dance does not necessarily deconstruct the African American dance it references, but enables a discussion about folk culture as a contested model for expressing minority culture. The dance asks performers to mask emotion through careful monitoring and regulation of internal and external parts of the body. The performers' mask is constituted by even-keeled energy and repressed external "naturally" expressive movement. On the one hand, insomuch as robots are seen as ideals of efficiency and perfection, this might be read as the transcendence of the ego. On the other hand, in the context of PCN, robots highlight a lack of Philippine signifiers and ironically present a deracialized ideal.

More than counterposing controlled and natural, human and robot, this dance dramatizes the mind of a racialized body. In the context of PCN, where performing folk dances is usually driven by modernist expression (external expression of internal emotion), the robot gives us a peek into what kind of cognitive work might replace that expression in the "unmarked" body.

First, the robot dancers establish their robot-ness by performing slides, "sac'ing," (pronounced "sacking"), Fillmore phrasings, and the signature hinged elbow swing gesture (see Figure 3.7).[85] This section appears generic, lacks a clear narrative or concept, and seems ambiguously representational. Far from setting up an ideal of virtuosity, the vocabulary, with little hip emphasis and flat dynamics, seems to sit at a low enough technical level to be inclusive for dancers that are not necessarily experienced in hip-hop. Indeed, while dancers underwent an audition process in order to be in "Assembly Line," choreographers actually selected those with a lack of "showy style."[86] The ideal that these robots set up is one of uniformity to an "unmarked" shell. This aesthetic echoes with what critical race scholar Patricia J. Williams describes as "visual ideology" in the first hiring of a Black dancer by the Radio

Figure 3.7 *Home*, Pilipino Culture Night (2000)—Robots in "Assembly Line," screen still. Dancers articulate estrangement from diversity management through roboting.

City Music Hall Rockettes in October 1987.[87] Williams discusses this controversial hiring, the arguments justifying the reluctance of hiring nonwhite dancers, as a way of underlining how so-called neutral or post-racial remedies fail. Williams revisits the company director's arguments for maintaining an all-white cast based on aesthetics of uniformity and precision, such that according to the Rockettes spokesperson, the Black body "definitely" equals ugliness, imbalance, and distraction from whiteness.[88] At the same time, if the institutionalism of the Rockettes is valued strictly based on its original intent, such "aesthetics" punish racialized bodies auditioning for a so-called equal opportunity employer. In "Assembly Line," post-raciality is choreographed as a departure from a Filipino-specific multiculturalism, by which unisex Black sleeveless vests and uniform choreography replaces traditional coupled dances in cisgendered Filipiniana costumes (*ternos, bahag,* and *barongs*).

The second section of "Assembly Line" begins when robots leave and re-enter, pushing the seemingly empty boxes onstage. When the automata rise up from the boxes, the robots begin to mime the actions literally involved in the factory assembly line packing process (see Figure 3.8). This section of dancing defines the robot as "factory worker," active only in relation to the automata as passive. This dynamic indicates that post-raciality not only allows us to

Figure 3.8 *Home,* Pilipino Culture Night (2000)—Robots packing automatons in "Assembly Line," screen still.

move differently from multiculturalism's essentialist choreography, but also allows us to act as managers of mediators—highlighting processes of managing "diversity" or those that adhere to the multiculturalist ideology. In this theory, post-raciality promotes and rewards denial or suppression of all types of difference—cultural, racial, and gender. In their movement, the robots have some power in their occupational function of assembling the automata and show how post-raciality privileges deracialized bodies.

Earlier I discussed how Proposition 209 drafters and its proponents held that U.S. society must act in a post-racial fashion and race should not play a part in educational policy. By replicating a type of post-racial ideology similar to the logic behind affirmative action punditry, the dancers embodied a statement regarding the terms of their own inclusion on the university's stage, spotlighting how post-raciality asks us to ignore hyper-racial realities of institutional racism and potentials for racial agency. This performance exposes the faults of post-raciality by centering a "neutral" dance like the robot at a Filipino time and place like PCN, when people expect Filipino markers of choreography, and thus, suggesting that ignoring one's racial realities results in estrangement. For PCN subjects, at stake is the ability to assess the work minority subjects must psychically perform amidst institutional racism and deploy PCNs to counter the reductionist notions of "inferiority complex," "white preference," and assimilation with a better understanding of negotiating communal grief.

The Balikbayan Box (Remittance Parcel)

Since "Assembly Line" allegorizes the mechanistic packaging of "culture in a box," balikbayan boxes are appropriate props for the robots and automata in "Assembly Line." Literally naming those who are returning to the Philippines for vacation or retirement, *balikbayan* translates from Filipino language to English as "return nation" or "homecoming."[89] There are even special Philippine immigration visas for processing Balikbayan.[90] Returnees use the large cardboard boxes, or balikbayan boxes, to pack souvenirs, gifts, clothes, candies, and supplies for friends and relatives in the Philippines.[91] It is important to note how the contents rarely change: usually, canned goods, candies, undergarments, instant coffee, and items thought to be either unobtainable or difficult to purchase in the Philippines. Given increasing access to American products in the Philippines, sociologist Anthony C. Ocampo observes, balikbayan boxes have little economic logic and no real use for their recipients.[92] For example, rice is one of the common items sent from the U.S. to the Philippines, a country famous for its rice production.[93] Some claim that the products, when attainable in the Philippines, simply "taste different" or cost too much. The boxes are considered markers of wealth, indirectly reminding the sender and recipients of the returnee's social capital in America.[94] With the social practice of balikbayan boxes in mind, we can better appreciate how "Assembly Line" integrates Black dances with balikbayan boxes, which function in an affective economy to maintain diasporic relations, in ways that generate social critique of said economy.[95]

By situating popping and roboting dances in relationship to the Filipino social practice of balikbayan boxes, the performers enable an explication of Black dance in transnational Filipino culture. Initially, the "packages" are seen rising from the depths of their respective boxes and rotating left and right across the audience, but immobile and confined to their containers. The automata perform their respective folklore dance moves, while the other robots rotate the boxes that house them to spell out "CULTURE," "FILIPINO," and finally, "PILIPINO" from the lettering on the sides (see Figure 3.9). The literal signification of Filipino culture

Figure 3.9 *Home,* Pilipino Culture Night (2000)—Balikbayan boxes in "Assembly Line," screen still.

and Filipinoness on the boxes attempts to physically turn a phrase. On the surface, the performers' statement is about one's role in the process of packaging multiculturalist commodities. Through this performative industrialization metaphor for the traditional PCN process, the performers suggest that the ways Filipinos re-assemble and name Filipino identity are unfixed. By the end of the dance, the robots seem either unable or unwilling to manage the job at hand, which suggests that they embody a theoretical stance, not about identity-in-motion, but one that lays bare identity-going-through-the-motions.

The boxes can be interpreted to have at least three levels of meaning. First, the boxes represent their literal usage as shipping containers retooled for the functions of dance. While the boxes act like props for the robot packers furthering their role as active, for the automata, the boxes objectify and act as a performance space from which they cannot escape. The boxes serve as a physical divide between the robots and automata, meant to materially render the differences between performing modernity/future and performing tradition/past. In the service of performance, balikbayan boxes are "delivered" to the audience members watching the PCN, *Home.*

Second, these cardboard boxes represent the dance suites, structural legs of PCNs that strictly adhere to a PCN canon, inspired by the Philippine's Bayanihan Dance Company. Recalling how critics viewed the PCN as inhibiting a more productive engagement with Filipino culture, the robots packing automata represent the PCN participant preparing the annual production of Barrio, Muslim, Spanish, and Mountain Suites. Like balikbayans, or returners, sending predictable contents overseas, PCN participants are tasked with the duty of packing a predictable set of cultural "traditions" expected for receipt by PCN audiences (family members of the cast, alumni, social networks, and non-Filipinos). Choreographically, the robots as factory workers highlight the process of selecting "what goes inside" PCN. They accomplish this by constructing themselves as PCN participants arranging the standardized repertoire of "traditional" Filipino dancing bodies into linear, geometric formations that signify their bound and stale traits. As a self-aware version of this PCN paradigm, the ominous feeling evoked by the dancers seems to warn about the desiccation of Philippine culture into mere commodities. The automata as balikbayan box contents draw a connection between the candies, SPAM, and underwear usually packed in balikbayan boxes and the standardized dance repertoire of Tinikling and Singkil. The automata reference the constraints of being the package, auto-exotification, or what they render as commodifying one's self within a touristic multiculturalist PCN canon. This effect is a re-staging of what is often presented by multiculturalist PCNs as authentic cultural heritage, as a cold, estranging manufacturing process.

Third, the boxes enable "Assembly Line" dancers to appropriate the robot and popping, the Black popular dances, as the social practice of packing balikbayan boxes, a particularly Filipino practice. Just as the balikbayan box has been critiqued for its irrelevance to recipients, "Assembly Line" problematizes the relevance of "traditional" cultural repertoire and Bayanihan-inspired PCN formulas (represented by the literal boxes) to their audiences. The "Assembly Line" draws a parallel between criticism about the economic logic of the boxes (i.e., sending rice to the Philippines) with concerns about PCNs and their increasing costs of time, money, and academic success of its participants. Similarly, the boxes represent how multiculturalist PCN deals with culture as celebratory moments that are apportioned as discrete in time and space. The boxes, representing both the social practice of in-kind remittance and the social practice of PCN, cast a cloud of doubt about the relevance and cost-effectiveness of cultural shows and Filipino diasporic culture.

Beyond the insights drawn from the literal and figurative ways of interpreting balikbayan boxes—performance space and prop, ideological divide, PCN canon, Filipino social practice—we might also add intra-racial class hierarchy. As discussed earlier, balikbayan boxes are considered social capital for recipients vis-à-vis their neighbors and indirect reminders of socioeconomic stratification between diasporic senders and Philippine-based recipients. Like the brand-named toothpaste, underwear, and other commodities sent overseas, the standardized repertoire that automata portray reminds audiences what is essential and daily necessity. By featuring the standard repertoire, not only as essential but also as commodities being exchanged between two subjects, "Assembly Line" riffs on the function of the standardized repertoire and PCNs as a marker of wealth, privilege, and transnational social capital. At the same time, by portraying balikbayans that dance robotically, the performance destabilizes the narrative of return and refigures scholarly critiques of "traditional" PCN participants (as returners) engaging in relationships with a romanticized, multiculturalist Philippines, frozen in its past.

Conclusion

When reading how Filipino dancers redefine Black social forms as American folk dance, one recognizes how the robot serves as a euphemism, generating a social critique against the mechanical reproduction of culture. Ironically, unfeeling robotic dancers use PCN to criticize the continual commodification of traditionally lively, soulful folk dancers. Whereas automata and robots execute seemingly forced labor, they also lay bare the drudgery of previous PCNs, full of exhausting personality and portraits of folk life. In this sense, these dancers speak to how PCNs echo divisions between the psychic and material conditions of Filipino diaspora. As automata, Filipinos theorize an "authentic" transnational heterogeneity and de-naturalize the boundaries of Filipino dancing bodies. Whereas folk dancers in previous PCNs embodied canonical forms to physically bring them closer to their "roots," the automata and robots refract their cultural amnesia and the subsequent "search for one's roots." Whereas automata speak obliquely to the epistemic violence confluent between Filipino folk suites and liberal multiculturalism pre–affirmative action, the robots reference post-racial ideologies that were promoted successfully by the anti–affirmative action movement.

As the third of four case studies that illuminates how individuals constitute Filipinoness through Black dance, this chapter points to the particularly regional and middle-class contexts within which the Filipino dancing body phenomenon is embedded. Against the setting of U.S. higher education and social engineering of resegregation at the turn of the twenty-first century, Filipino and Black peoples faced similar conservative reforms but in very different ways. "Assembly Line" highlighted how Filipino American students addressed Proposition 209 through dance. By allowing individuals a space for creative expression, PCNs and robots undermine the expectations of the model minority, and rather, recode critiques of their racial and ethnic struggles and how this enables rather than obscures the deeply vexed and complicated issues of educational segregation on campus. Their dancing relieved pressures to re-manufacture liberal multiculturalist products and redefined dance as a set of choreographic (and thus politically agentive) decisions, rather than something unquestionably passed down through ethnic and racial genealogies.

Although PCNs usually perpetuate liberal multicultural essentialism, *Home* offers proof that the genre is flexible enough to rehearse race-conscious agency. By examining the automata, robots, and balikbayan boxes, the dance enables criticism of the alienating and disembodying effects of multiculturalism and neutrality as reigning racial ideologies. Making ominous and robotic gestures of dance in the so-called post-racial era, Filipinos appropriate the conventional mode of PCN—an attempt to search for one's roots—and productively question the very concepts of home-making and model minority that diasporic practices such as Culture Nights often presume.

4

Judges and International Competitions

You're not just here to judge a routine.
You're taking people on a journey.[1]
 —Technical Director, Hip-Hop International

A successful competition is where you have a really well bonded panel,
who are on the same wavelength, who are in a great scoring range,
giving really accurate scores. And the results are all correct, I guess.
And you have a great feedback session where people are informed and
they come back with a better understanding than what they had be-
fore. A competition where the judges have a great experience and a
great knowledge of what they're doing. 'Cause then it's a nice smooth,
smooth ride. It's just from beginning to end it's peaceful, basically. It's
peaceful. But that rarely happens.[2]
 —New Zealand Judge, Hip-Hop International

In August 2015, the *Atlantic* issued a proclamation about the dance world—
the American dance critic is dead.[3] The unsteady industry and terminations
of dance critic positions at several U.S. presses drove the steady decline in
print coverage of dance over the last twenty years.[4] The apparent death also
traces back to the historical development of the art form and a short-lived
surge of companies, choreographers, and federal support since the 1960s
and 1970s.[5] Since then, we are told, critical discussion fixed its center on
pop culture instead of dance. "Kim Kardashian's selfies tend to get more serious coverage than dancers who have dedicated their lives to their form,"
the essay's author Madison Mainwaring says, and the extinction of critics
amounts to "a blow to the art form itself."[6] Using Misty Copeland as an
example, Mainwaring cites the lack of critical ink spilled on the African
American ballerina's technique.[7] Critics rightly celebrated Copeland because she and Filipina American Stella Abrera broke a major color barrier

Choreographing in Color. J. Lorenzo Perillo, Oxford University Press (2020). © Oxford University Press.
DOI: 10.1093/oso/9780190054274.001.0001

in the ballet world by becoming principals of American Ballet Theatre—but the public sees athleticism, not artistry.[8] The death of critics is built partly upon the classist and exceptionalist claim that critics alone have the capacity to intellectualize Copeland's artistic worth.[9] In contrast to this anxiety, this chapter begins with the premise that a more comprehensive portrait of the state of dance criticism, one inclusive of hip-hop dance, must also reckon with the omission of competitions and increasing complexity, if not vitality, of judging. Judging is a form of dance criticism. Attention to judging, as an invaluable aspect of cultural production, offers evidence at odds with criticism's absolute hold over dance intellectualism and its perpetuation of high-/low-brow inequalities. Questions of dance intellectualism should seriously consider competitions, particularly for transnational Filipino dancers systematically excluded from the ballet and modern dance worlds. In fact, competitions, not concerts, are major factors deciding how dancers of color gain "prestige, recognition, and validation," and their extensive system of evaluating performance underscore the unwillingness of prevailing dance criticism to attend to issues of race, gender, and technique.[10] Without understanding competitions, we risk continued exclusion of dancers of color from the scope of mainstream dance criticism and an unrepresentative understanding of the impacts of hip-hop's globalization.

The processes of hip-hop competition provide a means to acquire cultural capital that is readily legible across multiple national and linguistic borders. In the last chapter, the inclusion of Black dance as an advancement of Philippine-based expressions of dance was limited to the relatively insular space of Filipino American institutions and audiences of Pilipino culture nights (PCNs). Competitions accomplish a different kind of racial and gender articulation by providing a common ground for dancers from heterogeneous sexual, national, socioeconomic, and ethnic groups. Unlike multiculturalist PCNs, where street and hip-hop dances serve as foils and alternatives to Filipino folk forms, in competitions, they displace the colonial white aesthetics of European dance.[11] In competitions, judges from a variety of countries like Trinidad and Tobago, the Philippines, the United States, Japan, Brazil, New Zealand, and Italy index corresponding racial and gender histories, exchange ideas about dance, and work together to recognize street culture's intrinsic value in a bid for international belonging. By transmitting and standardizing ethnicity-specific and "traditional" dancing, and what constitutes a winning dance, they exercise control over how competition shapes and is shaped by competing markers of difference.[12] Also, unlike most concert forms of dance, which are largely based on a performer–audience dynamic, competition dances gain their significance from the complex processes of meaning-making between performers, audiences, *and* judges. As such, the adjudication system and standards play an often neglected role in manifesting participants' ability to parlay competition dance into other forms of social and economic mobility. Filipino dancers in international competition move laterally alongside dance "delegates" of other countries like New Zealand, Canada, India, and Romania in their efforts not just to bring prestige to their countries, but also to collaborate in advancing the second-class status of street dancers and the form of street dance cultures.

This chapter continues the book's theorization on the cultural politics of euphemism by arguing for recognition of systems of judging, the neoliberal economic contexts that structure them, and the roles they play in relation to expressions of artistic, political, and embodied potential.[13] In the previous chapters, we looked at how dancing bodies from within the prison industrial complex, labor brokerage system, and PCN community intersect with Black dance history across the Philippines and its diaspora. They draw upon embodied histories of colonialism, war, slavery, and racialized and sexualized labor to elude literal translation ("dancing a political message"), while simultaneously creating new stories and alternative humanities, and recoding them as "part and parcel" Filipino expression. This chapter develops the argument that competition dance reflects a racial project that underscores the contradictions in evaluating race, gender, ethnicity, and technique, in a global context.[14] It reveals how the scoring systems, selection criteria, and judging practices themselves, rather than the content of the dances, reflect problematic post-1970s neoliberal logics of technical solutions to political problems, even as they defy the dominant U.S.-versus-the-rest dichotomization and verbal paradigm of hip-hop that obscures race. It departs somewhat from the previous chapters, which focus on figures of euphemism—the zombie, hero, and robot—because it conceives of the judge as an agent of euphemism, standardizing hip-hop dance in competitions to reveal the possibilities and limitations of the form. As such, dance criticism is far from "endangered" but rather thrives in adjudication. In the traditional sense of "euphemism," competitions regulate offensive hip-hop performances and make them suitable for a particularly mainstream audience (family, international). Performance studies scholar Christine Balance writes on disobedient listening as "a method that aims to denaturalize tropes surrounding Filipinos' relationship to United States popular music and, in turn, Filipino music," and enables us to rethink "musical performances previously dismissed as merely imitative, abstract, or multicultural [that] unsettle dominant discourses of race, performance, and United States popular music."[15] Similarly, exploring judges as agents of euphemism decenters the trope of Filipinos as natural dancers and opens up ambivalent spaces for reading competitive dance, particularly in the blending of social and technical commentary, something that often escapes mainstream dance criticism.

According to existing frameworks of hip-hop studies, the standardization of hip-hop, or implementation of technical standards and rules, presents both a negative act of censorship (e.g., explicit language and lewd gestures) and mainstream commodification that effectively ruins the raw, street authenticity, and soul of the dancers who participate.[16] Reading rules and regulations in judging "against the groove," however, enables our recognition of their dances and activities as an opportunity to crack open new ways of world-making, beyond the dance's direct message (or lack thereof). To speak to the paradoxical decline in criticism and rise of competitions, this chapter highlights how the internationalization of hip-hop competition is characterized by the regulation, inclusion, exclusion, elevation, and depreciation of national, traditional, racial, gender, and creative differences. In particular, this chapter focuses on two aspects of judging that fill the gap in our current understanding of cultural criticism. The first aspect is judging criteria as an alternative site and object for analyzing dance and the disciplinary nature of judging. The second aspect is the conundrum around standardization. Judges offer crucial views into the ways that Filipino dancers gain authority and worldwide recognition in Black dance, but also in the ways that traditional markers of Filipinoness (music, chant, attire, language, humor, folk dance, indigeneity) are situated vis-à-vis other national forms of hip-hop. In turn, judges affirm the Filipino dancing body as a constituent element in manufacturing hip-hop as an international commodity.

The Opening Ceremonies: Making Hip-Hop Dance International

In the 2000s, Filipinos gained increasing international viability with critics and audiences in ways unseen in nearly a century of Hollywood. For example, Filipinos like Napoleon D'umo, Keone and Mari Madrid, Gil Duldulao, Cris Judd, Shaun Evaristo, Phil Tayag, Lyle Beniga, and Gigi

Torres have produced, conceptualized, and shaped the choreographies of Janet Jackson, Jennifer Lopez, Madonna, Justin Timberlake, Justin Bieber, and Bruno Mars, theatrical stage and television shows like Cirque Du Soleil's *Viva Elvis* and *Michael Jackson: The Immortal World Tour, So You Think You Can Dance, World of Dance*, and K-Pop groups like 2NE1, GOT7, Taeyang, and BTS (Beyond the Scene). The visibility of choreographers and dancers from the Philippines and its diaspora is attributed partly to the shifting practices of competitions and judging and partly due to the increasing number of dance directors, judges, and competition founders who identify as Filipino.[17] In the 1960s through 1980s, competitions were limited to underground parties, nightclubs, formal and informal contests, and television shows. After this time period, which itself expanded upon the funk and disco era television shows—*Soul Train* (United States) and *Penthouse 7* (Philippines) in particular—when dances at parties and bboy battles were evaluated by peers, the increasing professionalization of street dancers in private studios and entertainment industries influenced the trend in the culture to skew toward increasingly "official" judges whose authority was constituted by private dance studio ownership and recording artist credits.

During this time, from the 1970s until the late 1990s, judging was marked by unregulated invitation, lack of training, and simple scoring. In the 1990s, competitions continued growing through the networks of high school and university dancers that sought ways to collaborate across schools and beyond studio jazz- or drill team-centered worlds of Sharp and Miss Dance USA, leading to dance groups like 220 (San Diego).

Also, since the 1990s, international bboy competitions have proliferated like Battle of the Year (BOTY since 1990 in Germany), UK B-Boy Championships (since 1997), The Notorious IBE (a festival in the Netherlands since 1998), Red Bull BC One (since 2004), and R16 Korea/Taiwan (since 2007). Most recently, breaking was included in the Youth Olympics in Argentina (2018) and Southeast Asian Games (2019). The sport is also planned to be included in the Olympics in Paris (2024). Filipinos—like Daniel "Cloud" Campos (U.S.), Ereson "Bboy Mouse" Catipon (Funkstylers UK/United Kingdom), Rèo Canonoy Matugas (DYO/Norway), and Logan "Logistx" Adra (Red Bull BC One All Stars/U.S.)—have achieved visibility in breaking perhaps more than other style of hip-hop dance.[18] Filipinos have often played critical roles in international breaking competitions. For example, Karl Olivier "Dyzee" Alba (Supernaturalz Crew), a renowned Filipino Canadian bboy from Toronto, is the organizer for R16 (Korea/Taiwan) and created O.U.R.

System, a points system for bboying that was featured in the documentary *Meet OUR Bboys* (2012).

Parallel to the history of bboy competitions, there ran a stream of street dance competitions not limited to bboying forms of movement emerging from multiple origins themselves. Some competitions grew from talent shows held by college fraternities like Vibe (est. 1995).[19] Some competitions like Prelude Urban Dance Competition Series and World of Dance were developed by producers of youth culture who cultivated their early choreographic skills in garage sessions, cotillions and debuts, Air Band competitions, nightclub promotions, and import car shows. Others, like Bodyrock (formerly Bustagroove), created by San Diego–based Filipina American and dance community legend Anna Sarao, sprouted out of multinational corporations and their ventures into hip-hop dance, like Culture Shock Dance Company, which was initially part of Nike's Participate in the Lives of America's Youth (P.L.A.Y.) initiative to encourage sports and fitness in youth communities.[20] These events became interwoven with the dancing already in development in PCNs' Modern and American Suites (see Chapter 3), as the latter began outgrowing their university student organizations, booking paid gigs, entering these competitions, and expanding from their original Filipino-centric purposes. From these events, and drawing from dance aesthetics popularized by artists like Michael Jackson, Janet Jackson, and Missy Elliot, participants cultivated what they commonly called "choreo," "choreo dance," or "urban dance," a shorthand for a dance culture of many styles that ironically occurs in typical suburban contexts. "Choreo dance" is inclusive of, but does not center hip-hop dance forms and cultures.[21] As competitions and culture nights increased in scale and overlapped in the early 2000s, another major shift occurred when some judges took an active role, leading workshops in scoring, debating criteria, and judging demonstrations. By these demonstrations, or "demos," judges constitute their authority not by studio ownership and recording artist credits, as in the past, but by their own live dancing.

Here, I am interested in thinking through the case study of Hip-Hop International (HHI), a production company and competition franchise. Influenced by exposure to showcases and competitions organized by Angie Bunch, a white, out lesbian community leader of hip-hop dance in San Diego, California, Culture Shock Dance Company, Howard and Karen Schwartz produced dance and fitness events that informed their founding of HHI in 2001.[22] The physical fitness foundations of the internationalization of hip-hop resonate with the ways that physical education predominates dance education in the Philippines, a vestige of American colonial schooling. Similar to the ways the "PE paradigm" frames the Cebu Provincial Detention and Rehabilitation Center's "Thriller" dance's geometric design and reception (see Chapter 2), the neocolonial fitness aura haunts the technocracy of dance at HHI and limits its sociopolitical horizons. Nonetheless, HHI has grown to be one of the most influential competitions on the globe, where youth from South Africa to Thailand can compete in street dance.[23] Allegedly borrowing from the groundbreaking labor of Filipina American Anna Sarao and the choreo dance community, the Schwartzes created and produced HHI as a way to bring opportunities, exposure, and respectability to street dancers.[24] Throughout the year leading up to the annual event, official licensees hold national competitions to select up to three crews to represent their country.[25] Mostly occurring in the Southwest United States in early August, HHI boasts its ability to attract more than three thousand individual dancers from over fifty countries.[26] As part of HHI's week-long activities, the company also produces the U.S.A. Championship, the World Battles (with breaking, popping, locking, whacking, and All-Styles divisions), and Urban Moves Dance Workshops. HHI is best known for producing MTV's *Randy Jackson Presents America's Best Dance Crew* (*ABDC*), a program that has elevated the exposure of prominent Filipino American dancers such as Rynan "Kid Rainen" Paguio, Chris "ChrisStyles" Gatdula, Phil "SB" Tayag, Brian Puspos, and Dominic Kyle "D-Trix" Sandoval, dance crews with origins in PCN like Kaba Modern (Season 1), and crews with one or more Filipino members like SoReal Cru (Season 2), Quest Cr3w (Season 3), and Hype 5-0 (Season 5).[27] HHI has had a massive impact on popular dance and it is partly responsible for elevating the exposure of the Jabbawockeez (Season 1), a group claimed by Filipinos despite its multiethnic and racial composition, which is one of the few non–Cirque du Soleil, family-friendly dance groups with a Las Vegas Strip residency.[28] HHI also makes a point to include the recognized pioneers of street dance, mostly African American and Latino men, as battle judges and consultants.

HHI features battles (breaking, locking, popping, whacking, and all-styles) similar to other international hip-hop competitive events like Juste Debout in France, R-16 in Korea, and Battle of the Year in Germany.[29] At the same time, HHI departs significantly from these versions of international hip-hop competition because it focuses on groups or crews that draw upon a wider variety of dance styles—like swag, krump, stepping, and folk

Figure 4.1 The World Hip-Hop Dance Championship presented by Hip Hop International—Opening Ceremony

dance—in four age categories—Junior, Varsity, Adult, and Mega crew.[30] Moreover, consistent with the perception of HHI as the Olympics of hip-hop dance, a particularly nationalist and internationalist atmosphere is achieved through several formal and informal rituals. The modern Olympic framing includes opening and closing ceremonies in which each country's delegates brandish their respective national flags and perform a short dance, and a medal award ceremony involving winner's podiums and national anthems (see Figure 4.1). As crews step upon the competitive stage or as they are applauded post-performance, African American emcee Mookie Washington usually leads chants that permeate the arena and individualize certain countries (Canada, New Zealand, Japan, The Philippines, Australia, United States, and Russia). For Philippine teams, for instance, the war-like chant is an eight-count "Pin-oooy! Pin-oy-oy-oy!" which unlike the other countries' chants, illustrates a type of auto-exotification and tribal quality used to make hip-hop both international and raw. For many judges and dancers I spoke with, the prospect of Filipinos competing on America's "home court" is like David taking on Goliath. With the rituals enacted and foreign media poised with tales of their favorite underdog, it's as if an Olympic torch is lit and judges take their seats.[31]

The Preliminary Round: Judging as Discipline

A competition can have up to three rounds (Preliminary, Semifinal and Final) depending on the total number of entries and the time

*available. The decision shall be determined by the event organizer and
conveyed to all participants with ample time prior to the start of the
competition.*[32]

When I danced in Southern California in the late 1990s, judges would often
provide a cassette tape of their real-time criticisms. Competing in the high
school dance team circuit, our group of mostly Filipino Americans would
gather together to listen to these tapes and place ourselves back in the dance,
hearing the music in the background, with the judge's voice directing our
minds (and sometimes animating our bodies) to relive each gesture. These
personal experiences would inspire me to enroll in HHI judges' training
nearly twenty years later as another way to understand how dancers engage
in hip-hop. Set against the early blushing hues of an August morning, the Red
Rock Hotel and Casino, Las Vegas, stood as the venue for the 2013 World Hip-
Hop International (HHI) competition. I made my way through the smoky
hotel lobby, not yet filled with packs of dancers roaming around as they did
during the previous night's U.S. Championships. About twenty vendors had
assembled booths of street-style merchandise that lined the third floor of the
hotel and flanked the halls leading toward the main ballroom-turned-dance
competition area. It was eight o'clock when I approached the HHI headquar-
ters and asked for directions to the judges' panel workshop. A few others also
inquired, and an event staff member directed us toward the Ridges Room
back by the escalators. We loitered outside the room and met Tony "Go-Go"
Lewis Foster, a member of the famed dance group the Lockers and master
teacher in Japan for over thirty years.[33] We received our rules and regulations
packets and checked in. I sat beside a leading member of Canada's BluePrint
Cru, one of the first non-U.S. crews on *America's Best Dance Crew*, as the
room slowly filled with crew managers, judges (new and experienced), HHI
national directors, and dancers eager to train in the official judging system
of HHI.

The technical director of HHI served as the judging workshop in-
structor. "You're not just here to judge a routine. You're taking people [the
competitors and audiences] on a journey," he said.[34] He proceeded to address the participants that traveled from their respective hip-hop communities in Argentina, Australia, Canada, Columbia, the Dominican Republic,
Guam, Hungary, Paraguay, Mexico, New Zealand, Sweden, Switzerland,
South Africa, Thailand, the United Kingdom, and the United States.[35] The
workshop that the director led sought to transmit information regarding

the event, the roles and expectations of judges, and standardized criteria for judging.[36] This experience is an entryway for a consideration of how performance practices in particular and competitions in general influence everyday life for street dancers and the value with which it is recognized. After going through the certification process for judging, shadow-judging HHI rounds in 2013 and 2014, and interviewing several judges and competitors involved since the mid-2000s, I have come to see the judging practice as another space of Filipino cultural flows.

Judging is sometimes misunderstood as a blend of snap judgment and what dance scholar Julie Malnig calls a "'thumbs up, thumbs down,' consumer variety of connoisseur criticism."[37] In actuality, judges and dancers exist within a system of checks and balances. First, the process of "taking people on a journey" begins with the step of seeing judging as independent from dancing. Judging is a system by which agency and influential power is mutually shaped by individual and collective identity formation, personal knowledge-seeking, external discipline, and evaluative protocol belonging to private and nonprofit organizations. To understand how this relational system operates, it is important to initially identify how the competition constructs the judge's role and identity. For HHI, judging is both systematic and subjective, as nominees are selected by national HHI directors based on their relationship to the dance community or prior involvement with HHI. Thus, while judge panels vary in ethnicity and racial background, most panels comprise of cis-gendered middle-class men. Then nominees undergo training, which can consist of attending workshops and competition events. The trained judges then enter a pool of eligible judges, and if selected by event organizers, judge at national or international events. There are many dancers in one crew (from five to forty members), multiple crews in one round, and a few rounds in one competition (preliminaries, semi-finals, and finals). Given this volume of dances and information, the work of judging is overwhelming. Over the course of eight hours, one judge may be charged with actively watching and assessing around one thousand dancers. In 2013, World HHI Adult crews went from sixty-two then thirty-one and then eight crews from preliminaries to finals.

There is a science to judging dance and a recipe for winning routines. It is impossible for one judge to watch everything. To make the evaluation system more manageable and uphold the social contract between competition participants (judges, dancers, audiences, event organizers, and such), judges are assigned to evaluate discrete areas of each dance (see Table 4.1).[38] One

Table 4.1 Official Rules and Regulations of Hip-Hop International Crews of 5–8 Crewmembers - Amended for 2013, Hip-Hop International, 2013

Performance Judge	Skill Judge	Head Judge
Creativity (10%) • Moves • Music • Transitions	Musicality (10%) • Beat Technique • Syncopation • Instrumentation • Rhythmic Patterns	• Confirm performance of street dance styles • Evaluate discrepancies, deductions, and disqualifications
Staging (10%) • Staging • Spacing • Formations • Level Changes	Synchronization (10%) • Complexity • Speed • Timing • Range of Moves	• Observe attire and music violations • Notice and evaluate falls • Assess stage procedure and conduct
Showmanship (10%) • Showmanship • Intensity • Confidence • Projection/Presence	Execution (10%) • Execution • Controlled Mobility • Stabilization	• Monitor Performance and Skill Judges and score patterns
Street Presence (10%) • Presence • Attire	Difficulty of Execution of Authentic Street Dance Styles (10%)	
Entertainment (10%) • Entertainment Value • Audience Appeal	Variety of Street Dance Styles (10%)	

fellow shadow judge, Liz Rifino, demonstrated the benefit of such attention when she pointed out to a competitor where to put their weight when they entered a leap.

From the dancer's perspective, the judging criteria might evoke the quantitative, linear, orderly, forces of standardization that hamper innovation. From the judge's point of view, the components are tools for ensuring an environment where creativity can overcome popularity as the driving force of the culture. Judges favor dance creativity, or innovative movements, musical arrangements, and bodily formations, over a performance to the latest Billboard topper. HHI parses the dance to spread the evaluative labor amongst a judging team—the four performance judges, four skill judges, and head judge.[39] In fact, restricting one's judging to a discrete assigned sub-area, as opposed to judging the performance as a whole entity and experience, is noted by the director as one of the more challenging aspects of the system. In addition to its imitation of the language and rituals of Olympic sports, the system gains the appearance of fairness and myth of meritocracy by its application to each dance crew. The system functions like a script for judges to perform their own choreography. The disciplinary system of judging reflects the neoliberal logics of addressing political problems with technical approaches, and regulates the viewing body by mandating technical expertise, directs competing bodies toward these specific criteria, and acts as an exclusionary mechanism discrediting any claims by amateur viewers.

Reinforcing the distinction between types of judges, event organizers require that performance and skill judges physically occupy alternate seats on the panel to ensure fair practices. This surprising detail, what might be called "judge staging," carried out to preempt any allegations of "shared answers," indicates a heightened awareness of the surveillance by audience members, dance crews, and managers of judges. Perhaps to preserve their sense of authority, judges are also prohibited from competing and judging at the same event. If someone wanted to judge a Junior or Varsity division, for instance, they would not be able to compete in the Adult or Mega-Crew category, thereby restricting their role to one from the perspective of evaluation, not dance-making. Since organizers seem especially aware of those watching judges, it might puzzle readers to learn that at HHI, judges are not only allowed to evaluate their own crew but also encouraged to do so.[40] The fact that there is a presumed absence of any conflict of interest in their judges, HHI organizers claim, demonstrates their confidence in the system.[41] This contrasted with my own experiences outside of HHI contexts when apparently organizers of the University Athletic Association of the Philippines Street Dance competition considered but eventually decided not to invite me as a judge due to my research collaborations with the University of the Philippines Street Dance Club. Overall, the practice at HHI, along with assigned criteria, seating, and ineligibility from competition, only further drives the judge toward a stable identity category, upholding the image of the judge as a judge, not dancer or crew leader, and supports the feedback process between the international panel and the national crews.

While performance and skill judges supply the dance with points to produce a score, the head judge plays the "villain" and deducts points from that score. More interestingly, the head judge also exercises authority by disciplining "bad judges" in a type of quality control of judges' work.[42] What makes a "bad judge" eligible for removal by the head judge? Beyond the self-evident violations of having one's phone on the table or inattention to the routine being performed, "bad judge" practices also relate to the grayer areas of hip-hop. Skill judges are at risk of "bad judging" in two related categories: Difficulty of Execution and Variety of Street Dance Styles (see Table 4.1).[43]

Let's consider the Variety of Street Dance Styles. Skill judges are required to have knowledge of a majority of the ten styles listed in the rules in order, identify those performed, make a decision about whether enough elements were executed and danced to "count," and assess their difficulty level.[44] This shows just how high the bar is for judging and how much the judges need to know about hip-hop dance to treat the evaluated dance fairly. This also deters experienced dancers who specialize in one style (e.g., breaking or new school), but who appear less open to being judged in other styles. With the necessary evidence of erroneous scoring, head judges must assess the scoring styles of each judge, examine inconsistencies, and challenge a judge's score if necessary. This evaluation all happens in 45 seconds to a minute after a crew has performed and before the next crew is announced. In 2014, when I shadow-judged the junior prelims, we judged thirty-one crews from fifteen countries (see Figure 4.2). After ten crews, my ears started to feel warm and heat up. I felt increasingly powerless to keep up and catch up when I fell behind because of particularly challenging criteria. For Performance, Showmanship, and Staging, I felt most shaky and blurry, partly because each performance had three or four components within the single ten-point category and required parsing out 2.5 points. In comparison, I felt that the Street Presence and Entertainment Value were the easiest. We were instructed to shadow judge for Skills with the next ten crews. The Variety points required the least effort and the most challenging were the musicality and difficulty criteria. While dancers on stage certainly are the stars of the show, I felt a type of adjacent performance anxiety as a judge that mirrored that which comes from dancing.

This elaborate system is part of a wider set of practices and behaviors employed to advance particular principles held essential for "good judging"—consistency, rigor, transparency, and reciprocity. In terms of consistency, for example, head judges promote "blank slate" judging, which resonates with the neoliberal logic and meritocratic myth espoused by Prop 209 proponents and has two such aspects. First, scores from a previous qualifying round are not factored into the next round. Second, judges are directed to approach each crew within rounds and particular crews as they advance through

Figure 4.2 Judging panels spend more than eight hours per day judging over one-thousand dancers and rewarding creative, groove-based, multi-style dances over popular, over-edited, cheer routines (2014).

rounds with a completely "blank slate." The former means that two consecutive crews should not be compared with each other, regardless of any similarities in moves, music, transitions, nationality, and such. Similarly, if a crew advances from semi-finals to finals, head judges discourage panelists from using the memory of the semi-formal version to score the final performance. The "blank slate" principle goes against the reputation-based power dynamics that often govern street culture. Previous success or failure of a crew should not influence the judge's expectations of their dance.

Joel Gallarde, director of HHI Australia, relayed another example of consistency. In line with the Petisyonado dynamics I described in Chapter 2, in 1998, Gallarde's family had been waiting for a visa to the United States for twenty years, when his father decided to apply for a visa to New Zealand, with hopes of being a stepping stone to America. Gallarde moved to New Zealand in 1998 and brought his experience gained from dancing with Company of Ateneo Dancers (CADS) to Auckland by starting Company of University Dancers (CUDS), and since then has been director of Boogiezone New

Zealand/Australia, Triple 8 Funk.[45] According to Gallarde, often a group will compete with a dance that in and of itself is impressive but meets few of the criteria. In this instance, he and other judges are disciplined to refrain from giving points to such performances, which they call "showcase" routines, no matter how much they were swept by the dancing, simply because the group apparently has not read or followed the guidelines.[46] According to Joel, to award showcase routines puts the fairness of the competition into question.[47]

In some ways, the principle of consistency is outweighed by the looming sense that one's evaluative labor might be wasted. The highest and lowest scores of each judging type are discarded, a practice the organization offers as proof of the "Olympic-style" of competition, further mediating the judge's agency. This factor also creates a dynamic by which judges inadvertently "seek the middle" to avoid being the judge whose score is "dropped" the most in a round, and avoid being seen as overly critical, relaxed, or even worse, unqualified. After one round of preliminary competition, I walked over with judges to view the posted scores, and they proceeded to look for their own scores to see how they fared. Interestingly, they bragged and teased each other depending on whether their scoring was consistent, dropped, or consistently dropped, creating a sense of peer pressure between judges to perform well. Judges are also given instructions on *how* to judge to avoid charges of incompetence. They are warned against scoring the first crew lower simply because they danced earlier, and then judging the later crews based on an average from the earlier crews evaluated. Finally, judges should stick to their style— either strict or loose—and evaluate that way for all the groups. Despite the seeming resistance to subjectivity, judges are finally advised to pick what criteria means the most to them personally and score accordingly. The detailed rubrics and guidelines we were provided on how to judge, social interactions of judges, and personal and social pressures to perform well support the idea that judging is a practice of Foucaultian discipline.

Despite the increasing standardization and limits of technical solutions to political problems, judges can still find themselves at the center of conflict in some competitions. For smaller-scale industrial competitions, judges tend to be local leaders, professionals, and as before, past winners or celebrities. In Guam, Mary Anne Bordello is artistic director for Step Up Crew, who were competitors at HHI's World Hip-Hop Dance Championship in 2014. Resonating with the Insular Cases (see Introduction), Guam's foreign status afforded them an opportunity to compete on the world stage and bypass HHI's United States nationals competition. Like many Filipinos in the

United States, her father was petitioned by her grandmother to emigrate from the Philippines.[48] Bordello, who is a teacher by trade and ballroom dancer, recalls a popular local competition in which judges were not street dancers, but had some other dance background and were known as island celebrities or former stars from the Philippines that had since retired in Guam. Judges were allowed to discuss with each other, and Bordello saw this as a weakness in the competition as it allowed for the potential for domineering judges to persuade others.[49] These circumstances suggest the problematic potential for members of dominant racial, gender, ethnic, and style groups to reconsolidate their dominance through judging.

For larger competitions, enlisting judges affiliated to particular "schools" of hip-hop or non-hip-hop dance can raise questions amongst participants about bias in the results. In Las Vegas, Arnel Calvario, head organizer for the HHI World Battles, remembers one year that battlers criticized the Popping panel because it was mostly made up of people associated with Electric Boogaloo styles of the dance.[50] Although he felt that the results did not justify this criticism, the following year, Calvario still actively sought to address this issue by inviting a clearer diversity of Popping judges. These examples suggest that despite the authority of organizers and judges to determine how dances are evaluated, it's important for the audience and competitors to have space to voice concerns about real and perceived transgressions. Individuals and groups of judges navigate contemporary theoretical and practical issues of performance and shift the ever-changing value of dance that exists within, beside, and outside of the actual dancing aesthetics.

The Final Round: Standardizing Difference

Crews are permitted to use more than one routine or variations of the same routine at an HHI championship event. Keeping the routine fresh when performed in front of the same panel of judges throughout preliminary, semifinal, and final rounds is acceptable and encouraged.[51]

In the Fall of 2013, I conducted an exploratory workshop on judging amongst a group of interdisciplinary scholars, teaching them how to be hip-hop dance judges, in which several participants astutely asked about standardization and institutionalization, and the ramifications thereof. For them and perhaps many audiences, the discipline of judging, as a type of dance criticism that is generative outside of the proper "doing" of dance, is less interesting than the question of hip-hop's standardization.[52] In the framework of performative euphemisms, the institutionalization of hip-hop culture is more than a sad, multi-pronged process of domesticating something that is best left untouched, in its "pure," unregulated, spontaneous form. Rather than seeing standardization as simply a dulling of hip-hop's hard edges (i.e., curse words and lewd gestures), there is a story between the development of rules and regulations that centers their performative euphemism, or their opening up of an ambivalent space capable of layering social and technical commentary.

Central to standardization are the dance elements discouraged by judges, or those punishable red flags, which are emblematic of traditional notions of euphemism. If the head judge sees lewd gestures, like the crotch grab popularized by Michael Jackson, or dancers tossing clothes into the audience, he gives a 0.05 deduction.[53] In these ways, standardization enforces respectability politics that inhibit the "free" expression of gender, race, and class, while attracting investment in and circulation of Black dance forms to whiter, wealthier, more Northern, and normative audiences. If the head judge hears offensive lyrics, he gives a 0.1 deduction.[54] The issues of inappropriate lyrics and language demonstrate how within their events, organizers uphold a particular respectability, what they view as the right way to promote hip-hop culture. Before the event, both organizers and crews have a responsibility to preview the music. If crews come with a non-English song, then it is the responsibility of the head judge to check if there are any offensive lyrics in that language. Conversely, if there is a song with English lyrics, the crew (regardless of their native language) is responsible for finding an English speaker to check for obscenities. In the rules and regulations and judging workshops, organizers expressed particular interest in lyrics that discriminate based on religion, gender, and race, such as the N-word. For people married to an NSFW version of hip-hop filled with expletives and video vixens, this might further prove the competition's inauthenticity. At the same time, this mitigation of "explicit language" opens up an ambivalent space that is neither completely positive nor negative. On the one hand, this space is characterized by virtues of inclusivity of varieties of traditional dance, continuity, musicality, and flexibility, and on the other hand, problematic areas around the treatment of gender, traditional dance judging, and assumptions around regulations.

Part of the uniqueness of judging hip-hop relates to the high bar set for judges, and one's immersion in as much hip-hop dance history and experience as possible. "Exposure is really key," says the head judge for HHI, while describing a contemporary heated debate over the difference between tricks and dance (to be discussed later). Since much of early bboying and bgirling styles drew inspiration from a wide spectrum of sources like gymnastics, cartoons, and martial arts, judges have to be able to identify how dancers signify, reference these historical formations, and innovate. The more exposure a judge has, the more that judge can situate the dance in a specific history and know what has been and could be accomplished under the conditions of that particular competition. At the same time, the more exposure a judge has, the more they will be able to predict what move will come next, "control" their own emotions produced by watching dance, and reflect upon the gradations of dance over other forms of physical activity. Exposure, thus, is key for judges to evaluate creativity in dance. Again, this goes back to the wide spectrum of popular culture, artistic, and sports sources that street dance styles have been known to draw from. The gymnastic "Thomas flair," (also spelled "flare") invented by Kirk Thomas, involves someone balancing on their hands and rotating their lower body while their legs fly in the air. If a competitor were to step back and start flair-ing, that would not be dance. If someone were to dance footwork, execute a flair, and then dance more footwork into a freeze, then the flair approaches something closer to dance. Competitors can actually execute tricks musically (i.e., the lyrics call for a flip) or in character and also be considered at the dance end of the spectrum. The difficulty of this task is that often, the tricks please crowds and receive the most audible reaction from viewers. Nonetheless, organizers advise that it is a judge's responsibility to make the assessment rather than allow their score to be swayed by the audience.

To what degree is the institutionalization of hip-hop dance actually a barometer for the very things that its rules struggle against—a static culture filled with cookie-cutter routines, inauthenticity, and the lack of an individual style-based identity? In addition to the advocacy of the more conventional aspects of dance, what HHI judges advocate and what they discourage offer remarkable views into the increasing institutionalization of difference—different styles, genders, ethnicities, dimensions of performance, ages, and groupings—in street dance culture. This institutionalization is particularly useful as current scholarship on street dance tends to rely on "close readings" of dances and limit the racialized and gendered dynamics in either the identity formation of the dancers or the expressive representations they stage. Judging and standardization give us an alternative perspective. For example, judges advocate that crews perform a mixture of old school—defined as bboying or bgirling, popping, and locking—and new school styles of hip-hop. Also, in tune with the Olympic and multiculturalist framing of the competition, judges encourage the incorporation of "traditional," indigenous, and folk movement forms like capoeira, Bollywood, and salsa into their routine. These movement vocabularies are seen as part of a flavorful routine by amplifying a crew's individuality, as long as they are integrated within "reasonable" limits and a majority of the choreography is hip-hop.[55]

In this rule, the multiculturalism of PCNs by which Filipinos perform both traditional folk and Black dance to be legible, modern subjects (see Chapter 3), finds a parallel by which all delegates, Filipino and non-Filipino, are instructed to blend so-called traditional dances and hip-hop. Apart from a few examples the Philippine's competing crews generally do not draw from Filipino rap artists, folk dances, or costumes to compete at HHI. Some exceptions are when in 2006, the Philippine Allstars' choreography utilized musical samples from pioneering Filipino rapper, Francis Magalona, and his "Mga Kababayan Ko," (My fellow Filipinos) as well as Black Eyed Peas' "Bebot" (Filipino for babe) in which Apl.de.Ap chants "Pilipino! Pilipino!"[56] In 2009 Allstars demonstrated astig, or Filipino cool aesthetics, by drawing attention to their muscular chests and arms adorned with pre-colonial indigenous henna tattoos. Allstars member Maya Carandang designed indigenous warrior body ornaments, similar to the sixteenth-century Visayan "Pintados" for whom tattoos symbolized strength and intimidation. The tattoos were a way to draw a throughline from Filipino resistance against Spanish colonizers to contemporary hip-hop resistance. For judges, traditional elements are Othering markers and useful for identifying and individuating crews from one another. To award creativity in how dancers engage music, judges encourage an empathetic response, valuing records and their surprising sampling and sequencing. It is important to note the different expectations judges have around the Creativity of Moves versus Music. Part of evaluating Creativity of Music is based upon how unique the sequencing and sampling of music sounds to judges. However, and despite encouragement for crews to display an individuating "signature move," the sequencing of moves is not generally an area for awarding points for Creativity of Moves. Also, judges do not ask crews to utilize "authentic" hip-hop music or, more importantly, local, native language records, unlike the prerequisites for authentic, pioneer-conscious hip-hop moves. The lack of an emphasis on music and its indigenized, linguistic varieties in the music component of the

Creativity category might help explain why a majority of crews conform to the U.S. practice of relying on African American hip-hop and pop music.

Standardization has also illuminated a principle of continuity whereby judges require that dances feature one segment of continuous music— uninterrupted, unedited, and free from added sound effects.[57] The continuous music rule is so important that crews must indicate the time mark on the compact disc of their music for head judges to inspect. Judges believe that "[o]verusage of edits and sound effects often leads to a no music, no dance outcome."[58] At first, this might sound like a nod to Black noise, or American studies scholar Tricia Rose's identification of flow, layer, and rupture in hip-hop music.[59] Alternatively, perhaps this reminds us of dance exhaustion, or what performance theorist André Lepecki identifies in critics' anxiety of dance's futurity in light of "hiccupping" North American and European choreographers.[60] The continuity principle, as emphasized by judges, partly seeks to safeguard the viewing body's ability to apprehend the dancer's moves and interpret the concepts that dancers simultaneously enact and comment upon, as well as the dancer's ability to demonstrate their dancerly musicality. Judges deploy the continuous music rule to prevent crew choreography from sounding like cheer routines, which commonly add sound effects with each stunt. The continuity principle, when considered alongside the explicit regulations against the excessive display of cheer and gymnastics moves, constructs a subtext that defines HHI as strategically racialized and gendered. The regulations reflect anxiety about groups who perform in ways that resemble mostly white commercial cheerleading and drill team competitions—an anxiety expressed in the rules themselves and by a few of the senior judges during the training workshop. In other words, the rules define hip-hop dance over and against the figure of the white cheerleader, a trope of American femininity and bland white aesthetics, and mark its space with a particular type of multiracial Black masculine cool aesthetic, legitimacy, and flavorful originality.

The inclusion of Musicality as a criterion for standardization has also led to the development of and attention to more sophisticated music-dancer relationships. One head judge explained:

> Some dancers are actually not in the record at all; they're doing a complementary rhythm pattern, as if you were a musician, adding to a band. Not to be confused with, "Every sound in the record I hear, I have to dance those sounds." That doesn't necessarily mean superior musicality. Superior

musicality means appreciating downbeats and especially ingesting the music, this inward feeling [he bobs his head] is the most soulful thing you can do in hip-hop, soul, and in funk music. To be able to receive the music, and the movement from your neck to your waist, shows that you're dancing. Not foot movement, foot movement, foot movement, arm movement, arm movement. It has to be the total body dancing. And that's what really needs to be your basis for choosing and judging musicality.[61]

This head judge's theory on musicality places dancers inside or alongside the record and encourages judges to recognize Black musical soulfulness to look beyond a short-circuit link between the dancing body and music. In the tone of his voice, there was a sense of advocacy and caution toward judges that might otherwise underestimate the dancers' rhythmic skills. In some ways, musicality is an opportunity for judges to focus on rewarding the connection between the dancing body and the music incorporated.

The emphasis on "total body dancing" brings us to another concept that gained traction in hip-hop dance judge circles—the notion of the "missing" groove element. While they acknowledge how dancers have intensified the development of sophisticated isolations, intricate footwork, and Tutting (a finger/hand/arm-centered dance style), some judges worry that the emerging generation cannot groove and dance with one's total body (head-to-toe dancing). This "missing" groove is explicitly addressed in the official regulations:

Frequently overlooked or forgotten by crews is finding "The Groove." The groove is the dancer's reaction to the beat and the undertone of the music. It helps a dancer to improvise and express their dancing more from the inside out. The groove exists in all types of music and dance and certainly within all styles of street dance. It's what makes the dance "funky." Find the groove in your music and express it in your crew's routine. It's another opportunity to showcase the dance and be rewarded by the judges.[62]

In this narrative, judges see themselves as uniquely poised to define what is "dance," on the one hand, and what is physical movement that lacks dance, on the other hand.[63] Like a canary in a coal mine, the "missing" groove indicates when the performer and dance group has sacrificed its cool factor for overuse of cheer or drill-team moves. To this point, judges rely upon "Controlled Mobility," one sub-area within the "Execution" criteria of skills judges, to manage their anxieties about the "just arms" or "just legs" dance culture. Controlled mobility evaluates one's ability to maintain composure and cool while both locomoting and executing a movement (beginning, middle, and exit). While controlled mobility allows skill judges to guide the dance community toward more groove-based, whole-body dancing, it also further distances them from white, cheer stereotypes of lacking rhythm. These anxieties and the ever-changing rules that judges erect in an attempt to ease them, are symptomatic of the ways that embodied gesture and movement, unlike rap lyrics, theatrical scripts, and visual graffiti, have often escaped scholarly studies of hip-hop.

Let's consider an example of a dance group from the Philippines that illustrates head-to-toe groove in their choreography—University of the Philippines-Street Dance Club (UPSDC). In addition to a slow motion back flip "signature move" and "the Groove," another thing that UPSDC excels at in their bronze medal dance from HHI in 2013 is identifiably performing a variety of different street dance styles. Donning vests with indigenous Filipino script, or Baybayin, UPSDC dancers incorporated various Black dance forms including breaking, popping, locking, house, waacking (or whacking), and swag hip-hop choreography.[64] These dance forms emerge out of different Black dance historical and social contexts that provide subtext to the staged performance. House is a footwork-centered dance form that originated in nightclubs of Chicago and New York in the 1970s, with moves like "jacking" shaped by the techno sounds and rhythmic beats of pioneers like deejay Frankie Knuckles. In the queer of color communities of Los Angeles nightclubs, waacking was cultivated by dancers in the early 1970s and often included punctuated arm gestures and references to Hollywood films, martial arts, and popular culture. This brings us back to the evolution of Variety Points, which quintessentially reflects how judges continue to insist on the merits of standardization, even in the face of the fast-changing landscape of styles that seems to resist this process. Originally, to ensure variety and preserve the styles judges see as foundational to hip-hop dance, organizers required that crews include all old-school styles, defined as bboying or bgirling, popping, and locking, and any new school styles. However, the problem arose where dancers were proficient in new school styles and substandard in old-school styles. A few years of this noble system and crews began looking cookie-cutter—there was little to no creativity and choreography that judges could predict based on the musical arrangements. Then event organizers redefined Variety Points so that crews could perform any styles under the "hip-hop umbrella" regardless of their periodization. Judges required crews to perform at least three styles and awarded another point for each additional style they demonstrated.

In theory, this would allow crews to dance what they know and also inspire them to learn new styles outside their skill set. In practice, there were problems: First, crews would attempt to get the maximum ten percentage points by performing eight styles, but perform them poorly. Some crews would showcase only one eight-count of a style and expect to get a point. Another problem related to the judges' training and the period when multiple styles proliferated under the hip-hop umbrella. Judges claimed they only saw two or three styles when crews claimed to dance eight. Finally, event organizers adjusted the regulations again to their current structure. The current Variety Point rule is that judges will award crews the full ten percentage points as long as they execute three styles of any street dance style: locking, popping, bboying/bgirling (breaking), wacking/punking, vogueing, house dance, party dances or club dances, hip-hop dance/choreography, krumping, stepping/gumboots, dancehall, and "traditional dance" and "folklore." On the one hand, crews can focus on the styles they do well and not worry about competing with their weaker styles. On the other hand, one can imagine the scenario where the older styles decline further from the spotlight if crews only embrace the latest styles. The evolution of the Variety Points reflects the malleability of standardization, benefits of innovative difference, and drawbacks of hip-hop dance's plurality.

For many practitioners, the standardization process is inevitable, seen as a necessary process for legitimating the marginalized form. The "missing" groove and Variety Points help elucidate the promise of standardization. However, standardizing hip-hop dance is not so straightforward. Most judges acknowledged their mixed feelings about standardization, even while they participated in the process, in part, by voicing concerns about the artistic qualities of dance. For critics, standardization impedes the evolution of the art form and dancers' artistic expression, thus producing instrumentalization.[65] One such judge adds:

> Well obviously, it's a competition, and when you're putting standards to it, and a system to it, people are just going to do what it takes to win. So, what it does, it kind of limits the artistic value, I feel, because they're not really being true to themselves or what they want to express because they're just doing what they think is gonna score points, basically.[66]

The styles and types of movement that dancers choose to perform are not only related to standards but the reality that styles are fundamentally different. In a type of "comparing apples to oranges" dilemma, competitions ask judges to subscribe to the same criteria to evaluate incomparable things. This can also be a sensitive issue as more than one judge confided to me that they feel that despite the fact that different styles like bboying and vogueing hold equal value per regulations, they recognize that individual judges still tend to favor particular styles over others—masculine over feminine styles, high over low beats per minute, aggressive over smooth textures, old school over new school, and bboying over non-bboying.[67]

Also, it has already been mentioned that judges encourage the use of traditional, cultural, and indigenous dances to help identify, individuate, and promote inclusivity among dance crews. However, from a tribal critical race studies perspective the lack of acknowledgement or engagement with the original peoples who inhabited the lands on which the competition takes place or the relation between hip-hop and Indigeneity reflect the limits of a hip-hop settler colonial approach to internationalization. Moreover, there is neither designated criteria nor a requirement that judges attain qualification to evaluate traditional dance forms like Brazilian capoeira or the Maori Haka. For example, the Philippine Allstars felt that judges had failed to appreciate fully the message of resilience behind their incorporation of pre-colonial indigenous tattoos in their 2009 choreography. The encouragement of traditional dance without judge training creates situations for judges to exotify indigenous components and for competitors to culturally appropriate dances of ethnic minorities. Current standards also overlook the proximity of countries to pioneer dancers. Whereas there is an explicit directive that judges look to hip-hop dance legends (e.g., Don Campbell, Crazy Legs, Boogaloo Sam) and the ways they dance as benchmarks for evaluating execution, yet, the standardization process itself, lacks an apparatus for addressing the reality that most dancers recognized as pioneers are U.S.-based, Black and Latino cis-gendered men. Since event organizers acknowledge that each country has its own pioneers, yet only recognize the U.S. pioneers as legitimate standards for evaluating difficulty and authenticity, they create the dynamic in which Black and Latino masculinities function as American culture toward which dancers from the "Third World" are in perpetual "development" and playing catch up. Given this contradiction, the technical encouragement to dance one's own indigenous or tribal forms can have a patronizing tone and leave actual politics of inclusivity unresolved. It is important to recall here that at HHI, the discursive formation around the success of dance crews from the Philippines and Filipino diaspora is unfailingly a type of David versus Goliath matchup, and this framing is pivotal for neglecting both the structural dynamics of Filipino racialization and the social issues most commonly associated with hip-hop in the United States. Nicole R. Fleetwood writes on the iconicity of Black males in hip-hop and argues that "the black male body signifies within and outside of black communities a form of coolness through racialized and masculine difference and a diaphanous 'outlawness' that maintains an affective quality even as it functions as a highly reproducible and mass-marketed commodity."[68] Fleetwood's linkage of Black male figures of hip-hop to notions of "a new American dream" finds some resonance in HHI as dancers recognize the asymmetries regarding wage earnings and labor rights between the U.S. and their respective countries. Also, this form of outlawed coolness became more salient with the formation of the Black Lives Matter movement in 2013. In HHI, the competition and choreographies lack engagement with the movement for Black Lives, which raise questions about the role of dance and the criminalization of Black men in the United States.[69] Moreover, the questions converge with notions of global capital development, exoticism, assimilability, and the "foreign in a domestic sense," and AfroFilipino formations between the United States and the Philippines (see Introduction).[70] For example, there is a missed opportunity in HHI to catalyze a dialogue about the social status of Black Amerasians.[71]

Earlier I discussed the judging system's prohibition of music containing offensive language as it relates to gender, religion, and race as an example of euphemism. In contrast to this rule, the standards for the dancer's body insist on a gender-neutral approach. This neutrality inadvertently raises questions about the ways that gender differences in crew constitution influence the dance and what it's worth.[72] Imposing gender neutrality on judges actually prevents any substantial discussion about gendered choreography. While most crews are coed, there are also many "all-male" crews and a few "all-female" crews who perform a variety of gendered representation from celebrations of racialized femininity to provocative code-switching. As seen with groups like Prestige (Australia), whose 2013 Hip-Hop International Adult Finals dance involved a Beyoncé "Single Ladies" interlude where the cisgendered all-male crew ripped open their vests to reveal shirts tied up like bras, there have also been problematic dances that seek to capitalize on hip-hop transphobia. The use of drag and femme choreography as comic gimmicks, and the transphobia it calls upon, suggest the failures accompanying gender neutrality as a principle of competition. The problem of gender neutrality is made more salient when considering that HHI invites and brands itself upon difference and purports fairness and a "one love" brand of social equality.[73] These instances point to the critical ways that normative notions of gender continue to shape the sexual exclusiveness of transnational dance circuits. In contrast to the ideals reflected in anti-discrimination policy around music, there are no clear guidelines around judging choreography with issues regarding misogyny, Orientalism, cultural appropriation, biting (intellectual property theft), ageism, settler colonialism, or disability. These omissions ironically reproduce the dominant paradigm that defines a "conscious" hip-hop artist as one that only *speaks* to power in lyrics rather than embodiment.

To these issues, one might add the *a priori* assumptions about criteria and competitions at large. As one national head judge put it, "I think we've got to a stage now where everything is so systematic. And we're at this kind of level where everything's been thought about already, and nobody has any real reason to question it."[74] This assessment puts forward another weakness associated with standardization and thus neoliberal logics of using technical solutions for political problems. Generally, there is lack of discussion among judges and dancers on how certain criteria came to exist in the first place. For example, in the HHI rules and regulations workshop, no one questioned the origins of the criteria in the workshop, and the New Zealand head judge notes that while trainee judges and competitors sometimes dispute interpretations of criteria, rarely do they question why these criteria are utilized and not some others.[75] Maria, a Los Angeles–based veteran street dancer who identifies as Puerto Rican and Italian, was called to judge a U.S. competition in which the organizers directed her to judge mainly on the dancers' use of music, costume, and personality, inadvertently neglecting key criteria, in her view, like foundation and technique. Maria's account reveals that criteria and evaluative systems, when taken as a given, have potential to hinder judges' agency and their ability to assert both their individual opinions and their acquired knowledge of cultural norms and standards.

In a practical sense, one gets a better understanding of the virtues of standardization after several events and witnessing the recycled choreographic ideas and general redundancy that can afflict competitions like a nagging cough. In the case of HHI, criteria systems have enabled judges to clarify their ideas around dance. The function of music in a dance competition is a fitting example. In response to the repetition generated by multiple crews incorporating the same songs owed to nothing but their radio play and style-song affiliation (i.e., New Jack Swing dancing is often accompanied by DJ Kool's "Let Me Clear My Throat"), judges discourage that using a trendy and current song to dance might garnish some audience appeal but doesn't necessarily demonstrate creativity. As judges in HHI 2013 have suggested, Creativity of Music can take many forms like Brotherhood's (Canada) humorous juxtaposition of a cheeky white boyband record amidst tough African American rap, Royal Family's[76] (New Zealand) thoughtful sampling of pop songs, or EleColdXHot's (Malaysia) audacious decision to use a single, instrumental, Western classical song throughout their dance.[77] Through standards, judges maintain (and sometimes question) the porous border and hierarchies between popularity and creative musical choice, indigenous and street gestures, white feminine ideals and Black masculine "outlawness," triviality and legitimacy, anti-discrimination and gender neutrality, and non-dance and "dance."

The Awards Ceremony: Between Unity and Distinction

What are the material and figurative rewards for making the decision to enter international competition? Since HHI is one of the biggest international competitions, it provides a meeting ground for Filipino dancers from not only the Philippines, but also diasporic Filipino dancers from the United States (Quest Crew), Germany (Team Recycled), Guam (Step Up Crew), Australia, Canada (Praise Team and Brotherhood), Ireland (Infinite Dance Styles Crew), and New Zealand. HHI played a vital role in the popularization of Philippine-based crews like the Philippine Allstars, The Crew, the University of the Philippines Street Dance, La Salle Dance-Street, Addlibs, A-Team, Legit Status, Tha Project, and The Kingsmen. Former overseas entertainers and some Petisyonados like Bgirl Tzy (see Chapter 2) have strived to overcome the complicated immigration and economic hurdles to compete in HHI since the mid-2000s. For those in the Philippines unable to view the live performances, crewmates hold viewing parties and post videos with up-to-the-minute reporting of competitive dances on social media sites.[78] The year 2013 was the first year HHI charged a fee for online viewing (which began in 2011), subsequently garnering criticism from past competitors and would-be spectators that the organization was overly interested in profit-making through hip-hop.[79] For many dancers that reside outside the United

States, there is added incentive to participate in the opportunities to meet U.S.-based pioneering figures (e.g., Don Campbell, Toni Basil, Zulu Gremlin, Ana "Lollipop" Sanchez) and choreographers that garner billions of views on Youtube and Facebook (e.g., Parris Goebel, Ian Eastwood, ChaChi Gonzalez) (see Figure 4.3). Filipino dancers usually maximize their visas and spend time in Las Vegas, Los Angeles, and New York training in dance studios with popular choreographers, touring sites of hip-hop historical importance, and sometimes even auditioning.[80] Filipino dance crews have even parlayed their success and collaborated with local social organizations and private studios to produce their own concerts and workshops independent of HHI.[81] Similar to Battle of the Year (and equally depressing), HHI prize money is only a few thousand U.S. dollars per group. Given that the modest monetary prize does not come close to offsetting the costs for competing for Filipino crews, then the proximity to hip-hop resources, opportunity to be physically awarded medals by pioneering dancers, social capital, and chance to boast

Figure 4.3 Don Campbell with author (2014).

world-level ranking are actually the incentives to raise travel funds, apply for visas, train year-long, and compete at HHI.[82] As told to me by Filipino choreographer Vimi Rivera, member of HHI competitors The Crew and coach of Legit Status, the reward comes when you return to the Philippines as world champions or even contenders. It is not uncommon to see champions and contenders feature credits about past HHI participation, when publicizing workshops in the Philippines upon their return. They exemplify what James English calls "capital intraconversion," whereby competitive dancers, judges, and event organizers act as institutional agents who facilitate exchange between cultural capital in the field of hip-hop dance and other forms of capital in the world.[83]

Thus, Filipinos, non-Filipinos, and HHI alike enable reaffirmations of the exceptionalism of the Filipino dancing body. For the first six years that crews from the Philippines competed in HHI, not a single judge represented the Philippines.[84] The fact that Filipino crews won gold several times without having a judge representing their country dramatizes their winnings. This started to change in 2013. According to Nesh Janiola, technical director of HHI Philippines, from April to August 2013, Big Shift Studios, partly owned by Jhong Hilario, member of the television dance group Streetboys, became an official HHI licensee.[85] In 2013–14, Janiola—along with Xernan Alfonso from The Crew, and Benjamin "Benjo" Madrigal—worked through Big Shift to bring HHI to the archipelago's different regions (five regional legs)—Cebu, Davao, North Luzon (Baguio), South Luzon (Rizal), and NCR (National Capital Region—Manila).[86] Janiola described that, with fifteen to forty crews in each division from October to January, the top three qualifiers gained entrance into the grand finals in Manila in May.[87] A month before the regionals, HHI Philippines sends representatives to conduct workshops in the local areas on the HHI rules and regulations and hip-hop foundation.[88] The first year of HHI in Cebu, they had to reschedule the competition because of an earthquake and typhoon Yolanda (Haiyan) in 2013. In August 2013, prior to their first year of competitions, HHI Philippines flew out the HHI technical director, who stated, "I certainly believe the rest of the world is going to have some catching up to do, as far as competing is concerned," during his visit to the Philippines.[89] After completing the first ever HHI judging workshop in the Philippines, the director reflected:

> Whenever I teach I always tell people that I learn. I always learn when I teach. Because I learn from the interaction so much important and so much

interesting things come out when the students start to interact. And never have I ever learned as much as I have learned in this particular workshop. We had over forty persons attending this course and the enthusiasm, the questions, the interactions were superior. It was nothing like I've ever seen. And the questions that they asked challenged me, because it showed me that they were really interested in learning, really interested in knowing, how does HHI judge a routine, why does it judge it this way? I had to be on my toes.[90]

While the director, who happens to be Afro-Trinidadian, constructs a narrative by which hip-hop's history, "true essence," and fundamental values are passed from him to the Filipino judges to their students, it is interesting to imagine the workshop as a site of Black dance and Filipino exchange in the ways that workshop participants took the opportunity to learn from, share with, and question his authority. While most judging panels comprise of middle-class men, many Filipina competitors and choreographers—like Mycs Villoso, Lema Diaz, and Angelica Arda—found success at and further international opportunities through HHI. Given the successful experiences of Filipino dancers who have already won several times at HHI, their development as judges signals a new era, one that promises to continue evolving the next generation of dance champions.

These new forms of encounters also blend with the ways Filipino dancers, without eschewing the HHI narrative of unification, see themselves as distinct from other hip-hop dancers based in the "developed" world. One example is the integration of distinct Filipino dance styles like budots, a kind of social dance that originates in Davao City in Southern Philippines and mixes indigenous dance, techno music, and the social "deviances" of loitering and drinking. But most Filipino groups, like the U.P. Street Dance Club, A-Team, The Crew, UPeepz, and Addlib, actually do not draw on national symbols in their competition choreography, costume, or music, in a conventional sense (props, attire, and movement vocabulary). Unlike the mimicry of the zombie and the postracial critique of the robot (see Chapters 2 and 4), HHI dancers mainly construct Filipinoness in their representation, as delegates of the Philippines. While the Philippines as a nation ranks 47 out of 140 nations in the Global Competitiveness Index (GCI) rankings, Filipino dancers draw from their hip-hop experiences to place themselves, and by extension the Philippines, within other value structures.[91] Philip "Adrum" Pamintuan, one of the leading street dancers in Manila, describes how he sees his dancing in developmental contexts (see Figure 4.4):

Figure 4.4 Philip "Adrum" Pamintuan and Roz Manlangit—Operation Blessing Philippines.

Well, one thing is for sure, Filipinos have a lot of soul. We may lack in technique but we are full of soul. So that's what's inherent in Filipinos all around the world. Though speaking on my own experience, and as I've seen it there, the less you know, like knowledge-wise, the more soul you have. Because sometimes knowledge can be limiting. So *yun* (there) for me, Southeast Asia, not just Filipinos, Southeast Asia would be Singapore, Indonesia, Malaysia, Vietnam, Philippines, . . . These five countries who know not so much have a lot of soul and at the same time except for Singapore, I could say that these four countries especially the Philippines are not that well off. And it's that conflict and struggle that you put more value to dance. Because if you have something already given to you, it's nothing to you. But when you work hard for it, there's more value. More soul into it. There's more heart into it.[92]

Adrum is a dedicated krumper, or active practitioner of krump, a street dance form that evolved from Black vernacular dance, Thomas "Tommy the Clown" Johnson's "clowning," and marginalized communities shaped by the 1992 LA uprising, and policing of South Central Los Angeles.[93] Adrum, also member of Tha Project, an HHI competitive group based in Quezon City, naturalizes Filipinos and other Southeast Asians as exceptionally competitive or primed for hip-hop because of harsher living and training conditions than those in the Global North. Countering both an inclusive hip-hop world cypher and judge's desire for knowledge, Adrum constructs an alternative value structure wherein knowledge of proper technique is undesirable and redefines competitiveness in terms of social struggle, national infrastructure, region, and "the less you know."[94]

This account resonates with what American studies scholar Antonio T. Tiongson Jr. calls the authenticating strategy of lived experience.[95] Tiongson describes how, after acknowledging its foundational narrative as African American, San Francisco Bay Area–based Filipino American DJs foreground their early embrace of hip-hop to claim legitimacy in a culture that they believe to be as authentic as traditional Filipino expressive forms.[96] As Tiongson's respondents naturalize hip-hop as Filipino, Adrum similarly asserts a Third World fitness for its cultural practices, distinguishes Filipinos from Filipino Americans, and intimates technique as a class and racial euphemism that reifies risky ties between neoliberal order and competitiveness. Apart from association with the Philippine national flag during pre- and post-dance rituals or native language shout-outs, dancers primarily become legible as Filipinos by anchoring their practices in Filipino-specific struggles—thus connecting both hip-hop and Filipino transnationalism.

Conclusion

The standardization of difference in hip-hop resonates with the challenges faced by grant-awarding agencies. At a recent Mellon-sponsored dance studies book club meeting, I met a woman fortunate enough to sit on what sounded like several major arts grant selection committees. After the book club, we both caught the Red line, moving farther away from the meeting and deeper south into Chicago. I listened to her disdain of the competitions produced by Red Bull, a popular energy drink corporation that organizes a highly regarded international tournament. She confessed to me the low literacy levels of such committees for evaluating street dancers, who list competitions instead of critics' blurbs on their prospective grantee applications—and my heart sank. The death of the American dance critic heralded by the *Atlantic* is more than a straw man simply bested by judges. As judges and dancers see themselves advancing the hip-hop culture in international competitions, these competitions are not equally valued, misunderstood, or snubbed by cultural outsiders. Yet they should be seen as crucial interracial spaces for thinking through the very questions that dance criticism holds dear, particularly, the valuable ways performance operates beyond the doing of the dance. The internationalization of hip-hop, the discipline of judging, and debate around standardization provide many options besides dance's "endangered" modes of criticism that traditionally value technical merits over social impact. Rather, the judges of HHI offer important perspectives on the role of Filipinos and competition as a pivotal mode of contemporary dance discourse. Filipino dancers triangulate their self-representations, like that of indigenous warriors and soulful Southeast Asian counter-technicians, adjacent to the aesthetics of Black criminalized masculinity and white cheer femininity encoded within the judging system. From another perspective, the indigenous dancing body serves as an Other against which the organizers' hopes of elevating and promoting hip-hop dance forms are internationalized. This dynamic reminds us of how Overseas Filipino Worker (OFW) dancers are sought after as racial Others in Asian markets (see Chapter 2). Whereas the pre-migration training of OFW dancers to Japan mitigated the racial and sexual stigma of the Filipina dancing body with the promotion of white dance aesthetics, the judge training of national HHI delegates celebrates Black dance across multiple national contexts with discouragement of white dance aesthetics.

This chapter has sought to identify the euphemistic role of judging, a long overlooked component of competitions. For HHI judges, the job description is less about assuming universal and expert authority and the determination of champions, and more about engaging in cultural stewardship, identity formation, disciplinary measures, endogenous cultural and artistic conflicts, visual mechanization, and institutionalization. More importantly, the mutual benefits judges and participants gain are not innately progressive. The historical formations within physical fitness (as opposed to theater) of manufacturing hip-hop as an international product remind us of the "PE paradigm" that calisthenically frames the CPDRC's "Thriller" (see Chapter 2), or Filipino dance education as a shadow of American colonial schooling. In regards to the exceptional success of Filipino dancers at HHI, these formations offer up an explanation grounded on the structural dynamics of race and gender and internal logic of street dance rather than essentialism. These ideological junctions also elicit questions about the relationship between hip-hop, neocolonialism, and corporealities in the contexts of the other fifty countries and territories at HHI like New Zealand, Guam, Argentina, and India. These formations manifest in the technocratic solutions to the stigmatization of Black dance and limitations of standardizing an otherwise unregulated and improvisational dance. The shiny allure of unity at the end of these competitions is all but certain. Judges have the most sophisticated standards but doing justice to the dance is predicated on finding ways to maintain the ethos of speaking truth to power and the social struggles to which the dance moves.

In terms of developing hip-hop guidelines, the overall effect it has on the dance community remains an open question. On the one hand, judges advocate for a system of standardization that diversifies dance and encourages creativity over popularity. On the other hand, competitors demonstrate how judges still fail to engage issues around social justice, indigenous dance, and gender. Nor do they adequately address questions around dancers' agency and rights, "it is what it is" assumptions of criteria, and artistic expression. But maybe they could. After all, "how do you judge a competition?" if not by striking a balance between the contradictions of performance—multidirectional transnational flows of culture, history of its pioneers, and the ongoing emergence of new styles and technology—to reward, rather than stifle innovation. For some, guidelines seem to domesticate rather than transform and liberate bodies. But with a little creativity, to borrow from Theodore Parker, maybe the long moral arc of judging could bend toward justice.

Conclusion

Hip-Hop Ambassadors and Conventions

Choreography empowers Filipinos to re-orient themselves when they're lost, forgotten, or misunderstood. When I struggled to find my bearings in Manila while conducting fieldwork for this book, the dance community was a source of clarity and familiarity. The viral videos, migrations, culture nights, and international competitions this book has examined thus far exemplify this phenomenon. Across the previous chapters, the professional artists of *Penthouse 7* (Introduction), inmates of CPDRC (Chapter 1), diasporic dancers of PCN (Chapter 3), migrant dancers (Chapter 2), and HHI judges (Chapter 4), show how Filipino identity intersects with Black dance. Similar to the way that euphemisms provide hip-hop emcees with a way to express the ineffable, euphemisms provide Filipinos a way to convey themselves in gesture when the neocolonial, neoliberal stereotypes of Filipinoness—mimics, superhuman exports, model minorities, and natural dancers—fall flat. Here, one sees beyond lenses of mimicry and appropriation and toward notions of Filipinoness, which have long been informed by structural dynamics of race, gender, and colonialism. This panorama appreciates how these processes have been instrumental in making hip-hop a truly global entity, thereby enabling a critical aspect of hip-hop (dancing), whose multivalent significance and intellect has been heretofore virtually ignored.

I close by returning to the event which introduced this book, "America in 3D," the U.S. Embassy convention which took place in March 2012, in SM City North EDSA, Quezon City, Philippines.[1] Choosing to end this book with powerful women artists, I engage in conversation with Black feminist theory through "Pinays Rise," a striking dance component within the diplomatic event, and the concept of 3D (stereopsis), or three-dimensional depth visuality, to disentangle the gender, racial, and class heterogeneity underlying the bodily labor of Pinays (Filipino women) inscribed within a broader

Choreographing in Color. J. Lorenzo Perillo, Oxford University Press (2020). © Oxford University Press.
DOI: 10.1093/oso/9780190054274.001.0001

hip-hop horizon. While "Pinays Rise" demonstrates Filipina hip-hop as multiple and contradictory, the diplomatic context reveals the tensions between state-enacted euphemism—emphasizing familiarity between Filipinos and U.S. culture while redacting U.S. defense maneuvers—and non-elite, artist-enacted euphemism—provincializing U.S. hip-hop while collaborating with the U.S. State Department. Therefore, this case study demonstrates the ongoing intricacies of advancing the development of Black dance in the Philippines and its diaspora.

Performing Pinay as Euphemism

As a main stage event for "America in 3D," Chelo A.'s "Pinays Rise" was a four-minute live performance that blended pop music and hip-hop dance, featuring twelve dancers dressed in red and black from Stellars, a women's street dance collective, and produces a compelling view into the complicated role for Filipinas within global hip-hop culture. The song was released on Chelo's first solo album, *Love, Life, and D'Light* (2011). The strength of "Pinays Rise" lies in its ability to articulate a no-nonsense understanding of otherwise complicated racial, gender, and class politics within hip-hop while simultaneously expressing a modern Filipina point of view. The choreography holds onto enough of the album's lyrical structure to feature different street dance styles and formations as it progresses through intro and outro, verse, chorus, and bridge. A triptych of street dancers—krumper, swag dancer, and bgirl—reflects multiple gender presentations in the hard female masculinity of krump, pleasurable referentiality of swag, and cool finesse of bgirling. Each form of street dance embodies a different type of hip-hop feminism involved with reclaiming male-dominated genres. For example, according to Jason Cruz (Skittles Crew), "In a society like the Philippines, girls are not expected to bboy, krump, etc."[2] When teaching women essential krump movements like jabs and foot stomps, Cruz found himself faced with the task of undoing their preexisting habituations of gingerly stepping in ballet toe shoes and everyday high heels. According to Bgirl Beatch, there are only a few active bgirls in the Philippines, and thus entering a cypher, or breakin' competitive space, means higher risks of potentially violent sexual harassment, pseudo-sexual burns (or gestural insults), and "easy props" (recognition of her dancing based on assumed gendered weakness and without actual engagement of its merit).[3] Although the swag style of hip-hop choreography is less codified than krumps and breakin', many of the interviewees considered the low-effort, high-attitude, loose, hip-centric style to be a decidedly masculine one. This trifecta of movement and its inscribed struggles is counterbalanced by the feminine type of wacking-inspired dancing in the first two choral sections. The choreography redirects the traditional bodily expectations of Pinays and normative notions of global hip-hop and instead lands somewhere between irony and hip-hop "authenticity."[4]

In the "Pinays Rise" music video ⊙, Chelo dons a modernized version of the Filipina *traje de mestiza* [traditional dress]: an exposed midriff with butterfly sleeves.[5] But in the "America in 3D" live performance, Chelo rocks a tight-fitted black leather jacket, chains and studs galore, black tight pants, a reddish-black mesh tube top, and her signature bleached undercut.[6] The direct and sarcastic choreography—batted eyelashes in an exaggerated, punctuated fashion—playfully challenges the heteropatriarchal gaze with an unapologetic essentialism of its own (see Figure C.1). Affirming this reading, Chelo said "For too long I observed Filipinas being objectified as subservient wives of foreigners or playboy Filipinos."[7] Directed by Treb Monteras II, the "Pinay's Rise" music video is rendered in a *komiks* [Filipino comic book] style that visualizes Filipina gender politics.[8] A comic book aesthetic of lyrics, sound effects, and framed text boxes overlay its characters' dialogue and thoughts. The serial nature of the narrative of this video holds particular weight in the context of Filipino culture because it evokes the gendered

Figure C.1   Chelo A. in "Pinays Rise" (2011), screen still.

desires and shift in popular reading practices in the postwar era, dynamics that Filipino literature scholar Soledad R. Reyes has understood as a moment that created icons of Filipina representation.[9] For a brief shot in the video, the graphic crown of Darna is superimposed on the real image of Chelo (see Figure C.2). Created by Mars Ravelo, Darna is the Filipino superheroine from komiks and movies whose popularity began in the 1950s and continues today. Narda, a komik character from a *barrio* [rural town], transformed into Darna when she swallowed a white stone and thus gained the superpowers of flight, the strength of twenty men, and near invincibility.[10] While Darna's cultural significance during the anxiety-ridden and tumultuous postwar presidencies of Elpidio Quirino and Ramon Magsaysay may have articulated an implicit desire or served an escapist function for the reading public, Chelo's cultural meaning explicitly plays with the genre borders of social realism and fantasy.[11] By reference to Darna, Chelo summons an iconic Pinay potency and desirability to her work, and by doing so she accentuates the social realism and populism that overlap hip-hop and komiks as colorful cultural practices.[12]

In the live performance, during the final lyric, "Pretty, intelligent, nice, and why? Because I'm a Filipina," Chelo and Stellars curtsy, each of their knees awkwardly turned inward. Some dancers top off this darling-ness with a shoulder dip, others hold the seams of their long shirts—each winking at the subordinate role and limited mobilities of women in society at large. At

Figure C.2 Chelo A. as Darna in "Pinays Rise" (2011), screen still.

one point, Chelo draws our eyes to her black mid-top boots with a high kick to accent the break in the lyric, "You ain't gonna find girls like us." When read alongside Black feminist theory, the dance's naming of exploratory desire as a constituent aesthetic feature for the construction of Brown native women elaborates on a particular type of relational construction—bell hooks' "Eating the Other"—which bears upon women of color's affective interventions around the material analyses of race and gender inequality.[13] hooks argues that viewing the process of seduction as based upon two racializing bodies—the commodifying body and the commodified body—can help insert political critique into the economics of racism. hooks states:

> The commercial nexus exploits the culture's desire (expressed by whites and blacks) to inscribe blackness as "primitive" sign, as wildness, and with it the suggestion that black people have secret access to intense pleasure, particularly pleasures of the body. It is the young black male body that is seen as epitomizing this promise of wildness, of unlimited physical prowess and unbridled eroticism. It was this black body that was most "desired" for its labor in slavery, and it is this body that is most represented in contemporary popular culture as the body to be watched, imitated, desired, possessed. Rather than a sign of pleasure in daily life outside the realm of consumption, the young black male body is represented most graphically as the body in pain.[14]

Reading the Pinay body alongside "Eating the Other" reminds us of the ways the Western and Asian heteropatriarchal gaze naturalizes Filipina bodies.[15] This gaze touches upon the issue of "marriage brokers"—some Filipino themselves—operating for-profit businesses that offer a Filipina to a foreign national in Japan, South Korea, China, or the United States, for marriage or partnership, a practice which was outlawed in the Philippines in 1990 with the Anti-Mail Order Bride Act (Republic Act 6955).[16]

Nonetheless, the contentious practice continues with spouses from the Philippines and other developing regions, with reports of Filipina brides to South Korea as vulnerable to abuse.[17] In 2016, a revised law was passed; the Anti-Mail Order Spouse Act (Republic Act 10906) included stricter penalties, ranging from deportation of foreigners to twenty years imprisonment for syndicates, and included Filipino men.[18] "Eating the Other" and the plight of mail-order spouses thus enables us to see the lyric "You ain't gonna find girls like us" anew as commentary on the ways race, capitalism, gender, and desire perpetuate anti-Filipina oppression.

The "show and prove" activities around the many ways Filipinas move also inadvertently address a particular racialized, classed, and gendered heterogeneity that draws together the paradox of Brownness across the subjects of this book and which I read alongside the overdetermination of Black women in diaspora. In the lyrics of "Pinays Rise"—"Mestiza, Chinita, Morena, let me hear ya?" for example—Chelo's roll-call names and calls to action a liberal multiculturalist racial array of Filipinas: Mestiza are mixed-race women of Native and white descent; Chinitas are mixed-race women of Native and Chinese descent; and Morenas are mixed-race women of Native and Hispanic descent. While the acknowledgment and centering of mixed-race Filipinas counters the singularity of white feminine beauty ideals institutionalized through Spanish and American colonialisms and reflected in the Philippine's skin-whitening and entertainment industries, the absence of Black Filipinas warrants exploration. In response to the YouTube version of "Pinays Rise," one user alerted Chelo that she neglected to include *Negrita*, a Spanish colonial term that describes the archipelago's dark-skinned first inhabitants (see Introduction), to which Chelo responded and expressed fear that Negrita would likely be confused with racism and the pejorative N-word in U.S. society.[19] Drawing from the metaphor of grammar, or what is allowable in language and U.S. racial discourse, Hortense Spillers responds to the overdetermination of Black women as a pathological burden as depicted in the Moynihan Report, sociologist Daniel Patrick Moynihan's *The Negro Family: The Case for National Action* (1965).[20] Dealing with the "interruption" of the African past, American Grammar argues that the processes of social, cultural subject-formation for African and indigenous subjects means revisiting if not undergoing processes of theft, mutilation, dismemberment, and exile. Drawing precisely upon Spiller's rendering of the multiplicity of flesh brings into relief the ways the U.S. state deployed Blackness to bring Filipina women into the common sense of white supremacy (see Introduction).[21]

Given the contentious topic of the use of the N-word within Black and non-Black communities in the United States, as well as hip-hop music's role (mostly pertaining to rap), Chelo's lyrical and choreographic choices mark the problematics of imperial amnesia and acknowledging Filipino heterogeneity to non-Filipino audiences.[22] Even though adding Negrita to the "Pinays Rise" roll-call would more accurately reflect the heterogeneity of Filipinas and verbally reclaim the neocolonial space of Filipina representation that marginalizes Black and dark-skinned Filipinas, Chelo believed it would also risk criticism from those who staunchly uphold Filipino respect-ability and the many people unaware of the Philippines' multiple colonial histories. From a lyrical perspective, Chelo's decision to leave out Negrita in the roll-call (1) suggests a self-awareness of her own image as a light-skinned non-Black Cebuana (native of Cebu, Philippines) using Negrita, and (2) resounds with Spiller's attention to what is allowable in language, or a certain type of imperial grammar. From the perspective of represen-tation, the video centers the triumph of Naomi Tamayo-Jackson, a dark-skinned Filipina protagonist, and inclusion of mixed-race Black and Filipina American artist, Rachel Razon, and a transFilipina artist, Tzielo, while cen-tering Black dance forms (see Figure C.3). Still, the verbal omission reaffirms American grammar in the dismemberment of Black women from collective Filipina womanhood, forgets AfroFilipino formations and the ways that American occupiers historically used the N-word to render indigenous peo-ples of the Philippines within white supremacist logic, and, thus, underlines the simultaneous presence and absence of Black peoples and Blackness in contemporary representations of Filipino culture.

"Pinays Rise" shares much of the same multi-style hip-hop dance vocab-ulary that HHI judges evaluate (see Chapter 4); there is a great distance be-tween the images these groups construct and the once commonplace image of Imelda Marcos waltzing in her infamous shoe collection.[23] Since the mid-1990s, Filipinas have used popular dance to work against neocolonial tropes

Figure C.3 "Pinays Rise" battle featuring Naomi Tamayo-Jackson, screen still.

of womanhood. Philippine Allstar Leal Marie "Lema" Diaz first brought Stellars, a community of Filipina dancers, together in 2007, to combat internal gender bias in hip-hop. Diaz spoke of the deliberate use of hips (balakang) but a conscious attempt to steer clear away from kendeng-kendeng.[24] An example of a longer pattern in popular dance that has yet to relinquish the spectacle of a woman's waist (bewang), kendeng-kendeng can consist of hips moving side-to-side, bouncing, or shaking.[25] Kendeng-kendeng was popularized on noontime television programs by spokesmodels and William Revilliame on *Will Time Big Time* (2011). Kendeng and other dance crazes—like the twisting about of shembot and swaying backsides of kembot—usually have their own songs and semi-cute, semi-sexual choreographies.[26] These dances are highly visible entities of Filipino culture and considered playful "novelties" and easy for people to embody; an ease that is cumulative in the ways each seems to remake its precedent in gesture and name. It is not uncommon to see adults prompt their pre- and grade school children to perform these dances as entertainment during familial gatherings and community festivities. The novelty dances of the late 1990s and 2000s were staged on massively popular television programs and owe their success to audience relatability. Novelty dancing demonstrates how media corporations and Filipinas employ popular dance to make household, food, and beverage products relatable and accessible to a broad consumer class. These representations share commonalities with the colonial linkage between black women dancing bodies, hypersexuality, and bottoms.[27] Diaz aptly points out that it is the daily noontime show ritual of attractive Filipinas grinding and gyrating their hips that degrades women— and that her own choreography eschews.[28] This patriarchal ideology informs the "You think that's all we can do?" attitude that infuses Stellars dance choreography—and much of hip-hop dance.[29]

This attitude resonates with Chelo's own lived experiences with Filipina gender and class stereotypes—"Everywhere I traveled, I often would get asked, 'Are you a nurse?' Or someone would tell me, 'Oh, my nanny was Filipino.' I understand that Filipinas are nurturing and make ideal wives or caregivers. . . . But besides that, Filipinas can be more. Filipinos can be more . . . thus, I pushed for that 'Rise.'"[30] This speaks to the ways that lexicographers—such as in the Oxford English and Greek Dictionaries in 1989 and 1998, respectively—have defined the term Filipina as a maid and domestic helper rather than a woman from the Philippines. Chelo's own mother worked as a caregiver and this upbringing fundamentally shaped her views on womanhood, some that may be perceived as conservative. The dance accomplishes this by bridging the Filipina woman and hip-hop dancer as laboring bodies. It does so in the company of lyrics that spell out the racial and occupational diversity under the banner of "Pinay."

> We nurses, care-takers, the lovin', lovin' don't stop
> We business-women and dancing traffic cops
> There ain't nothing a Super Pinay can't do
> We ruling nations, while lookin' fly-high-high too![31]

In the music video, Chelo and Stellars portray characters in various employment settings and must abandon their duties to help support a fellow Filipina who is out-numbered by an all-male dance crew in a cypher.[32] Lyrical references to global Filipina labor offer a multi-faceted "we" (i.e., "We nurses," "We business-women," "We ruling nations") that is ordinary to Filipino culture and extraordinary for hip-hop culture. Ethnic studies scholar Catherine Ceniza Choy speaks to the inextricable roots of U.S. imperialism (i.e., Americanized nursing schools and English language curriculum in the American colonial period) as fundamental for explaining the normalcy of "we" and the fact that Filipinas comprise the largest population of overseas nurses.[33] By emphasizing the role of Filipinas in a care chain, Chelo further encircles the Filipina hip-hop dancing body within the colonial violence and neoliberal developments that laid the groundwork for global Filipino labor.[34] This dancing and the message of women's empowerment it delivers seek to actively re-make Filipinas.

Stereoscopic Relations

A few days before the "America in 3D" convention at SM City North EDSA, Quezon City, Philippines, I met one of the main organizers, the Public Affairs Officer for the U.S. Embassy in Manila and Philippine-American Educational Foundation (PAEF) Board Chairman, Rick Nelson.[35] Upon seeing me in the crowd at the Allstars concert portion of "America in 3D," Nelson invited me to sit in the front row and introduced me to the U.S. Ambassador and Honorary PAEF Board Chairman, Harry Thomas.[36] As a representative of the U.S. State Department, Thomas personally represented one of the three main bodies of U.S. presence in foreign nations like the Philippines.[37] The Department of State, along with the Department of Defense and U.S. Agency for International

Development (USAID), plays a pivotal role in advancing national security policy. In 2009, then–Secretary of State Hillary Clinton invoked the three-word alliteration, "Diplomacy, Development, and Defense," in her testimony before the Senate Appropriations Committee to underline the affinity between armed forces risking their lives and civilians in the State Department and U.S. Agency for International Development (USAID).[38] The United States seeks to integrate the efforts of the Department of State, Department of Defense, and USAID to effectively promote U.S. interests, both domestically and abroad. Nonetheless, this 3D foreign policy has not been without criticism. For instance, Nafees Asiya Syed highlights budgetary and expense differences between agencies: "The emphasis on defense at the expense of development and diplomacy raises serious questions about whether American foreign aid can achieve its stated goals and whether America is most effectively promoting peace and stability throughout the world."[39] Clinton, in fact, conceded that diplomacy and development amount to only 6 percent of the national security budget.[40] The gross disproportionality between defense spending and that of diplomacy and development has only escalated under the Trump administration.[41] Still, according to Nathan Finney, military writer for *Small Wars Journal*, the counter-insurgency-focused online magazine, the 3D foreign policy provides "a national security tool chest that has been enhanced with a wide variety of capabilities which would flow from the integration of our nation's soft power."[42] Finney's point is instructive because it frames the cultural work of Filipino dancers as not simply a matter of asserting a global visibility for the heretofore invisible (see Chapter 1) or carving a space in a postracial or international context (see Chapters 3 and 4), but also embedded in securing U.S. global military dominance.

If Finney were to experience the road show, "America in 3D," he might argue that the convention all but confirms his views on soft power. The Quezon City version of "America in 3D" enlisted the talents of several cultural resources for a three-day program including Martin Nieverra, who had hosted *Penthouse Live* in the 1980s (analyzed in "Introduction"). After *Penthouse*, Nieverra became a singer/actor popularly known as the "concert king" of the Philippines. He opened the weekend's program with Jaya, a mixed Jamaican and Visayan platinum soul singer. The Manila Hoedowners, a square dance club, taught square dance and tapped into the popular Filipino love for line dance. Workshops entitled "The Visa Process Demystified" and "Learn How to Study in the United States" ran several times throughout the weekend. Musical and vocal performances across the weekend featured a remarkable genre diversity: country music of Miles Poblete "Asia's Ambassadress of Country Music," Broadway and Popular music of Stephanie Reese, Gospel by the Greenhills Christian Fellowship Chancel Choir, Jazz by the University of Santo Tomas Jazz Ensemble, and American Pop by Jed Madela. The Block Cinemas housed films/discussions in three theaters on subjects like "Trafficking in Persons," "Freedom of the Press," "U.S-Philippine History," "Strengthening Democracy," "Protecting Labor Rights," and "Families in America."[43] The Philippine Basketball Association coaches and players offered an extensive two-day youth basketball clinic that was organized in three age categories in the Sky Dome.[44] Former White House Executive Chef Cristeta Comerford conducted a digital video-conference on Saturday morning to inform people about important things like "What's President Obama's favorite meal?" This exhaustive (and exhausting) itinerary of events was intent on demonstrating that the U.S.-Philippine relationship was un-deniably in-sync, at least in cultural terms (see Figure C.4). In other words, American culture was deeply integrated and perfected by Filipino bodies and Filipino culture (and cuisine especially) had infiltrated the upper echelons (and intestines) of American society. Yet, if defense is the main tool of foreign affairs—and 94 percent of the national security budget—what is to be sur-mised by the seemingly heavy hand of America's soft power in the "America in 3D" road show? What narrative energies does this 3D foreign policy draw upon to achieve its intended effects?

While "America in 3D" does not exactly parallel the examples of previous chapters, as the former is an approach rather than figure, like the zombie, hero, robot, and judge, it still exemplifies the performative euphemism. While the three "D's" in "America in 3D" point to the collective efforts of the Department of State, Department of Defense, and U.S. Agency for International Development (USAID) to effectively promote U.S. interests, these interests in the Philippines are shaped by the archipelago's position as an Asian ally, similar to Japan, South Korea, Australia, and Thailand.[45] This relationship is different from the relationship between the United States and China, India, or Russia—countries that the United States sees as "21st Century Centers of Influence." From the dominant Americanist hip-hop standpoint, the difference between Asian allies and "Centers of Influence" point to key fissures of any imagined homogenous, monolithic Asian hip-hop culture.[46] Given that the United States sees the Philippines as an im-portant figure in its plan to "pivot" to Asia and manage relations with these "21st Century Centers of Influence," "America in 3D" warrants a new attempt

Figure C.4 "America in 3D" poster captures a heavy-handed soft power.

to re-brand the U.S.-Philippine relationship and American image to the Filipino public and points to further differences underlying hip-hop and other Asian contexts.

In the late twentieth century, 3D connotes paper-framed glasses with red and blue (cyan) color filters, or "anaglyph glasses," used for American comic books, movies, or cereal boxes, and the nostalgia of childhood. Essentially, 3D works by viewing two slightly different versions of the same scene—taken together, the human body creates for itself an illusion that the two-dimensional image is three-dimensional through *stereopsis*, a sense of depth produced by psychological and physiological depth cues.[47] Resurfacing in the 2010s, 3D has had a mixed reception from critics and public alike.[48] 3D has generally been accepted as a technological upgrade, to give audiences a sense of image realism. According to journalist Dan Engber, when applied to films with unusual or exotic landscapes, 3D has the ability to create a new cinematic space.[49] But in cases such as Star Wars and Disney movies where 2D films have been re-released in 3D format, experts have expressed disappointment in how this usage fails to shift the cinematic paradigm or create new worlds but instead merely passes off something old for something new and more costly.[50] Still, Engber holds out hope for stereoscopic experiences: "[3D] has or had the possibility (unrealized as of yet) to be more of a paradigm shift than an upgrade in cinema. It has the possibility of something deeper, more complicated, and more mind-bendingly awesome."[51] That being said, 3D strikes me as a particularly useful metaphor for this book and the false sense of depth constructed by the common dichotomous view of the U.S.-Philippine relationship (native and foreign, pre-colonial and post-colonial, traditional and modern, and Filipino and American). If one follows the historical lineage of 3D as a medium for perceiving reality, the "America in 3D" road show only seems to gain more persuasiveness.[52] In this sense, it serves U.S. interests to ride the wave of 3D's resurgence in American popular cinema in an attempt to recreate a landscape of an imagined America that Filipinos could enter.[53]

These formations of stereoscopy shed light on my own mixed reaction to "America in 3D," made up of part skepticism and part hopeful possibility. Part of the questions surrounding the efficacy of the event originated from its own promise to effectively champion U.S.-Philippine relations. On the one hand, in its use of a variety of cultural agents and career fair resources, the road show was both broad and transparent in its attention to cultural production and labor migration as integral sites for fortifying the diplomatic and development aspects of U.S.-Philippine relations. On the other hand, the activities that directly related to the third "D"—Defense—in "3D" remained unclear and a far cry from the paradigm-shifting potentials of visual 3D.[54] Absent from this conversation was the history of U.S. militarism in the Philippines (and across other hip-hop communities), beginning with the Philippine American War, participation of Filipinos in the U.S. Navy and other branches, and contemporary activities in the Southern Philippines. For many progressive activists in the Philippines, the reopening of U.S. military bases in the Philippines is less than welcome and symbolizes contemporary neocolonialism and perpetual precarity of Philippine sovereignty.[55]

Lest one mistakes dancers such as the Philippine Allstars as pawns of U.S. foreign policy, they saw state collaborations as extremely useful when qualifying for visas that are necessary for competing in the annual U.S.-based world championship of hip-hop dance, World Hip-Hop Dance Championship presented by Hip-Hop International (HHI) (see Chapters 3 and 5). Indeed, it is in part due to their success from winning gold medals at HHI in 2006 and 2008 and folk hero–like popularity at the global level of hip-hop dance that the U.S. Embassy benefited from their participation. Moreover, it is no small point that the Allstars used their dance concert and workshop as a space to address widespread misconceptions about hip-hop cultural codes in places like Quezon City, Cebu, and Laoag, among *masa* [non-elites, social masses] who have little access to hip-hop workshops and classes outside the Philippines. Allstars see this as a critical platform to address a general societal prejudice against hip-hop and street dance as *jologs* [pejorative for lower class] or *patapon* [like trash], unlike other dance genres like ballet, modern, and folk. This is linked to how hip-hop dancers are discriminated against as second-class artists without labor rights, even as hip-hop has gained mainstream acceptance in the 2010s compared to previous decades.[56] By providing these classes for free, they challenged these dynamics and increased access to people usually excluded from formal hip-hop education. As one point of social and economic context, 28 percent of the population lives below the poverty line.[57]

For example, the Allstars produced instructional videos that were projected onscreen before different dance components of the concert took the stage. Before the Pinoy House Community took the stage, a video introduction to house—a Chicago-born club style of dance that blends industrial electronics, spirituality, and fast-paced upright footwork—gave audiences a glimpse of the dance as it was featured in recent international competitions in France and Singapore. These short but significant video essays, paired with live performance, seemed to signal to the Filipino public that these dances are part of a larger system of global hip-hop culture, thereby provincializing American hip-hop and challenging the U.S.-centricity offered up by the rest of the road show. This maneuver resonates with the way some Filipino street dance educators refer to certain styles of choreography as "LA style." Their ability to use source materials from their own battles enabled the Allstars to speak from their experience, rather than from some ur-text of hip-hop. For them, it seems clear, whether dance diplomats for the Philippines or United States, at the end of the day, any move toward advancing a better understanding of hip-hop is a step in the right direction.

The Colors of Change

Although the dances by Chelo and the Philippine Allstars in "America in 3D" remake Filipino identity through, against, and alongside Black dance and elucidate strategies to regain and assert authority in relationship to the Philippine and U.S. state, industry, and community, one must move both inside and outside of the Philippines to understand how such actions align with a particularly globalized Filipino struggle. Inspired in part by ethnomusicologist Joseph Schloss's call to "put theory back in the hands of practitioners," this book has asserted the performative euphemism is a mode of social critique articulated across the historical and contemporary development of Filipino hip-hop.[58] Erstwhile studies of the postcolonial production of racial knowledge and how multiple colonialisms shape Filipino identity formation and continued struggles for self-determination often marginalize Blackness in the Philippines. Within these pages, I historicized the simultaneous development of Filipino popular dance and Filipino experiences in Black dance in the contexts of prison rehabilitation, migration, educational segregation, international competition, and cultural diplomacy. In effect, AfroFilipino formations were and continue to be principal to the ways Filipinos engage histories of American imperialism and contemporary conditions of neoliberalism *regardless* of whether they occupy local or global cultural spaces and regardless of whether they constitute the racial minority or majority.

To begin with the assumption that race is irreducible gives us a space to understand how hip-hop dance operates as part of a race-making process for Filipinos. As the significance of the Filipino body lends itself to misunderstandings, miscasting, or illegibility, it is important to ground our understanding of its dancing in relationship to the ways American imperialism and neoliberal restructuring racialize the Filipino body. A complicated colonial history of Black social dance, whitewashed folk dances, and Black dance in the neoliberal era precedes Filipino hip-hop, and informs how and why Filipinos identify with hip-hop culture. A variety of indigenous and syncretized foreign dances, and their institutionalization under American colonialism and military expansion, laid the groundwork for Filipino masses' early adoption of hip-hop. In the United States, Pilipino culture nights (PCNs) emerged as community-based events of celebratory multiculturalism for West Coast Pilipino youth and the 1990s emergence of hip-hop dance in PCN Modern Suites reflects another site for racial agency based not upon folk, indigenous, and ethnic roots but in Filipino-American domesticity. *Home* (see Chapter 3) points to PCNs' potential, beyond representation, of engaging systemic forms of race and illuminating the intra-racial relations between Filipinos in the Philippines and diaspora. While poppin' and robotic dancing enabled critiques of multiculturalism, post-raciality, and the affirmative bodied/disembodied dichotomy, the show itself was an exception. Nonetheless, with a critical race approach to hip-hop dance, one begins to uncover the ways in which Filipinoness, as it is understood by Filipinos and non-Filipinos, has been informed by Blackness and also fully appreciates how Filipinos have been instrumental in making hip-hop a truly global entity.

In light of the ongoing implementation of neoliberal "free market" economic policies, enabling of multinational corporations, and divestment of the state's role in providing public goods for its people, Filipino dancing renders visible a crucial aspect of hip-hop's emancipatory power, understood intersectionally and intellectually, whose significance has been heretofore virtually ignored.[59] In some ways, the dance-based approach to hip-hop has revealed to be consistent with extant theories of hip-hop and globalization, as an antidote for the negative effects of economic globalization or the performative site of cultural globalization (the heightened connectivity of cultures, people, and ideas across borders and intensifying processes of local/global signification). Filipino hip-hop offers particular examples: *Home* functioned to address the removal of affirmative action and dancers simultaneously localized hip-hop within Manila while utilizing international hip-hop codes. The commodification of prisoners' dancing, discourse of exporting the labor of migrants, and the corporatization of hip-hop competitions reflect the convergence of capitalist demands for low-cost, low-status workers and a Filipino global labor force "naturalized" to meet those demands. Far from being symptomatic of the implementation of neoliberal structural adjustments, dance refracts how people make sense of these changes. The terms "modern," "street," "urban," "community," and "choreo" gain momentum, as categories for euphemizing the politics of Filipinoness and Blackness behind dance nomenclature, virtue and/or vice signaling devices, and constitution of new forms of racial and cultural capital; such forms are notably still reliant upon older notions of heterogeneity, usefulness, and authenticity. Still, these categories point to the ways Filipinos conceive of dance, beyond the dominant colonial paradigms of physical education or enlightenment art, as useful for expressing, escaping, and transforming Filipino corporeality and the material conditions within which they exist.

These choreographies of hip-hop's globalization are not without their contradictions. The locking in the United States serves as an index of the ascendant Black pride in the 1970s. Ironically, the legislative gains that informed the colorful U.S. versions of locking find an antithesis in the dictatorial oppression of civil rights during martial law—which set the stage for *Penthouse* dancers to introduce an upper-class version of Locking in Manila. Decades later, hip-hop dance in PCNs underscores meritocracy as a system used to walk back legal guarantees of equity. More recently, hip-hop is seen as a contemporary global cultural movement and dance of which Filipinos in Manila are exceptional champions.[60] Even so, the successes of Filipinos in hip-hop dance and other areas of popular culture have yet to yield a substantive cultural shift, in the way that the public and mass media talks about global hip-hop, systematically forgets empire, and reads dance. As diasporic Filipinos represent countries and territories like Germany, Finland, Guam, Australia, Canada, Ireland, and New Zealand at the World Hip-Hop Dance Championships, the international presence and success of Filipinos further evidences the limitations of nation-bound approaches to global hip-hop and the need for judges to lead a shift toward an understanding of the unequal power relations and racial, postcolonial, gendered, and settler dynamics of hip-hop.

The ethos of euphemism, or articulation of the relationship between corporeality and its recoding, precedes and permeates hip-hop's circulation. Queer dancers in CPDRC's "Thriller" and *Prison Dancer* make light of the seriousness of everyday queer life by playing with historical and contemporary gendered essentialisms. Immigrants and migrants from the Philippines circulate Black dance forms against a backdrop of "dance drain" shaped by the Philippine state's labor brokerage, Asian demands for "desirable, cheap labor," and the racial exclusivity of the U.S. dance market. Robots in *Home* are performative euphemisms for the lack of Filipino content in U.S. public education and the prevalent "search for one's roots" narrative of PCNs. In HHI, judges bring to bear a type of affirmative choreography that resonates with statist codes in higher education as the institutionalization of hip-hop dance forms for international competition led them to open up an ambivalent space capable of blending social and technical commentary. By underlining the potentials and limits within euphemism, I also recognize their uneven and unfinished nature. While the CPDRC discontinued its dance rehabilitation program, affirmative action continues to be debated across the United States and the government continues to divest itself of public education.[61] Even though folk dances returned to Berkeley PCN since *Home* (2000), students there continue to play around with the form and function of the show. I was invited to deliver the keynote speech to the community dinner that followed the April 2010 PCN, *Check-it*, a show that incorporated a public service campaign advocating for Filipino participation in the U.S. Census. Filipinos continue to have a strong presence at HHI. In 2017, three out of the six finalists in the megacrew categories were Philippine delegates (The Alliance, Legit Status, and Upeepz), with the gold medal going to Upeepz.

In August 2017, Chelo released a single, "Historic," that features garments from her clothing company, Barong Warehouse. In Manila in April 2008, *Penthouse* dancers—then in their fifties—gathered for a live reunion show; many had long since migrated from the Philippines across the globe. According to Sandy Hontiveros, they are always "threatening" to do another reunion show. Through performative euphemism one can understand Filipino hip-hop and street dancing as an attempt to navigate and challenge empire, neoliberalism, state-sanctioned violence, and more, thereby creating a space where Filipinos participating in hip-hop through dance can be regarded as something beyond mimicry or, even still, appropriation.

I began the study with doubts going into "America in 3D," but my cynical impulses were gradually replaced with ambivalence. So much about what characterizes these dancers' polyform practices comes from histories of imperialism and the polysemy of "Filipino." With broad strokes, one could consider how the processes of AfroFilipino formation are inherently historically contingent. In the 1970s, Filipinos were sponsored by the Philippine government to emigrate and thus circulated various forms of Black dance not only amidst the Marcos dictatorship, but in part, enabled by it. In the 1980s, as Filipino and Filipino American youth popularized popping and pop dance on Philippine television shows like *Dance10*, *Student Canteen*, and *Eat Bulaga*, youth in California came together to celebrate Filipino heritage through music and dance popularized by Philippine dance companies, like the ones that facilitated *Penthouse* dancers' exposure to Black dance forms in the 1970s. The 1990s witnessed the birth of PCN Modern Suites (a vehicle for incorporating hip-hop dance) in the U.S. West Coast and the institution of street dance in universities in Manila. "Hip-hop" finally crossed over into the Manila lexicon in the 1990s, although bboyin', poppin', lockin', and other forms were already present. In the 2000s, PCNs saw radical changes and PCN Modern Suites outgrew the original genre conventions. In the second half of the 2000s, Filipina hip-hop dancers in Manila demonstrated overt engagements with postcolonial gender tropes and Manila-based crews flourished inside and outside universities, competed internationally, hosted foreign choreographers, and collaborated with the nation-state, even while they challenged American hip-hop discourse.

Although I went into "America in 3D" thinking it would confirm the criticisms of Filipino scholars and activists calling for real decolonization and independence, I came away with a much more ambivalent response about the neocolonial, neoliberal, racialized, and gendered relationship between the Philippines and the United States. Part of this response had to do with the message of women's empowerment, specifically through the rejection of demurity and objectification as constitutive of Filipina womanhood delivered by "Pinays Rise." Another part of my reaction is attributed to the evident labor of hip-hop practitioners, many of whom saw this opportunity as a means to build better relations with the U.S. Embassy in Manila. At the same time, state collaborations undermine the spirit of the dance or the notion of self-determination that hip-hop promises. These formations tell us that self-determination is not possible in isolation, especially when considering extrinsic factors like cultural globalization and state actors. Moreover, "America in 3D" and its dancers both seem to problematically omit the historical and contemporary formations of Blackness in U.S.-Philippine and global Filipino relations, while simultaneously legitimizing Black dance in the context of the Philippine's long colonial legacy of whitewashed, yet multicultural dance culture.

The case of "America in 3D," and the many examples of ambivalence within Filipino hip-hop, point to a necessary reluctance to assume hip-hop to be inherently resistant, and an uneasy need to see hip-hop as having operated and emerged in tandem with both American imperial expansion and Philippine neoliberalism. Even so, "America in 3D" alludes to how hip-hop practitioners and national leaders can reach mutual agreements and in turn spark meaningful dialogues about the lived practice of hip-hop, *and* in its own terms and discourse. While the colors of change that euphemism produces—much like the anaglyph glasses—are not exclusively red or blue, they nonetheless hold potential to shift paradigms and offer insight into "something deeper, more complicated, and more mind-bendingly awesome."[62] Just as 3D technology is insufficient in changing the story it frames, the violence of U.S. empire remains. Thankfully, there are choreographers and communities creating work that inspires views besides the reds and blues, to wider frames and deeper hues.

Notes

Introduction

For this book, I define hip-hop inclusively and polysemously as a competitive dance culture, improvisational and choreographed bodily movement, postcolonial expressive form, and metonym for marginalization and struggle. Hip-hop dance as artistic practice includes a variety of dance genres depending on context and ranging from bboying, bgirling, popping, locking, New Jack swing, party/fad dances, and dance crazes. Hip-hop events may also include other street dance or social, popular, and urban dance forms like krump, house, waacking (whacking), vogueing, footwork, tutting, j-setting, step, stroll, strut, tricking, dancehall, experimental dance, and dance challenges. Filipino hip-hop dance may also include native, indigenous dance forms and variations like folk and festival dances, "LA-style," popular dances like kembot, gumiling, budots, as well as Japanese and Korean pop dances.

1. The jeepney is a colonial relic of transportation, repurposed and radiantly appropriated for modern uses. Modeled after leftovers from World War II, these US military jeep-like buses seat fifteen to twenty passengers and derive their popularity from their low cost (compared to buses, taxis, and personal vehicles), kitschy character, and pervasiveness on urban streets.
2. At the time of my 2011 fieldwork, fare was eight pesos or about 20 cents in U.S. currency. There is usually a fee reduction for students.
3. SM stands for Shoe Mart.
4. EDSA is short for Epifanio de los Santos Avenue.
5. The Block is an annex of the SM City North EDSA Complex, one of the largest retail shopping malls in the Philippines.
6. Consider the title of Roland Tolentino's *Sa Loob at Labas ng Mall Kong Sawi / Kaliluha'y Siyang Nangyayaring Hari: Ang Pagkatuto at Pagtatanghal ng Kulturang Popular*, in which he replaces "bayan" (nation) with the "mall" (popular culture) from a canonical line in Philippine poem by Francisco Balthazar. Roland Tolentino, *Sa Loob at Labas ng Mall Kong Sawi / Kaliluha'y Siyang Nangyayaring Hari: Ang Pagkatuto at Pagtatanghal ng Kulturang Popular* (Quezon City: University of the Philippines Press, 2001).
7. Bakla is a Tagalog word with contested origins and definitions that may coexist and conflict with concepts including but not limited to gay male identity, lower class homosexuality, trans male-to-female identity, corporeal, performative, and affective signification, cross-dressing, and effeminate Filipino modernity. See Martin F. Manalansan IV, *Global Divas: Gay Filipinos in the Diaspora* (Durham: Duke University Press, 2003).

8. The broader event took place March 18–20, 2011. The concert was held at 7:00 pm on Friday night and the workshop took place on Sunday at noon.

9. Thousands of fans had experienced the Allstars' concert and workshop online; some uploaded videos to YouTube and some viewed the live-streaming of the events on the U.S. Embassy's Ustream channel. Beyond the strong live and online hip-hop presence, "America in 3D" was not just about hip-hop. Celebrity musicians and vocalists performed across an impressive range of genres.

10. SM City Baguio on July 8–10, 2011; Robinsons Place, Ilocos Norte on August 25–26, 2011; SM City Cebu on September 16–18, 2011; SM City Iloilo on March 2–4, 2012.

11. Anna Romina Guevarra, *Marketing Dreams, Manufacturing Heroes: The Transnational Labor Brokering of Filipino Workers* (New Brunswick, NJ: Rutgers University Press, 2009); Robyn Magalit Rodriguez, *Migrants for Export: How the Philippine State Brokers Labor to the World* (Minneapolis: University of Minnesota Press, 2010).

12. George E. Marcus, "Ethnography in/of the World System: The Emergence of Multi-Sited Ethnography," *Annual Review of Anthropology* 24, no. 1 (1995): 95–117.

13. Mimicry is "construed as a sign of inferiority borne out of racial [Oriental and Spanish mestizo] difference," for Filipinos, as Vicente L. Rafael observes. His analysis of surveys and censuses used as colonial weapons for neutralizing anti-imperialists and dehumanizing the countless killed by U.S. troops links the frequent categorization of the Filipino as "natural imitator" with justification for refusing to recognize Filipino rights to self-determination. See Vicente L. Rafael, *White Love and Other Events in Filipino History* (Durham, NC: Duke University Press, 2000), 34; David Harvey, *A Brief History of Neoliberalism* (New York: Oxford University Press, 2007).

14. In this book, I am using "Filipinoness" to refer to the multiple, ever-shifting notions and qualities attributed to "Filipino," including modes of self-identification in relationship to colonialism and neoliberalism, representation in media and popular culture, stereotypes linked to racial and ethnic markers, cultural belonging, and statist codes marking inclusion and exclusion.

15. Diana Taylor, *The Archive and the Repertoire: Performing Cultural Memory in the Americas* (Durham, NC: Duke University Press, 2003).

16. Maria P. P. Root, ed., *Filipino Americans: Transformation and Identity* (Thousand Oaks, CA: Sage Publications, 1997); Rafael, *White Love*; Antonio T. Tiongson, Edgardo V. Gutierrez, and Ricardo V. Gutierrez, eds., *Positively No Filipinos Allowed: Building Communities and Discourse* (Philadelphia: Temple University Press, 2006); Rick Baldoz, *The Third Asiatic Invasion: Migration and Empire in Filipino America, 1898–1946* (New York: New York University Press, 2011); Martin Joseph Ponce, *Beyond the Nation: Diasporic Filipino Literature and Queer Reading* (New York: New York University Press, 2012); Martin F. Manalansan and Augusto Espiritu, eds., *Filipino Studies: Palimpsests of Nation and Diaspora* (New York: New York University Press, 2016); Nerissa Balce, *Body Parts of Empire: Visual Abjection, Filipino Images, and the American Archive* (Ann Arbor, MI: University of Michigan Press, 2016).

17. See Vicente L. Rafael, *White Love and Other Events in Filipino History* (Durham, NC: Duke University Press, 2000); Anthony Christian Ocampo, *The Latinos of*

Asia: How Filipino Americans Break the Rules of Race (Redwood City, CA: Stanford University Press, 2016); Rommel A. Curaming, "Filipinos as Malay: Historicising an Identity," in *Melayu: Politics, Poetics and Paradoxes of Malayness,* (eds.) Maznah Mohamad and Syed Muhd Khairudin Aljunied (Singapore: National University of Singapore Press, 2011): 241–274.

18. For more on Joe Bataan's music and life, see Theodore S. Gonzalves, *The Day the Dancers Stayed: Performing in the Filipino/American Diaspora* (Philadelphia: Temple University Press, 2009); Tyrone Nagai, "An Interview with Joe Bataan: Torrance, California, February 14, 2013," *Kalfou* 1, no. 2 (2015); Raquel Z. Rivera, *New York Ricans from the Hip Hop Zone* (New York: Palgrave Macmillan, 2003); Oliver Wang, "Rapping and Repping Asian: Race, Authenticity, and the Asian American MC," in *Alien Encounters: Popular Culture in Asian America*, ed. Kevin Fellezs (Durham, NC: Duke University Press, 2007), 35–68.

19. Nagai, "An Interview," 198. Bataan writes that before, Asians were passive and did not "come out publicly" as Filipino or Asian, but "They're starting to understand that there's much more to the Filipino question, to the Korean question, to all these questions that can be done."

20. Grace Kyungwon Hong and Roderick A. Ferguson, "Introduction," in *Strange Affinities: The Gender and Sexual Politics of Comparative Racialization*, eds. Grace Kyungwon Hong and Roderick A. Ferguson (Durham, NC: Duke University Press, 2011), 9; Vijay Prashad, *Everybody Was Kung Fu Fighting: Afro-Asian Connections and the Myth of Cultural Purity* (Boston: Beacon Press, 2002); Bill V. Mullen, *Afro Orientalism* (Minneapolis: University of Minnesota Press, 2004); *AfroAsian Encounters: Culture, History, Politics*, eds. Heike Raphael-Hernandez and Shannon Steen (New York: New York University Press, 2006); Victor Román Mendoza, *Metroimperial Intimacies: Fantasy, Racial-Sexual Governance, and the Philippines in U.S. Imperialism, 1899–1913* (Durham, NC: Duke University Press, 2016).

21. Kimberle Crenshaw, "Mapping the Margins: Intersectionality, Identity Politics, and Violence Against Women of Color," *Stanford Law Review* 43 (1990): 1241–1299.

22. I also remove the hyphen to indicate a more porous rather than compound relationship between the two terms. There are important recent and forthcoming works at the intersection of Black Amerasians, African American Studies, and Filipino Studies including: Nicholas Trajano Molnar, *American Mestizos, The Philippines, and the Malleability of Race: 1898–1961* (Columbia, MO: University of Missouri Press, 2017); Martin Joseph Ponce, "Toward a Queer Afro-Asian Anti-Imperialism: Black Amerasians and US Empire in Asian American Literature," *Journal of Asian American Studies* 20, no. 2 (2017): 283–287; Angelica Allen, "Black Filipino Amerasian Identity," in *Filipinx American Studies: A Critical Registry of Terms*, eds. Rick Bonus and Antonio T. Tiongson Jr. (New York: Fordham University Press, forthcoming).

23. In this book, I build upon the conversations in dance studies about Black dance, prompted in part by the economic and symbolic theft Black people have experienced amidst popularization. My research follows Brenda Dixon's call for attention to Black original contexts, aesthetics, as well as culture-specific approaches, and furthermore,

builds upon her attention to Black/White American syncretism by centering Filipino cultural contexts. Brenda Dixon, "Black Dance and Dancers and the White Public: A Prolegomenon to Problems of Definition." *Black American Literature Forum* 24, no. 1 (1990): 117–123.

24. Allen, "Black Filipino Amerasian Identity."
25. I thank an anonymous reviewer for leading me to this insight. Global hip-hop scholarship might frame Filipino hip-hop as a part of a "global village," an iteration of Black popular culture's globalization, a resistant tool against economic globalization, and a performative site of cultural globalization in action. These four types of global hip-hop scholarship are particularly instructive yet risk assuming Filipino practitioners are not creating theories and meanings of their own. Imposing any of the existing global hip-hop frameworks says little about and does little justice to the actual political and global realities of Filipinos, like Clara Bajado (Juste Debout, France/UK), Joel Gallarde (Triple8Funk, Australia), Ricky Carranza (Style Dance Industry, Finland), Rosie Pajela-Marzan (Danz People, Singapore), and Ryan Ramirez (Animaneaux, UK), who reflect the realities of Filipino migration that exceed U.S.-non-U.S. models of global hip-hop. To varying degrees, these artists are transforming hip-hop and hip-hop mutually remakes them.

See, for example, Tony Mitchell, "Introduction: Another root—Hip-Hop outside the USA," in *Global Noise: Rap and Hip-Hop Outside the USA*, ed. Tony Mitchell (Middletown, CT: Wesleyan University Press, 2001), 2; Dipannita Basu and Sidney J. Lemelle, "Introduction," in *The Vinyl Ain't Final: Hip Hop and the Globalization of Black Popular Culture*, eds. Dipannita Basu and Sidney J. Lemelle (Ann Arbor, MI: Pluto Press, 2006), 1–15; M. T. Kato, *From Kung Fu to Hip Hop: Globalization, Revolution, and Popular Culture* (Albany, NY: State University of New York Press, 2007); Ian Condry, *Hip-Hop Japan: Rap and the Paths of Cultural Globalization* (Durham, NC: Duke University Press, 2006).
26. Lucy Mae San Pablo Burns, "'Splendid Dancing': Filipino 'Exceptionalism' in Taxi Dancehalls," *Dance Research Journal* 40, no. 2 (Winter 2008): 23–40.
27. A burgeoning group of scholars has already elaborated upon the potentials of "misrecognition," "disarticulation," and "playful exaggeration." For Filipino subject formation, see Allan Punzalan Isaac, *American Tropics: Articulating Filipino America* (Minneapolis: University of Minnesota Press, 2006); Sarita Echavez See, *The Decolonized Eye: Filipino American Art and Performance* (Minneapolis: University of Minnesota Press, 2009); Lucy Mae San Pablo Burns, *Puro Arte: Filipinos on the Stages of Empire* (New York: New York University Press, 2012).
28. Susan Leigh Foster, "Introduction," in *Corporealities: Dancing Knowledge, Culture and Power*, ed. Susan Leigh Foster (New York: Routledge, 1996), xi–xvii.
29. See also Yutian Wong, *Choreographing Asian America* (Middletown, CT: Wesleyan University Press, 2010); Priya Srinivasan, *Sweating Saris: Indian Dance as Transnational Labor* (Philadelphia: Temple University Press, 2012); Burns, "Splendid Dancing," 23–40; SanSan Kwan, *Kinesthetic City: Dance and Movement in Chinese Urban Spaces* (New York: Oxford University Press, 2012); Eng-Beng Lim, *Brown Boys and Rice Queens: Spellbinding Performance in the Asias* (New York: New York

University Press, 2014); Rachmi Diyah Larasati, *The Dance That Makes You Vanish: Cultural Reconstruction in Post-Genocide Indonesia* (Minneapolis: University of Minnesota Press, 2013).

30. Wong, *Choreographing Asian America*, 18–20; Srinivasan, *Sweating Saris*.

31. Wong, *Choreographing Asian America*, 14. See also Rosemary Candelario, *Flowers Cracking Concrete: Eiko & Koma's Asian/American Choreographies* (Middletown, CT: Wesleyan University Press, 2016).

32. Wong, *Choreographing Asian America*, 12, 15.

33. Jonathan Rosa, *Looking like a Language, Sounding like a Race: Raciolinguistic Ideologies and the Learning of Latinidad* (New York: Oxford University Press, 2018), 2–5.

34. See Nerissa S. Balce, "Filipino Bodies, Lynching, and the Language of Empire," in *Positively No Filipinos Allowed: Building Communities and Discourse*, eds. Antonio T. Tiongson, Edgardo V. Gutierrez, and Ricardo V. Gutierrez (Philadelphia: Temple University Press, 2006), 43–60; Burns, *Puro Arte*.

35. Luis H. Francia, *History of the Philippines: From Indios Bravos to Filipinos* (New York: Overlook Press, 2010); Janet D. Headland, Thomas N. Headland, and Ray T. Uehara, "Agta Demographic Database: Chronicle of a Hunter-Gatherer Community in Transition," accessed November 11, 2017, http://www.sil.org/silepubs/abstract.asp?id=49227.

36. Janet D. Headland, Thomas N. Headland, and Ray T. Uehara, "Agta Demographic Database," 3.

37. Janet D. Headland, Thomas N. Headlan, and Ray T. Uehara, "Agta Demographic Database," 7–8; Dylan Rodriguez, "The Meaning of 'Disaster' under the Dominance of White Life," in *What Lies Beneath: Katrina, Race, and the State of the Nation*, eds. the South End Press Collective (Cambridge, MA: South End Press, 2007), 133–156.

38. Abe Ignacio, Enrique de la Cruz, Jorge Emmanuel, and Helen Toribio, *The Forbidden Book: The Philippine-American War in Political Cartoons* (San Francisco: T'boli, 2004).

39. Ibid., 80–95; Paul A. Kramer, *The Blood of Government: Race, Empire, the United States, and the Philippines* (Chapel Hill: University of North Carolina Press, 2006); Balce, "Filipino Bodies, Lynching, and the Language of Empire"; Anthony Kwame Harrison, "Post-Colonial Consciousness, Knowledge Production, and Identity Inscription within Filipino-American Hip-Hop Music," *Perfect Beat* 13, no. 1 (2012): 29–48.

40. Unknown artist, *Boston Sunday Globe*, March 5, 1899, reprinted in Ignacio et al., *The Forbidden Book*, 80.

41. Ibid.

42. Brooke Baldwin, "The Cakewalk: A Study in Stereotype and Reality," *Journal of Social History* 15, no. 2 (1981): 205–218; P. Gabrielle Foreman et al., "Writing about Slavery/Teaching About Slavery: This Might Help," community-sourced document, April 9, 2019, 7:09pm, https://docs.google.com/document/d/1A4TEdDgYslX-hlKezLodMIM71My3KTN0zxRv0IQTOQs/edit.

43. Victor Román Mendoza, *MetroImperial Intimacies: Fantasy, Racial-Sexual Governance, and the Philippines in U.S. Imperialism, 1899–1913* (Durham, NC: Duke University Press, 2015), 105.

44. *The Philippine Exposition Souvenir Booklet*, 1904, 18, accessed April 9, 2019, https://humanzoos.net/?page_id=175.

45. Henry Theodore Johnson, "The Black Man's Burden," *Voice of Missions* 1 (1899); Willard B. Gatewood Jr., *Black Americans and the White Man's Burden, 1898–1903* (Urbana: University of Illinois Press, 1975); Michele Mitchell, *Righteous Propagation: African Americans and the Politics of Racial Destiny after Reconstruction* (Chapel Hill: University of North Carolina Press, 2005); Michele Mitchell, "'The Black Man's Burden': African Americans, Imperialism, and Notions of Racial Manhood 1890–1910," *International Review of Social History* 44, no. S7 (1999): 77–99.

46. Ignacio et al., *The Forbidden Book*, 82; Cynthia L. Marasigan, *"Between the Devil and the Deep Sea": Ambivalence, Violence, and African American Soldiers in the Philippine-American War and Its Aftermath* (PhD diss., University of Michigan, 2010). I thank Angelica Allen for this suggestion.

47. Brian Shott, "Forty Acres and a Carabao: T. Thomas Fortune, Newspapers, and the Pacific's Unstable Color Lines, 1902–3," *Journal of the Gilded Age and Progressive Era* 17, no. 1 (2018): 98–120.

48. Sarah Steinbock-Pratt, *Educating the Empire: American Teachers and Contested Colonization in the Philippines* (Cambridge, UK: Cambridge University Press, 2019), 169–172.

49. Ibid.; Basilio Esteban S. Villaruz, *Sayaw: An Essay on the American Colonial and Contemporary Traditions in Philippine Dance* (Manila: Sentrong Pangkultura ng Pilipinas Special Publications Office, Cultural Center of the Philippines, 1994), 4, 11. . Prior to vaudeville, American military (along with expatriates and Filipino natives) were entertained by imported minstrel troupes.

50. Reynaldo Alejandro and Amanda Abad Santos-Gana, *Sayaw: Philippine Dance* (Manila: National Book Store and Anvil Publishing, 2002), 135–137; Carolina de Leon San Juan, *From Vaudeville to Bodabil: Vaudeville in the Philippines* (PhD diss., University of California, Los Angeles, 2010); American military personnel were entertained by minstrel troupes, tap, blues, jazz, and other imported African American forms of popular culture.

51. Alejandro and Abad Santos-Gana, *Sayaw*.

52. Basilio Esteban S. Villaruz, "Tapping Thoughts on Black and Brown Dances in the Americas," in *Saysay Himig: A Sourcebook on Philippine Music History, 1880–1941*, ed. Arwin Q. Tan (Diliman: University of the Philippines Press, 2018), 339–346.

53. Basilio Esteban Villaruz and Ramon A. Obusan, *Sayaw: An Essay on Philippine Ethnic Dance* (Manila: Sentrong pangkultura ng Pilipinas, 1992), 4–9.

54. J. Lorenzo Perillo, "Embodying Modernism: A Postcolonial Intervention across Filipino Dance," *Amerasia Journal* 43, no. 2 (2017): 123–140.

55. Burns, "Splendid Dancing."

56. Baldoz, *The Third Asiatic Invasion*, 135–143; Santa Cruz Sentinel and Donna Jones, "Riots in 1930 Revealed Watsonville Racism: California Apologizes to Filipino Americans," *Santa Cruz Sentinel*, September 3, 2011, updated September 11, 2018, accessed April 19, 2019, https://www.santacruzsentinel.com/2011/09/03/riots-in-1930-revealed-watsonville-racism-california-apologizes-to-filipino-americans/.

57. White riots and anti-Filipino violence proliferated in a variety of rural places including Yakima Valley, Washington in 1927, Dinuba, California in 1928, Exeter,
California in 1929, and the bombing of the Filipino Federation of America
(FFA) clubhouse in Stockton, California. See Baldoz, *The Third Asiatic Invasion*,
135–143; Michael P. Showalter, "The Watsonville Anti-Filipino Riot of 1930: A
Reconsideration of Fermin Tobera's Murder," *Southern California Quarterly* 71, no.
4 (1989): 341–348. doi:10.2307/41171455.

58. Burns, *Puro Arte*, 50–62.

59. I discuss "Modern Suites" in more detail in Chapter 3.

60. See, *The Decolonized Eye*, xvii.

61. See also Burns, *Puro Arte*; Enrico Dungca, "The Forgotten Amerasians," *Asian
American Writer's Workshop—Open City*, February 11, 2016, accessed January 8,
2018, http://opencitymag.aaww.org/the-forgotten-amerasians/; Sunshine Lichauco
de Leon, "'Amerasians' in the Philippines Fight for Recognition," *CNN World*, March
3, 2012, accessed January 8, 2018, http://www.cnn.com/2012/03/03/world/asia/
philippines-forgotten-children/index.html; Rodriguez, "The Meaning of 'Disaster'
under the Dominance of White Life."

62. J. Lorenzo Perillo, *Hip-Hop, Streetdance, and the Remaking of the Global Filipino*
(PhD diss., University of California, Los Angeles, 2013); Arjun Appadurai,
"Disjuncture and Difference in the Global Cultural Economy," *Theory, Culture &
Society* 7, no. 2–3 (1990): 295–310.

63. Sandy Hontiveros, interview with the author, digital recording, Manila, Philippines,
May 14, 2011; Philippine Allstars, "Beyond Hip Hop - Penthouse 7: The Grand
Reunion," *Multiply* (blog), posted April 27, 2008, accessed February 26, 2011, http://
allstars2005.multiply.com/reviews/item/5. Multiply website is no longer available as
of April 8, 2020.

64. Hontiveros, interview.

65. Villaruz, *Sayaw*, 9. It is worth noting that unlike other dancers, Hontiveros views
locking and hip-hop as separate, the latter not becoming mainstream in the
Philippines until the 1980s.

66. Donald Campbell, interview with the author, digital recording, Ithaca, NY, March
22, 2015; Jorge Pabon, "Physical Graffiti: The History of Hip Hop Dance," in *Total
Chaos: The Art and Aesthetics of Hip Hop*, ed. Jeff Chang (New York: Basic Books,
2006), 18–26. The core unit of the dance—the lock—is a posture in which the
elbows are out at ninety-degree angles, one leg is bent, and the opposing hip juts out
laterally. The lock operates like a form of punctuation for each phrase and combination of points, twirls, and knee drops animating the funky dance.

67. Pabon, "Physical Graffiti"; James "Skeeter Rabbit" Higgins, Tony GoGo, and
Peekaboo Frenke, "The History of Locking Editorial: The terms or Dances Locking,
Roboting & "PopLocking" valid," *Locker Legends*, accessed March 27, 2013, http://
lockerlegends.net/?page_id=359.

68. Ibid.

69. Hontiveros, interview; "About," *Ballet Philippines* (website), accessed March 27,
2013, http://www.ballet.ph/about; Sam L. Marcelo, "Start Small but Start Well: Alice

Reyes and Ballet Philippines," *BusinessWorld Online Edition*, November 22, 2012, accessed March 27, 2013, http://www.bworldonline.com/weekender/content.php?id=61838. As of April 8, 2020, link no longer works.

70. Hontiveros, interview.

71. Edouard Glissant, *Caribbean Discourse: Selected Essays* (Charlottesville: University Press of Virginia, 1989); Homi Bhabha, *The Location of Culture* (London: Routledge, 1994); Philippine Allstars, "Beyond Hip Hop—Penthouse 7: The Grand Reunion," *Multiply* (blog), posted April 27, 2008, accessed February 26, 2011, http://allstars2005.multiply.com/reviews/item/5. Multiply website is no longer available as of April 8, 2020.

72. Eric Charry, "A Capsule History of African Rap," in *Hip-Hop Africa: New African Music in a Globalizing World*, ed. Eric Charry (Bloomington: Indiana University Press, 2012), 1–25. This partly resonates with the elite and middle-class pathways that hip-hop cultural practices took to Bamako, Mali, from the United States and France, and through Dakar, Senegal, and Abidjan, Ivory Coast. According to Amadou Philippe Konate, member of Bamako City Breakers, the economically comfortable, with access to travel and VHS recordings and players, were responsible for hip-hop's beginnings in 1983 (14).

73. Hontiveros, interview.

74. Teresita Gimenez Maceda, "Problematizing the Popular: The Dynamics of Pinoy pop(ular) Music and Popular Protest Music," *Inter-Asia Cultural Studies* 8, no. 3 (2007): 390–413. I am certainly not the first to note the contradictions. Maceda writes of the Broadcast Media Council's 1975 Memorandum Order No. 75–31 (and subsequent amendments in 1976–8) by which radio stations were to play at least one Filipino composition per hour and promote Pinoy pop music as "palliatives given by the dictatorship to create a semblance of an atmosphere of freedom for artists even as summary executions, unlawful detentions, food blockades and other violent measures continued to be imposed on the populace by the mailed fist of the dictatorship" (396).

75. Alexander R. Magno, "Tyranny Descends," Chap. 11 in *Kasaysayan: The Story of the Filipino People* (Hong Kong: Asia Publishing Company Limited, 1998), 150–151.

76. Ibid.

77. See Magno, "Tyranny Descends," 150–151.

78. Ibid.

79. Kale Bantigue Fajardo, *Filipino Crosscurrents: Oceanographies of Seafaring, Masculinities, and Globalization* (Minneapolis: University of Minnesota Press, 2011).

80. Neferti Xina M. Tadiar, *Fantasy-Production: Sexual Economies and Other Philippine Consequences for the New World Order* (Quezon City, Philippines: Ateneo De Manila University Press, 2004).

81. Pearlie Rose S. Baluyut, *Institutions and Icons of Patronage: Arts and Culture in the Philippines During the Marcos Years, 1965–1986* (Manila: University of Santo Tomas Publishing House, 2012), 44.

82. Marcos supporters might make the argument that he cared about the arts and artists by his presidential orders, decrees, and proclamations. For instance, Presidential

Decree No. 49 aimed to protect the intellectual property of Filipino artists and writers. For more examples see Baluyut, *Institutions and Icons of Patronage*, 26–27.

83. Tadiar, *Fantasy-Production*, 6.

84. For how the Marcos dictatorship shaped folk dance communities through Bayanihan Dance Company, see Gonzalves, *The Day the Dancers Stayed*; Christi-Anne Castro, *Musical Renderings of the Philippine Nation* (New York: Oxford University Press, 2011); Baluyut, *Institutions and Icons of Patronage*.

85. Hontiveros, interview; Pinky Nelson, interview with author, digital recording, Manila, Philippines, May 14, 2011.

86. Niels Mulder, "The Legitimacy of the Public Sphere and Culture of the New Urban Middle Class in the Philippines," in *Social Change in Southeast Asia*, eds. Johannes Dragsbaek Schmidt, Jacques Hersh, and Niels Fold (New York: Addison Wesley Longman Limited, 1998), 98–113.

87. Hontiveros, interview.

88. Ibid.

89. Philippine Allstars, "Beyond Hip Hop—Penthouse 7: The Grand Reunion."

90. Ibid.

91. Ibid.

92. Hontiveros, interview.

93. See J. Lorenzo Perillo, "Theorising Hip-Hop Dance in the Philippines: Blurring the Lines of Genre, Mode and Dimension," *International Journal of Asia-Pacific Studies* 9, no. 1 (2013): 93–94.

94. Dana Osborne, "'Ay, Nosebleed!': Negotiating the Place of English in Contemporary Philippine Linguistic Life," *Language & Communication* 58 (2018): 118–133.

95. Clod Yambao, interview with author, Quezon City, Philippines, December 9, 2017. The popularization of nosebleed traces in part back to celebrities Ruffa Mae Quinto and Ethel Booba on the Philippine television sketch comedy show, *Bubble Gang*, which was popular in the late 1990s and early 2000s.

96. Most performance studies trace performativity to the work of British linguistic philosopher J. L. Austin and the recognition of speech acts which perform a certain action, to the work of Judith Butler in theorizing gender performativity. See J. L. Austin, *How to Do Things with Words* (Cambridge, MA: Harvard University Press, 1962); Jill Dolan, "Geographies of Learning: Theatre Studies, Performance, and the 'Performative,'" *Theatre Journal* 45, no. 4 (1993): 423; Judith Butler, *Gender Trouble* (New York, NY: Routledge, 1990); Rebekah J. Kowal, *How to Do Things with Dance: Performing Change in Postwar America* (Middletown, CT: Wesleyan University Press, 2010).

97. Michel De Certeau, *The Practice of Everyday Life*, trans. Steven Rendall (Berkeley: University of California Press, 1984); Homi Bhabha, "Of Mimicry and Man: The Ambivalence of Colonial Discourse," *October* 28 (1984): 125–133; Burns, *Puro Arte*; Jill Dolan, "Performance, Utopia, and the 'Utopian Performative,'" *Theatre Journal* 53, no. 3 (2001): 455–479.

98. Thomas F. DeFrantz, "Hip-Hop Habitus v.2.0," in *Black Performance Theory*, eds. Thomas F. DeFrantz and Anita Gonzalez (Durham, NC: Duke University Press,

2014), 227. Thomas DeFrantz attributes the marginalization of social change-centered studies on Black social dance partly due to their undertheorization and pervasiveness in Europeanist and Africanist discourse respectively.

99. Jeff Chang, *Can't Stop Won't Stop: A History of the Hip-Hop Generation* (New York: St. Martin's Press, 2007); Perillo, *Hip-Hop, Streetdance, and the Remaking of the Global Filipino*, 14.

100. Siobhan Brooks and Thomas Conroy, "Hip-Hop Culture in a Global Context: Interdisciplinary and Cross-Categorical Investigation," *American Behavioral Scientist* 55, no. 1 (2011): 3–8. See Nelson George, *Hip Hop America* (London: Penguin, 2005); Mickey Hess, ed., *Hip Hop in America: A Regional Guide* (Santa Barbara, CA: ABC-CLIO, 2009); Tony Mitchell, ed., *Global Noise: Rap and Hip Hop Outside the USA* (Middletown, CT: Wesleyan University Press, 2001).

101. See H. Samy Alim, Awad Ibrahim, and Alastair Pennycook, eds., *Global Linguistic Flows: Hip Hop Cultures, Youth Identities, and The Politics of Language* (New York: Routledge, 2008); Basu and Lemelle, *The Vinyl Ain't Final*; Ian Condry, *Hip-Hop Japan: Rap and the Paths of Cultural Globalization* (Durham, NC: Duke University Press, 2006); Sujatha Fernandes, *Close to the Edge: In Search of the Global Hip Hop Generation* (New York: Verso Books, 2011); Halifu Osumare, *The Africanist Aesthetic in Global Hip-Hop: Power Moves* (New York: Palgrave MacMillan, 2007). Alim, Condry, Basu and Lemelle, Fernandes, Neate—all focus on rap emcees. Osumare's text is the exception as it highlights dance within an Africanist approach.

102. Joseph G. Schloss, *Foundation: B-Boys, B-Girls, and Hip-Hop Culture in New York* (New York: Oxford University Press, 2009), 8.

103. Schloss, *Foundation*, 4–5, 12; Osumare, *The Africanist Aesthetic*; Mohanalakshmi Rajakumar, *Hip Hop Dance* (Santa Barbara, CA: ABC-CLIO, 2012).

104. Brenda Dixon Gottschild, *Digging the Africanist Presence in American Performance: Dance and Other Contexts. No. 179* (Westport, CT: Greenwood Publishing Group, 1996); Brenda Dixon Gottschild, *The Black Dancing Body: A Geography From Coon to Cool* (New York: Palgrave Macmillan, 2003).

105. Gottschild, *The Black Dancing Body*, 86.

106. Thomas F. DeFrantz, "The Black Beat Made Visible: Hip Hop Dance and Body Power," in *Of the Presence of the Body: Essays on Dance and Performance Theory*, ed. Andres Lepecki (Middletown, CT: Wesleyan University Press, 2004), 67.

107. DeFrantz, "The Black Beat Made Visible," 68.

108. Ibid.; Thomas F. DeFrantz, "Hip-Hop Habitus v.2.0."

109. Jose Edmundo Ocampo Reyes, "Fungibility, *Dead Souls*, and Filipino OCWs," *Kritika Kultura* 8 (2007): 111–126; OED, "Fungible." By invoking "fungibility," I also draw upon the work of Jose Edmundo Ocampo Reyes, who writes about Filipino OFWs, saying: "I viewed them as being as fungible as Chichikov's dead souls or the Hong Kong Dollar bills I withdrew and spent in my three-and-a-half years of living there." As far back as the late seventeenth century, according to the *OED*, the word "fungible" has Latin roots in *fungi* ("to perform, enjoy") and *fungi vice* ("to serve in place of").

110. Chelo Aestrid and Michelle Salazar, "The Road to the 2008 World Hip-Hop Dance Championships," (Unpublished report, private collection of Chelo Aestrid, 2008) 4. This derision seems to have lessened from 2009 to 2019.

111. J. L. Austin, *How to Do Things with Words* (Cambridge, MA: Harvard University Press, 1962); Dolan, "Geographies of Learning, 423; Kowal, *How to Do Things with Dance.*

112. In this book, I adopt the terms bgirl, bboy, bgirling, and bboying without the hyphen in order to reflect and respect the way that subjects spelled their own names.

113. For a discussion on cultural appropriation of hip-hop in South Asian youth culture, see Sunaina Maira, "Henna and Hip Hop: The Politics of Cultural Production and the Work of Cultural Studies," *Journal of Asian American Studies* 3, no. 3 (October 2000): 329–369.

114. E. Patrick Johnson, *Appropriating Blackness: Performance and the Politics of Authenticity* (Durham, NC: Duke University Press, 2003), 243.

115. Johnson, *Appropriating Blackness*, 246; Allan Punzalan Isaac, *American Tropics: Articulating Filipino America* (Minneapolis: University of Minnesota Press, 2006), 23–47.

116. Gerald L. Neuman, "Introduction," in *Reconsidering the Insular Cases: The Past and Future of the American Empire*, Vol. 5, eds., Gerald L. Neuman and Tomiko Brown-Nagin (Cambridge, MA: Harvard University Press, 2015), xii–xvi.

117. Samuel Downes v. George Bidwell, 182 U.S. 244, 21 S.CT. 770, 45 L.Ed 1088(1901) at 372 . I thank Matthew Weyer for support in locating the original text of the ruling and my interpretation.

118. Ibid. at 251.

119. Thomas F. DeFrantz, "Unchecked Popularity: Neoliberal Circulations of Black Social Dance," in *Neoliberalism and Global Theatres: Performance Permutations*, eds. Lara D. Nielsen and Patricia Ybarra (New York: Palgrave Macmillan, 2012), 139. Popular television shows like *Soul Train* and *American Bandstand*, as Thomas F. DeFrantz argues, demonstrated a profitable market for black social dance in which neoliberal orthodoxy coopted "freedom" as the right and choice to dance "like a black American."

120. José Esteban Muñoz, *Disidentifications: Queers of Color and the Performance of Politics* (Minneapolis: University of Minnesota Press), 1999.

121. Prashad, *Everybody Was Kung Fu Fighting*; Mullen, *Afro Orientalism*; Raphael-Hernandez and Steen, *AfroAsian Encounters*.

122. Sunaina Maira, *Desis in the House: Indian American Youth Culture in New York City* (Philadelphia: Temple University Press, 2002); *Desi Rap: Hip Hop and South Asian America*, eds. Ajay Nair and Murali Balaji (Lanham, MD: Lexington Books, 2008); Nitasha Tamar Sharma, *Hip Hop Desis: South Asian Americans, Blackness, and a Global Race Consciousness* (Durham, NC: Duke University Press, 2010); Cathy J. Schlund-Vials, *War, Genocide, and Justice: Cambodian American Memory Work* (Minneapolis: University of Minnesota Press, 2012).

123. Linda Tuhiwai Smith, *Decolonizing Methodologies: Research and Indigenous Peoples* (New York: Zed Books Ltd., 2013), 149–150; Anthony Kwame Harrison,

"Post-Colonial Consciousness, Knowledge Production, and Identity Inscription within Filipino-American Hip-Hop Music," *Perfect Beat* 13, no. 1 (2012): 29–48; Antonio T. Tiongson Jr., *Filipinos Represent: DJs, Racial Authenticity, and the Hip-Hop Nation* (Minneapolis: University of Minnesota Press, 2013); *Empire of Funk: Hip Hop and Representation in Filipina/o America*, eds. Mark R. Villegas, Kuttin Kandi, and Roderick N. Labrador (San Diego, CA: Cognella Academic Publishing, 2014); Oliver Wang, *Legions of Boom: Filipino American Mobile DJ Crews in the San Francisco Bay Area* (Durham, NC: Duke University Press, 2015).

124. The controversy arose from Issa Rae's proposal for educated black women to date Asian men, but not Filipinos. While some read her work as satire, and others read her attempts to subvert caricatures as merely reinforcing colorism, anti-Black, and anti-Filipino sentiment, there is also a presumption of Filipinos as less educated. In her book, Rae states: "This is why I propose that black women and Asian men join forces in love, marriage, and procreation. Educated black women, what better intellectual match for you than an Asian man? And I'm not talking about Filipinos; they're like the Blacks of Asians. I'm talking Chinese, Vietnamese, Japanese, et cetera" (138).

Issa Rae, *The Misadventures of Awkward Black Girl* (New York: Simon and Schuster, 2016); Janice Williams, "Issa Rae's Book Calls Filipinos 'The Blacks of Asians'" *Newsweek.com*, May 1, 2018, accessed November 22, 2018, https://www.newsweek.com/issa-rae-book-asian-dating-906886.

125. Deirdre Sklar, "Five Premises for a Culturally Sensitive Approach to Dance," in *Moving History/Dancing Cultures: A Dance History Reader*, eds. Ann Dils and Ann Cooper Albright (Middletown, CT: Wesleyan University Press, 2001), 30–32.

126. Leo, interview with the author, June 20, 2015, Quezon City, Philippines.

127. This is particularly important not only because it doubled the amount of physical labor, sweat, and danger involved, but it helped me avoid the pitfalls of research reproducing the ongoing processes of cultural tourism that capture, sanitize, commodify, and ultimately objectify cultures.

128. Susan Leigh Foster, *Reading Dancing: Bodies and Subjects in Contemporary American Dance* (Berkeley: University of California Press, 1986).

129. Cynthia Novack, *Sharing the Dance: Contact Improvisation and American Culture* (Madison: University of Wisconsin Press, 1990).

130. As things go, this script inevitably imposed itself upon me and I found myself wielding it to render both my dancing body and my project legible.

131. Thomas DeFrantz, *Dancing Revelations: Alvin Ailey's Embodiment of African American Culture* (Oxford, UK: Oxford University Press, 2004); Susan Leigh Foster, "Choreographies of Writing," March 22, 2011, accessed April 29, 2019, http://danceworkbook.pcah.us/susan-foster/choreographies-of-writing.html; Randy Martin, "Overreading 'The Promised Land': Towards a Narrative of Context in Dance," in *Corporealities*, ed. Susan Leigh Foster (New York: Routledge, 1996), 177–198.

132. Halifu Osumare, *The Africanist Aesthetic in Global Hip-Hop: Power Moves* (New York: Palgrave Macmillan, 2007); Basu and Lemelle, *The Vinyl Ain't Final*, "Introduction," 1–15; Felicia McCarren, *French Moves: The Cultural Politics of Le Hip-hop* (New York: Oxford University Press, 2013).

133. John M. Liu, Paul M. Ong, and Carolyn Rosenstein, "Dual Chain Migration: Post-1965 Filipino Immigration to the United States," *International Migration Review* 25, no. 3 (Autumn 1991): 487–513.

134. bell hooks, "Eating the Other: Desire and Resistance," in *Media and Cultural Studies: Keywords*, eds. Meenakshi Gigi Durham and Douglas M. Kellner (Maldwell, MA: Wiley-Blackwell Publishing, 2006), 366–380; Hortense J. Spillers, "Mama's Baby, Papa's Maybe: An American Grammar Book," *Diacritics* 17, no. 2 (1987): 65–81.

135. Theresa C. Suarez, "Militarized Filipino Masculinity and the Language of Citizenship in San Diego," in *Militarized Currents: Toward a Decolonized Future in Asia and the Pacific*, eds. Setsu Shigematsu and Keith L. Camacho (Minneapolis: University of Minnesota Press, 2010), 181–201.

136. For Filipinos deejays, see Lakandiwa M. de Leon, "Filipinotown and the DJ Scene: Expression and Identity Affirmation of Filipino American Youth in Los Angeles," in *Asian American Youth: Culture, Identity, and Ethnicity*, eds. Jennifer Lee and Min Zhou (New York: Routledge, 2004); Tiongson, *Filipinos Represent*; Wang, *Legions of Boom*. For Filipino emcees, see Stephen Alan Bischoff, "Filipino Americans and Polyculturalism in Seattle, WA, through Hip-Hop and Spoken Word" (Master's thesis, Washington State University, 2008), http://search.proquest.com/docview/ 1032540568?accountid=14512; Mark Angelo Delacruz Bautista, "Through the Mic: Stories of Filipino American Emcee Crews in the Margins" (Master's thesis, San Francisco State University, 2005); Rachel Devitt, "Lost in Translation: Filipino Diaspora(s), Postcolonial Hip Hop, and the Problems of Keeping It Real for the 'Contentless' Black Eyed Peas," *Asian Music* 39, no. 1 (Winter/ Spring 2008): 108–134; Michael Viola, "Hip-Hop and Critical Revolutionary Pedagogy: Blue Scholarship to Challenge 'The Miseducation of the Filipino,'" *Journal of Critical Education Policy Studies* 4, no. 2 (2006): 171–194, http://www.jceps.com/index.php?pageID=article&articleID=71.

Chapter 1

1. In this chapter, I distinguish the CPDRC's "Thriller" from Michael Jackson's music video "Thriller" by using Jackson's name. For pragmatics and because it is the main object of analysis, I often refer to the CPDRC version simply as "Thriller."

2. Byron Garcia, "Thriller (original video upload to YouTube)," YouTube. July 17, 2007. http://www.youtube.com/watch?v=hMnk7lh9M3o; Associated Press (AP), "Smooth Criminals? Inmates Dance on YouTube: Millions Watched Filipino Prisoners' Version of Michael Jackson's 'Thriller,'" *NBCNews.com*, August 9, 2007, accessed April 28, 2008, http://www.msnbc.com/id/20203606/. In its YouTube category ("People and Blogs"), Thriller reached number 3 based on the number of viewers clicking "favorite," and separately, Thriller was deemed the fifth most viewable online video of 2007 by *Time* magazine.

3. While media reports tend to describe Resane with "he" pronouns, I will use "they" pronouns as I lack information on how they self-identify.

4. Qtd. in Margo Ortigas, "Philippine Prisoners: Performing to Reform," Al Jazeera via YouTube, July 29, 2007, accessed January 6, 2011, Video, 2:16, http://www.youtube.com/watch?v=R72kxZW1orE; "Philippine Jailhouse Rocks to Thriller," *BBC News*, July 26, 2007, accessed August 31, 2011, http://news.bbc.co.uk/2/hi/asia-pacific/6917318.stm. Garcia maintains this type of division between mind and body—the body as the key to the mind's deviance—as he states: "Using music, you can involve the body and the mind. . . . Inmates say to me: 'You have put my mind off revenge, foolishness, or thinking how to escape.'"

5. Mary Madden, "The Audience for Online Video," July 25, 2007, accessed April 12, 2019, https://www.rsis.edu.sg/wp-content/uploads/2015/04/Report-Workshop-on-Terrorist-Rehabilitation-Implementation-WTRI.pdf. Although limited to the U.S., an audience for an online video in 2007 is majority young adults (18–29), views and shares links of videos more than uploading them, mostly watches at home, mostly watches YouTube, and is mostly male, according to a Pew Internet & American Life Project Tracking Survey, February 15–March 7, 2007.

   Their effectiveness is also evidenced by the consideration of the CPDRC as a model for other institutions. After visiting the CPDRC, researcher Tuty Raihanah Mostarom recommended that the International Centre for Political Violence and Terrorism Research (Singapore) adopt its dance program for detained Islamist terrorists by using Quranic recitations. See "Workshop on Terrorist Rehabilitation Implementation (WTRI)," 25–30, November 2009, accessed January 9, 2011, https://www.rsis.edu.sg/wp-content/uploads/2015/04/Report-Workshop-on-Terrorist-Rehabilitation-Implementation-WTRI.pdf.

6. It is interesting to note that the username recalls the first native Filipino to write, print, and publish in the early 1600s. Tomaspinpin, comment on Thriller, YouTube, March 2007, accessed April 28, 2008, http://www.youtube.com/watch?v=hMnk7lh9M3o.

7. The CPDRC dancers were choreographed by Gwen Lador. Daniel Chu and Barbara Rowes, "Michael Peters Is the Hot New Choreographer Who Makes Dancers Out of Video's Rock Stars," *People*, published June 25, 1984, accessed December 6, 2017, http://people.com/archive/michael-peters-is-the-hot-new-choreographer-who-makes-dancers-out-of-videos-rock-stars-vol-21-no-25/.

8. Gail Mitchell and Melinda Newman, "Exclusive: How Michael Jackson's 'Thriller' Changed the Music Business," *Reuters.com*, July 6, 2009, accessed April 18, 2020, https://www.reuters.com/article/us-jackson-thriller-idUSTRE56300320090706.

9. Elizabeth McAlister, "Slaves, Cannibals, and Infected Hyper-Whites: The Race and Religion of Zombies," *Anthropological Quarterly* 85, no. 2 (2012): 457–486. McAlister writes, "Like the Haitian zonbi, the US film zombie must be understood as being embedded in a set of deeply symbolic structures that are a matter of religious thought. In both contexts, zombie narratives and rituals interrogate the boundary between life and death, elucidate the complex relations between freedom and slavery, and highlight the overlap between capitalism and cannibalism" (458–459).

10. Ibid. I would like to thank Mario LaMothe for his comments that led me to this reference.

11. Michel Foucault, *Discipline and Punish: The Birth of the Prison*, trans. Alan Sheridan (New York: Pantheon, 1977).

12. Byron Garcia, quoted in AP, "Smooth Criminals?"

13. In Michael Balfour's "Introduction" to *Theatre in Prison: Theory and Practice* (Portland: Intellect Books, 2004), he writes that "[t]he function of the aesthetic experience is therefore to re-engage with the decisions of a criminal act and highlight consequences of actions in order to encourage greater degrees of social responsibility and moral maturation" (9). Rather than grappling with criminal decisions and action consequences as Balfour suggests, the CPDRC discourse seems to emphasize escapism.

14. The human rights question could be further posed with data regarding individual assessments of inmate rehabilitation, recidivism, and the handling of donations. Unfortunately, the prison has not been transparent about such data. See Tracie Hunte, "Prisoners' Dance: Celebration or Human Rights Violation? Viral Video of Inmates Performing 'Thriller' Video Generates Concerns, Along with Clicks," *ABC News*, August 14, 2007, accessed January 16, 2011, http://abcnews.go.com/icaught/story?id=3478161&page=1.

15. See Username Pinoy Traveler, "CPDRC Dancing Inmates 5/29/2010 Version," *Philippine Travel Notes blogspot*, posted May 29, 2010, accessed February 6, 2019, https://philippinetravelnotes.blogspot.com/2010/05/cpdrc-dancing-inmates-5292010-version.html; Associated Press (AP), "Filipino Inmates' Video Is a 'Thriller' on the Web," *NPR*, August 9, 2007, accessed January 15, 2011, http://www.npr.org/templates/story/story.php?storyId=12643181.

16. Dale G. Israel, "Gwen Wants Donations to CPDRC Inmates Accounted for," *Inquirer.net*, February 13, 2010, accessed January 9, 2011, http://globalnation.inquirer.net/cebudailynews/news/view/20100213-252934/Gwen-wantsdonations-to-CPDRC-inmates-accounted-for. Link is no longer available per April 18, 2020.

17. Angela Yvonne Davis and David Barsamian, *The Prison Industrial Complex* (San Francisco: Ak Press, 1999); Ruth Wilson Gilmore, *Golden Gulag: Prisons, Surplus, Crisis, and Opposition in Globalizing California Vol. 21* (Berkeley: University of California Press, 2007); Julia Sudbury, *Global Lockdown: Race, Gender, and the Prison-Industrial Complex* (New York: Routledge, 2014).

18. Jhunnex Napallacan, "Cebu's Dancing Inmates Hit It Big Again," *Inquirer.net*, January 27, 2010, accessed January 15, 2011, http://newsinfo.inquirer.net/inquirerheadlines/nation/view/20100127-249691/Cebus-dancinginmates-hit-it-big-again. Article is no longer available at link as of April 18, 2020.

19. Byron Garcia, qtd. in ibid. See also "Cebu Dancing Inmates in 'This Is It' DVD Launch," *ABS-CBN News*, January 19, 2010, accessed January 21, 2017, http://news.abs-cbn.com/entertainment/01/19/10/cebu-dancing-inmates-it-dvd-launch.

20. Jhunnex Napallacan, "Inmates Do the 'Drill,' Another YouTube Hit," *Inquirer.net*, January 27, 2010, accessed January 15, 2011, http://globalnation.inquirer.net/cebudailynews/news/view/20100127-249702/Inmates-do-the-Drillanother-YouTube-hit. Article is no longer available at link as of April 18, 2020.

21. dor Vincent Mayol, "No Commercial Deal for Inmates," *Inquirer.net*, February 2, 2010, accessed January 9, 2011, http://globalnation.inquirer.net/cebudailynews/news/view/20100202-250835/No-commercial-deal-for-inmates. Article is no longer available at link as of April 18, 2020.

22. see also Suk-Young Kim, *Illusive Utopia: Theater, Film, and Everyday Performance in North Korea* (Ann Arbor: University of Michigan Press, 2010).

23. AP, "Filipino Inmates' Video."

24. Foucault, *Discipline and Punish*, 152, 215.

25. McAlister, "Slaves, Cannibals, and Infected Hyper-Whites," 472.

26. AP, "Filipino Inmates' Video."

27. Susan Leigh Foster, "Choreographies of Gender," *Signs: Journal of Women in Culture and Society* 24, no. 1 (1998): 5.

28. A growing yet marginalized scholarship on dance has addressed issues of choreography specific to Philippine cultural identity. See, for example, Sally Ann Ness, "When Seeing Is Believing: The Changing Role of Visuality in a Philippine Dance," *Anthropological Quarterly* 68, no. 1 (1995): 1–13; Basilio Esteban S. Villaruz, *Treading Through: 45 Years of Philippine Dance* (Diliman: University of the Philippines Press, 2006); Rina Angela P. Corpus, *Defiant Daughters Dancing: Three Independent Women Dance* (Diliman: University of the Philippines Press, 2007); and Patrick Alcedo, "Sacred Camp: Transgendering Faith in a Philippine Festival," *Journal of Southeast Asian Studies* 38, no. 1 (2007): 107–32.

29. Filipino mimicry, while not always termed this way, has been recognized in previous literature. Neferti Xina M. Tadiar, for instance, discusses Filipino mimicry as evidence of domination by "Americanization" and a possible form of agentive resistance; see Neferti Xina M. Tadiar, *Fantasy-Production: Sexual Economies and Other Philippine Consequences for the New World Order* (Quezon City: Ateneo de Manila University Press, 2004), 3.

30. Villaruz, *Treading Through*, 287.

31. I would like to thank Martin Manalansan for leading me to this observation.

32. see Philip Zimbardo, Craig Haney, and Curtis Banks, "A Study of Prisoners and Guards in a Simulated Prison," in *Theatre in Prison*, 19–34. In collaboration with Haney and Banks, Zimbardo conducted a study that found that prisoners' uniforms worked ideologically to promote anonymity and deindividuation, while guards' uniforms worked to reinforce group identity and status.

33. Balfour, "Introduction," 8.

34. Ibid.

35. Pico Iyer, *Video Night in Kathmandu and Other Reports from the Not-So-Far East* (New York: Knopf, 1988). As part of this maneuver, Iyer neglects native, Spanish colonial, Muslim, and any other influences on Philippine culture.

36. Ibid., 153.

37. Garcia, "Thriller." For instance, one viewer from Malaysia, on October 15, 2008, commented that "be it prison inmates or regular filipino [sic] citizens, they sure know how to dance, sing and perform! proud to be a person with filipino [sic] blood!" Other comments mention popular-culture Internet "sensations" such as Charice Pempengco and Arnel Pineda.

38. Clifford Coonan, "YouTube's Dancing Prisoners Denied New Licence to Thrill," *Independent on Sunday*, January 18, 2008, accessed January 9, 2011, http://www.independent.co.uk/news/world/asia/youtubes-dancingprisoners-denied-new-licence-to-thrill-770911.html.

39. Thomeczeck, qtd. in Lee Ferran, "Boogie Behind Bars: Inmates Dance the Days Away," *ABC News*, August 14, 2007, accessed January 9, 2011, http://abcnews.go.com/icaught/story?id=3415920.

40. Rubio, qtd. in ibid.

41. Balfour, "Introduction," 8.

42. bell hooks, "Eating the Other: Desire and Resistance," in *Black Looks: Race and Representation* (Boston: South End Press, 1992), 21–39.

43. I use the term "Filipinizing" to refer to a liberationist Filipino-studies social practice as described by Priscelina Patajo-Legasto's "Introduction," in her edited volume, *Philippine Studies: Have We Gone Beyond St. Louis?* (Diliman: University of Philippine Press, 2008), xvii.

44. As an alternative, Philippine media scholar Elizabeth Enriquez, citing Homi Bhabha, notes that representations of failed mimicry might decenter, clear discursive space, or mock colonial texts; see Elizabeth Enriquez, *Appropriation of Colonial Broadcasting: A History of Early Radio in the Philippines, 1922–1946* (Diliman: University of the Philippines Press, 2008). The Filipino mimicry stereotype I outline fails to accomplish these acts and works more as a nonstrategic essentialism.

45. One exception is the British/Australian documentary, *Jailhouse Rock* (2007), available on YouTube.com via "The Filipino Prisoners Who Dance to Thriller" posted by Journeyman Pictures, November 12, 2007, accessed January 21, 2017, Video, 20:38, https://youtu.be/wAjItY7X0Yc.

46. J. Neil Garcia, *Philippine Gay Culture: Binabae to Bakla, Silahis to MSM*, 2nd ed. (Diliman: University of the Philippines Press, 2008), xxiv.

47. Mark Johnson, *Beauty and Power: Transgendering and Cultural Transformation in the Southern Philippines* (New York: Berg, 1997); Fenella Cannell, *Power and Intimacy in the Christian Philippines* (Cambridge, UK: Cambridge University Press, 1999); Martin F. Manalansan IV, *Global Divas: Filipino Gay Men in the Diaspora* (Durham, NC: Duke University Press, 2003). The role of beauty is superficial, but is also a defense against gender discrimination. Cannell, for instance, interprets beauty as a protective tactic.

48. Cannell, *Power and Intimacy*, 216 (emphasis added).

49. Garcia, *Philippine Gay Culture*, xxi–xxii. Garcia sees the oppression of bakla in Philippine society as a consequence of several factors, including pre-colonial/indigenous subordination of the feminine, Spanish colonial views on sodomy, and Western colonial knowledge systems of homosexuality/heterosexuality.

50. Johnson, *Beauty and Power*, 32. The term used by Johnson's subjects for sexual minority is "bantut."

51. Ibid., 72.

52. Paul Kramer, *The Blood of Government: Race, Empire, the United States, and the Philippines* (Chapel Hill: University of North Carolina Press, 2006), 257.

53. Cannell, *Power and Intimacy*, 216. Cannell identifies beauty as an essential element for defining cultures of sexual minorities in the Philippines. She concludes that bakla

act as mediators of American Otherness, but more specifically American ideals of feminine beauty.

54. Ibid. Cannell reports that in everyday conversation, bakla often substitute "beauty" for pronouns.

55. Angela Y. Davis, "Foreword: A World unto Itself: Multiple Invisibilities of Imprisonment," in Michael Jacobson-Hardy, *Behind the Razor Wire: Portrait of a Contemporary American Prison System* (New York: New York University Press, 1999).

56. Resane, qtd. in AP, "Filipino Inmates' Video."

57. Suzzane Salva-Alueta, "Dancing Prisoners, Bonuses Mark Cebu's 438th Birthday," *Inquirer.net*, August 7, 2007, accessed January 9, 2011, http://globalnation.inquirer.net/cebudailynews/news/view/20070807-81088/Dancing_prisoners,_bonuses_mark_Cebu%27s_438th_birthday. This article is no longer available at link as of April 18, 2020. Inmates had been issued court orders allowing them to perform outside the confines of prison for certain events, such as the 438th anniversary of the founding of Cebu Province.

58. Michael Salman, "'Nothing without Labor': Penology, Discipline, and Independence in the Philippines under United States Rule," in *Discrepant Histories: Translocal Essays on Filipino Cultures*, ed. Vicente L. Rafael (Philadelphia: Temple University Press, 1995), 113–29.

59. Ibid., 116.

60. Michael Salman, "'The Prison That Makes Men Free': The Iwahig Penal Colony and the Simulacra of the American State in the Philippines," in *Colonial Crucible: Empire in the Making of the Modern American State*, eds. Alfred W. McCoy and Francisco Antonio Scarano (Madison: University of Wisconsin Press, 2009), 117.

61. Karapatan: Alliance for the Advancement of People's Rights, "The 2007 Year-End Report on the Human Rights Situation in the Philippines," *Karapatan.org*, January 20, 2008, accessed August 31, 2011, http://www.karapatan.org/2007-HR-report.

62. William Pesek, "Trump Engineers 'Dutertefication' of America," *Forbes*, March 28, 2019, accessed September 2, 2019, https://www.forbes.com/sites/williampesek/2019/03/28/trump-engineers-dutertefication-of-america/#483ba66f40c8; Emmanuel Tupas, "Drug War Death Toll Hits 6,847," *Philippine Star*, August 16, 2019, accessed September 2, 2019, https://www.philstar.com/headlines/2019/08/16/1943876/drug-war-death-toll-hits-6847.

63. see VONRAT, comment on Thriller, YouTube (video), September 2011, accessed September 25, 2011, http://www.youtube.com/all_comments?v=hMnk7lh9M3o.

64. Hortense J. Spillers, "Mama's Baby, Papa's Maybe: An American Grammar Book," *Diacritics* 17, no. 2 (1987): 65–81; Alexander G. Weheliye, "Pornotropes," *Journal of Visual Culture* 7, no. 1 (2008): 65–81; Keguro Macharia, "Queer Genealogies (provisional notes)," *Bully Bloggers* (2013): 150. Martin Manalansan discusses the formulaic portrayal of bakla in Philippine popular culture and how, in films, a sexual awakening to heterosexuality usually follows bakla bashing; see Manalansan, "Speaking of AIDS: Language and the Filipino 'Gay' Experience in America," in Rafael, *Discrepant Histories*, 193–223.

65. I would like to give thanks to Professor Victor Bascara for drawing my attention to Resane's nonprisoner attire, which led me to this insight.

66. User prisondancer, "Prison Dancer Episode 11: Finally Free," YouTube Video, published March 6, 2012, 5:25, accessed June 27, 2017, https://www.youtube.com/watch?v=N-BRNI94LQQ.

67. User byronfgarcia's last video upload was in June 2011.

68. Originally accessed at https://www.prisondancer.com/

69. Henry Jenkins, *Convergence Culture: Where Old and New Media Collide* (New York: New York University Press, 2006), 20–21.

70. Mizuko Ito, "Technologies of the Childhood Imagination: Yugioh, Media Mixes, and Everyday Cultural Production," in *Network/Netplay: Structures of Participation in Digital Culture*, eds. Joe Karaganis and Natalie Jeremijenko (Durham, NC: Duke University Press, 2005).

71. User prisondancer, "Episode 1: Choice Point: Lola," YouTube, published March 6, 2012, accessed June 27, 2017, https://www.youtube.com/watch?annotation_id=annotation_838234&feature=iv&src_vid=RQIG4IokRTI&v=uwGayqiMwH0.

72. See Constancio R. Arnaldo, *Embodying Scales of Filipina/o American Sporting Life: Transnational Sporting Cultures and Practices in the Filipina/o Diaspora* (PhD diss., University of Illinois at Urbana-Champaign, 2015).

73. In the credit screen, we hear from Lola that she survived bullies and thieves who attacked her beauty parlor and was charged with murder. User prisondancer, "Episode 1: Choice Point: Shakespeare," YouTube, published March 6, 2012, accessed June 27, 2017, https://www.youtube.com/watch?annotation_id=annotation_330632&feature=iv&src_vid=KX8bMDNzclA&v=RQIG4IokRTI.

74. User prisondancer, "Prison Dancer Episode 11: Finally Free," YouTube, published March 6 2012, accessed June 27, 2017, https://www.youtube.com/watch?v=N-BRNI94LQQ.

75. Ibid.

76. "Cast—Prison Dancer," PrisonDancer, accessed December 6, 2017, https://www.prisondancer.com/live/cast/.

77. Izobelle T. Pulgo, "Warden: No Monthly Dances by Inmates," *Cebu Daily News*, January 19, 2017, accessed February 28, 2018, http://cebudailynews.inquirer.net/119816/warden-no-monthly-dances-inmates.

78. "Cebu Dancing Inmates in 'This Is It' DVD Launch."

79. "Workshop on Terrorist Rehabilitation Implementation (WTRI)" (see note 5 above).

Chapter 2

1. Michelle "Bgirl Tzy" Salazar, interview with author, digital recording, Los Angeles, CA, May 28, 2014. In the United States, the Hart Cellar Immigration Act of 1965 began instituting family reunification policies under which family-sponsored preferences exist in four categories based on age, marital status, and relation: 1) unmarried sons and daughters of U.S. citizens; 2) spouses and children, and unmarried sons and daughters of permanent residents; 3) married sons and daughters of U.S. citizens; and 4) brothers and sisters of adult U.S. citizens.

2. This includes the only other three "oversubscribed" nations—China, India, and Mexico—where demand for preference visas exceeds the annual limitation set by law. Originally available on U.S. Department of State, "The Visa Bulletin," U.S. Department of State, *Travel.State.Gov*, https://travel.state.gov/content/travel/en/legal/visa-law0/visa-bulletin.html.

   Also available at Immihelp, "Visa Bulletin for May 1998," *immihelp*, https://www.immihelp.com/visa-bulletin/may-1998.html.

3. In 2009, a total of 15,277 immigrant visas (all five categories) were issued under family preference to the Philippines. This number has ranged between 13,000 and 20,000 annually since 2004. It is unclear how many petitions are pending each year. The cut-off date for November 2017 F4 preference categories was June 8, 1994, meaning only petitioners with priority dates earlier than that date would have visas available. In early 2017, the Trump administration expressed interest in removing family preferences.

   "Table V (Part 1). Immigrant Visas Issued and Adjustments of Status Subject to Numerical Limitations Fiscal Year 2009," U.S. Visas, U.S. Department of State, Bureau of Consular Affairs, https://travel.state.gov/content/dam/visas/Statistics/FY09AnnualReport_TableV_1.pdf.

4. "Push through" is a slang phrase that implies the notion of execution and "follow through" but with a sensitivity for keeping open the possibility for failure or the expectation for plans to work out the way one hopes.

5. Michelle Salazar, "After 10 Days of Being Uprooted," *And I Wander* (blog), February 27, 2011, accessed June 4, 2014, https://calvinswife.wordpress.com/2011/02/27/after-10-days-of-being-uprooted/. Link is no longer available per April 27, 2020.

6. In 1986, Uriel Policarpio started the group that would become Octo Manoevres with Jon Supan, neighbors, and cousins, "Parañaque boys," with the group name, Wea Dynamics, with Wea Recording Company, before moving to Octo Arts. Joshua auditioned for the group after his brother Jason had already been a member. The Octo Manoeuvres, deriving its name from an English new wave band, Orchestral Manoeuvres in the Dark, rose to success with Valenciano (Gary V) in this concert, in part because Valenciano's regular dancers, *Octo Mechanics*, were working abroad in Japan. Because both groups were managed by Octo Arts, Zamora's group was sent as a replacement.

7. The Philippine Allstars, the popular dance group I will discuss later, have a similar goal in their dancing.

8. Joshua Zamora, interview with the author, Quezon City, Philippines, July 11, 2011. There were also women's groups that performed jazz-based dances.

9. Jannis T. Montañez, Paulynn P. Sicam, and Carmelita G. Nuqui, *Pains and Gains: A Study of Overseas Performing Artists in Japan: From Pre-Departure to Reintegration* (Manila: Development Action for Women Network [DAWN], 2003). One of the major recommendations by conference participants was to stop using the term "overseas performing artists" or OPAs, "because calling Filipino women workers in Japan as such makes one part of the deception and misconception perpetuated by the government" (122). For this reason, I use the term overseas Filipino worker. Other recommendations included drafting an OFW rights Magna Carta, as well as educating OFWs and government leaders on human rights, women's rights, and migrant rights.

10. Anna Romina Guevarra, *Marketing Dreams, Manufacturing Heroes: The Transnational Labor Brokering of Filipino Workers* (New Brunswick, NJ: Rutgers University Press, 2009); Kale Bantigue Fajardo, *Filipino Crosscurrents: Oceanographies of Seafaring, Masculinities, and Globalization* (Minneapolis: University of Minnesota Press, 2011); Robyn Magalit Rodriguez, *Migrants for Export: How the Philippine State Brokers Labor to the World* (Minneapolis: University of Minnesota Press, 2010); Robyn M. Rodriguez, "Migrant Heroes: Nationalism, Citizenship and the Politics of Filipino Migrant Labor," *Citizenship Studies* 6, no. 3 (2002): 341–356; Jean Encinas-Franco, "Overseas Filipino workers (OFWs) as Heroes: Discursive Origins of the 'Bagong Bayani' in the Era of Labor Export," *Humanities Diliman: A Philippine Journal of Humanities* 12, no. 2 (2016).

11. Paul Scolieri, "Global/Mobile: Re-orienting Dance and Migration Studies," in *Choreographies of Migration: New Orientations for Dance and Migration Studies*, ed. Paul Scolieri. Spec. issue of *Dance Research Journal* 40, no. 2 (2008): v–xx.

12. Guevarra, *Marketing Dreams, Manufacturing Heroes*.

13. Richard E. Joyce and Chester L. Hunt, "Philippine Nurses and the Brain Drain," *Social Science & Medicine* 16, no. 12 (1982): 1223–1233; "How Philippines Can Reverse 'Brain Drain,'" *ABS-CBN News*, March 11, 2015, accessed October 30, 2017, http://news.abs-cbn.com/business/03/11/15/how-philippines-can-reverse-brain-drain.

14. See Christina B. Chin et al., "Tokens on the Small Screen: Asian Americans and Pacific Islanders in Prime Time and Streaming Television," September 2017, accessed October 12, 2017, http://www.aapisontv.com/uploads/3/8/1/3/38136681/aapisontv.2017.pdf.

15. As the phenomena of hip-hop diaspora and Filipino diaspora are two seemingly separate topics that are deeply linked, these varieties of dance migration counter the solidity of Filipino hip-hop as merely an additional case of the cultural globalization of hip-hop, one by which culture flows outward from the fountainhead of South Bronx to the streets of Manila. In part, this material argues against the ability of globalization as a concept to capture or speak to the realities of embodied practices as if they were analogous to other globalized objects, texts, and media.

16. The section heading was the title of an employment ad on an OFW website.

17. "OFW Statistics," Philippine Overseas Employment Administration (POEA), 2016, accessed May 19, 2014 originally but no longer available at http://www.poea.gov.ph/stats/statistics.html; accessed January 24, 2018, http://www.poea.gov.ph/ofwstat/ofwstat.html.

18. Ibid. In 2006, Japan revised its immigration policy, leading to a sharp decrease in Filipino dance migration there.

19. Ibid.

20. Ibid. There were 45,591 entertainers recorded migrating to Japan in 1994.

21. I am grateful to Robyn Rodriguez for encouraging me to clarify this point. For Filipino history, see Teodoro Agoncillo, *The History of the Filipino People* (Manila: University of the Philippines, 1960); Renato Constantino, *A Past Revisited* (Manila: The Author, 1975); Reynaldo C. Ileto, *Pasyon and Revolution: Popular Movements in the Philippines, 1840–1910* (Quezon City, Philippines: Ateneo de Manila University Press, 1979); Vicente L. Rafael, *White Love and Other Events in Filipino History*

(Durham, NC: Duke University Press, 2000). For Filipino dance scholarship, see Basilio Esteban S. Villaruz, *Treading Through: 45 Years of Philippine Dance* (Quezon City: University of the Philippines Press, 2006); Rina Angela P. Corpus, *Defiant Daughters Dancing: Three Independent Women Dance* (Quezon City: University of the Philippines Press, 2007); Lucy Mae San Pablo Burns, "'Splendid Dancing': Filipino 'Exceptionalism' in Taxi Dancehalls," *Dance Research Journal* 40, no. 2 (2008): 23–40; Theodore S. Gonzalves, *The Day the Dancers Stayed: Performing in the Filipino/American Diaspora* (Philadelphia: Temple University Press, 2009).

22. Following this labeling, entertainer immigration policy in Japan was revised. Maria Rosario P. Ballescas, *Filipino Entertainers in Japan: An Introduction* (Quezon City, Philippines: Foundation for Nationalist Studies, 1992); Aurora de Dios, "Japayuki-san: Filipinas at Risk," in *Filipino Women Overseas Contract Workers... At What Cost?*, eds. Mary R. Palma-Beltran and Aurora Javate de Dios (Manila: Goodwill Trading Co., 1992), 39–58; James A. Tyner, *The Philippines: Mobilities, Identities, Globalization* (New York: Routledge, 2009); Rhacel Parreñas, "Trafficked? Filipino Hostesses in Tokyo's Nightlife Industry," *Yale Journal of Law & Feminism* 18 (2006): 147–149.

23. Social scientists claim that Filipina migrant entertainers themselves dispute the assumption that they are "trafficked victims," a claim made by the United States and Japanese governments in the mid-2000s. Rodriguez, *Migrants for Export.*

24. Guevarra, *Marketing Dreams, Manufacturing Heroes.*

25. POEA. According to POEA data the amount remitted by OFWs steadily increased from 8,550,371 (2004) to 22,968,000 (2013). Across this period, the remittance figures saw a 5 to 14 percent growth rate annually, with a drop from 14 percent to 6 percent between 2008 and 2009 and average 6 percent to 8 percent growth each year since then.

26. This is when compared to Filipino workers in other host countries.

27. See Tyner, *The Philippines*; Parreñas, "Trafficked?" 145–180; Nobue Suzuki, "'Japayuki,' or, Spectacles for the Transnational Middle Class," *Positions* 19, no. 2 (Fall 2011): 439–462; Stephanie Ng, "Performing the 'Filipino' at the Crossroads: Filipino Bands in Five-Star Hotels Throughout Asia," *Modern Drama* 48, no. 2 (2005): 272–296.

An exception to this homogenization of performing artists is found in Stephanie Ng's essay on Filipino bands in Asia. Ng claims that they do not fit the same labor category as caregivers and construction workers because they have a "certain proximity to the kind of transnational mobility experienced by economic, social, and professional elites" (277). Yet Filipino musicians also experience similar working conditions as these other laborers, including transnational family life and residence in the workplace, as well as pressure to perform off-duty tasks by hotel employers.

28. Basilio Esteban S. Villaruz, "A Dancer's Fate," in *Treading Through: 45 Years of Philippine Dance* (Quezon City: University of the Philippines Press, 2006), 18.

29. Tyner, *The Philippines*, 163.

30. Ibid., 159.

31. Ibid., 170–171.

32. Montañez et al., *Pains and Gains*, 54–56. Another example lies in Montañez et al. which features dance in a short vignette, "Sidebar: False hopes, Shattered Dreams,"

about twenty-one-year-old "Twinkle." During her six-month contract in Japan, dance appears as a type of smokescreen for the real type of work that OFWs perform.

33. Suzuki, "Japayuki," 439–462. "Sex work" is an external label. Nobue Suzuki argues against the work of social scientists that only cherry-pick victim narratives to make OPA appear monolithic rather than portraying OPAs in the Japan realities, combating social injustices, or the reality that "most entertainers are actually hostessing in bars and clubs—which is itself strictly speaking illegal, since the workers' contracts are usually breached and the work is beyond what is stipulated in their entertainer visas. Though the workers may feel betrayed by this, they do not necessarily consider themselves victimized or their job assignments defiled 'sex work.' On the contrary, OPAs often call themselves 'talents,' as Japanese promoters use the word *tarento* (from the English word 'talent' to indicate performers with various levels and types of skill) to refer to these entertainers" (451).

34. Tyner, *The Philippines*, 147–176. Upon arrival in Japan and throughout her contract, Lisa was taught that dance was cheap bait for higher-valued commodities—drinks and afternoon dates. Moreover, dance was used by club owners and managers as a type of negative reinforcement for poor drink sales. From the club owners' perspective, dancing was merely the draw, for profits hinged on the purchase of drinks. Whoever sold the fewest drinks would be expected to dance more frequently. In Lisa's view, however, this was not entirely viewed as punishment. In general, she did not object to the dancing, but did complain of having to change costumes so often.

35. Ibid., 170–171.

36. *Choreographies of Migration: New Orientations for Dance and Migration Studies*, ed. Paul Scolieri, special issue of *Dance Research Journal* 40, no. 2 (2008). This discussion builds upon previous attempts to highlight the overlapping terrains of dance and migration studies. See Scolieri's edited collection of essays that proposes "choreography" as a critical lens for migration studies.

37. Lucy Mae San Pablo Burns, *Puro Arte: Filipinos on the Stages of Empire* (New York: New York University Press, 2012).

38. Burns, *Puro Arte*, 49–74.

39. For Burns, corporeality-based exceptionality is made up of dance virtuosity, mobility, intimacy skills, and spatiality.

40. Jorge "Popmaster Fabel" Pabon, "Physical Graffiti: The History of Hip-Hop Dance," in *Total Chaos: The Art and Aesthetics of Hip Hop*, ed. Jeff Chang (New York: Basic Books, 2006), 18–26.

41. Other test judges include: Professor Corazon Generoso Iñigo, influential Filipino dance leader since the 1950s, and Anamarie A. Quirino, daughter of prominent modern dancer Julie Borromeo.

42. Basilio Esteban S. Villaruz, interview with the author, Quezon City, Philippines, June 9, 2011; Parreñas, "Trafficked?" 27; Technical Education and Skills Development Authority (TESDA), "Training Regulations," *TESDA.gov.ph*, accessed December 17, 2017, http://tesda.gov.ph/Downloadables/TR%20Performing%20Arts%20(Dance)%20NC%20II.pdf.

43. Caroline Joan S. Picart, *Critical Race Theory and Copyright in American Dance: Whiteness as Status Property* (New York: Palgrave, 2013), 4, 25, 73.

44. Ng, "Performing the 'Filipino' at the Crossroads"; Villaruz, "A Dancer's Fate"; TESDA, "Training Regulations," *TESDA.gov.ph*. According to Villaruz, these examinations no longer take place. It remains unclear, however, because while the TESDA core competencies presently include ballet, jazz, and fundamentals of Philippine folk dances with written examination, demonstration, and observation, the site fails to list a single accredited assessment center that qualifies applicants in the "Performing Arts (Dance)" category.

45. James Tyner, "Constructing Images, Constructing Policy: The Case of Filipina Migrant Performing Artists," *Gender, Place & Culture: A Journal of Feminist Geography* 4, no. 1 (1997): 24.

46. These dancers include Hontiveros, Nelson, Dimalanta, and Zamora.

47. Suzuki, "Japayuki," 441.

48. Villaruz, "A Dancer's Fate," 17.

49. It is important to note that dance theater artists have experienced exodus and "dance drain" as well.

50. Catherine Ceniza Choy, *Empire of Care: Nursing and Migration in Filipino American History* (Durham, NC: Duke University Press, 2003); Mark Johnson, "Diasporic Dreams, Middle-Class Moralities and Migrant Domestic Workers Among Muslim Filipinos in Saudi Arabia," *Asia Pacific Journal of Anthropology* 11, no. 3–4 (2010): 428–448; Deirdre McKay, *Global Filipinos: Migrants' Lives in the Virtual Village* (Bloomington: Indiana University Press, 2012); Steven C. McKay, "Filipino Sea Men: Constructing Masculinities in an Ethnic Labour Niche," *Journal of Ethnic and Migration Studies* 33, no. 4 (2007): 617–633; Rodriguez, *Migrants for Export*.

51. Zamora, interview with the author.

52. Parreñas, "Trafficked?," 146–147.

53. Ibid.

54. Rhacel Salazar Parreñas, "Homeward Bound: The Circular Migration of Entertainers between Japan and the Philippines," *Global Networks* 10, no. 3 (2010): 301.

55. Jose Edmundo Ocampo Reyes, "Fungibility, *Dead Souls*, and Filipino OCWs," *Kritika Kultura* 8 (2007): 111–126. Reyes speaks about "fungibility" as a particular trait of neoliberalism that inhibits a person's individuality.

56. Montañez et al., *Pains and Gains*; Parreñas, "Trafficked?," 159.

57. POEA.

58. Some hip-hop dancers I met in 2009 have since emigrated for dance and dance-related work in Hong Kong, Dubai, and Singapore.

59. Ivy "Bgirl Eyevee" Lobrin, interview with author, digital recording, Manila, Philippines, August 9, 2011.

60. Love Sabio, interview with the author, Quezon City, Philippines, September 5, 2011.

61. Quoted in "Filipino Pride in Hong Kong Disneyland," *Manila Times*, February 28, 2015, accessed April 4, 2019, https://www.manilatimes.net/filipino-pride-in-hong-kong-disneyland/166282/.

62. Username: rwscooper, written by Grace K from Entertainment, "The Rockafellas Will ROCK YOU." Resorts World Sentosa Singapore Scoop blog, *Rwsentosablog.com*, January 26, 2010, accessed April 4, 2019, http://www.rwsentosablog.com/the-rockafellas-will-rock-you/.

63. Jesse "Bboy Reflex" Gotangco, interview with the author, Quezon City, Philippines, August 17, 2011.

64. "Filipino Pride in Hong Kong Disneyland.".

65. Chelo A., interview with the author, digital recording, Manila, Philippines, September 17, 2011.

66. Jerome Dimalanta, interview with the author, digital recording, Manila, Philippines, September 5, 2011.

67. Ibid.

68. Ibid.

69. Michelle "Bgirl Tzy" Salazar, email message to the author, April 27, 2019.

70. John M. Liu, Paul M. Ong, and Carolyn Rosenstein, "Dual Chain Migration: Post-1965 Filipino Immigration to the United States," *International Migration Review* 25, no. 3 (Autumn, 1991): 487–513.

71. In my interviews with dancers who have made the decision to migrate to the United States, the wider range of travel to foreign countries afforded to U.S. passports (172) in contrast to Philippine passports (58) was an added incentive to pursue U.S. citizenship.

72. Michelle "Bgirl Tzy" Salazar, e-mail message to author, June 9, 2015.

73. Dancers also place great value on the ten-year multiple entry U.S. visa over the short-term visa because it exempts or eases visa requirements for Filipino passport holders entering other select countries.

74. These competitions include Hip Hop International (U.S.), World Supremacy Battlegrounds (Australia), Astro Battlegrounds (Japan), R-16 (South Korea), Juste Debout (France), and Battle of the Year (Germany).

75. "Trump Wants to End 'Chain Migration,'" *ABS-CBN News*, January 31, 2018, accessed February 21, 2018, http://news.abs-cbn.com/overseas/01/31/18/trump-wants-end-to-chain-migration.

76. Jill Dougherty, "International Hip-Hop Artists Find Their Roots in U.S.," *CNN*, July 31, 2009, accessed June 4, 2014, http://www.cnn.com/2009/SHOWBIZ/07/30/international.hip.hop/index.html?eref=rss_us.

77. "Performing Artists Cultural Visitors Program," Explore the Arts, Kennedy Center 2009, June 4, 2014; Bureau of Public Affairs, Office of the Spokesman, "U.S. Department of State and the John F. Kennedy Center for the Performing Arts to Present Hip-Hop Artists from Argentina, Lebanon, the Palestinian Territories, the Philippines, and Vietnam on the Millennium Stage," *U.S. Department of State*, July 27, 2009, accessed May 4, 2019, https://2009-2017.state.gov/r/pa/prs/ps/2009/july/126510.htm.

78. See Clare Croft, *Dancers as Diplomats: American Choreography in Cultural Exchange* (New York: Oxford University Press, 2015); Clare Croft, "Dance Returns to American Cultural Diplomacy: The U.S. State Department's 2003 Dance Residency Program and Its After Effects," *Dance Research Journal* 45, no. 1 (2013): 22–39.

79. Hishaam Aidi, "The Grand (Hip-Hop) Chessboard: Race, Rap and Raison d'État," *Middle East Report* 260 (2011): 28.

80. Ibid., 26.

81. Ibid., 25–39.

82. Dougherty, "International Hip-Hop Artists Find Their Roots in U.S."

83. Michelle Salazar, "If Life Throws You Apples . . . It Means I Didn't Eat It," *And I Wander* (blog), July 14, 2010, accessed June 4, 2014, https://calvinswife.wordpress.com/2010/07/14/if-life-throws-you-apples-it-means-i-didnt-eat-it/. Link is no longer available per April 27, 2020.

84. *Black-ish*, television program, Season 1, Episode 1, performed by Anthony Anderson (2014; Disney-ABC Domestic television, 2014), 22:00, online streaming video.

85. Ibid.

86. Ibid.

87. Some of Bgirl Tzy's observations about racial expectations rang true with some of my own exposure to the dance industry. From 2007 to 2009, I trained in hip-hop at Debbie Reynolds's Studio in North Hollywood, where many of the industry's choreographers taught and occasionally casted. In one of Tricia Miranda's classes, a Japanese vocal artist visited with the intent of casting American hip-hop dancers for her music video. While the class was composed of dancers of Black, Latinx, white, and Asian and Asian American backgrounds, myself and other Asians and Asian Americans were excluded from auditioning.

88. Ana "Rokafella" Garcia, "Herstory," in *We B*Girls*, by Martha Cooper and Nika Kramer (New York: powerHouse Books, 2005), 9–10.

Chapter 3

1. Terry "Hitmaster Fish" Williams, personal communication with author, April 11, 2011. The robot is an American popular dance that consists of its own movement vocabulary including isolations, "dime stops," and "double dime stops." It has multiple origins in the 1970s during which individuals imitated various media representations of animated robots. According to Hitmaster Fish, the popping genre is defined as "the dancing robot," a phrasing which interestingly highlights the non-dance nature of the robot.

2. In this chapter, I adopt the convention of using "Pilipino," in respect to how the Filipino American community at U.C.–Berkeley self-identifies the show and student organization, but for clarity, I use "Filipino" with an "F" as the general term. A wider analysis of PCNs across the East, Midwest, and Pacific would provide additional insight into how Filipino performance practices integrated Black dance forms in their respective regions. Unfortunately, such a study is outside of the scope of this project. I thank James Zarsadiaz for this observation.

3. Theodore S. Gonzalves, "The Day the Dancers Stayed: On Pilipino Culture Nights," in *Filipino Americans: Transformation and Identity*, ed. Maria P. P. Root (Thousand Oaks, CA: Sage Publications, 1997), 173–176; Theodore Sanchez Gonzalves, *When the Lights Go Down: Performing in the Filipina/o Diaspora, 1934–1998* (PhD diss., University of California–Irvine, 2001).

4. Gonzalves, *When the Lights Go Down*; Theodore S. Gonzalves, *The Day the Dancers Stayed: Performing in the Pilipino/American Diaspora* (Philadelphia, PA: Temple University Press, 2009); Barbara Gaerlan, "In the Court of the

Sultan: Orientalism, Nationalism, and Modernity in Philippine and Pilipino American Dance," *Journal of Asian American Studies* 2, no. 3 (October 1999): 251–287; Michelle Bautista, "Philippine Cultural Nights," in *Fil-Am: Pilipino American Experience*, ed. Alfred A. Yuson (Makati City, Philippines: Publico, Inc., 1999), 157; Anna Maria Alves, "In Search of 'Meaning': Collective Memory and Identity in Pilipino Cultural Night at UCLA" (master's thesis, University of California–Los Angeles, 1999).

5. Alves, "In Search of 'Meaning.'"

6. Jerome Karabel, "Freshman Admissions at Berkeley: A Policy for the 1990s and Beyond. A Report of the Committee on Admissions and Enrollment, Berkeley Division, Academic Senate," University of California–Berkeley (1989), 20, 40–41. Filipinos, affirmative action students (Black, Hispanic, Native American students), rural students, disabled students, athletes, and "students with special talents in such fields as music, drama, and debating" formed the complemental groups of Tier 3 group of admits. By 1986, U.C. reduced the Filipino target because they viewed an increasing number of Filipinos qualifying for Tier 1.

7. For practicality purposes, traditional in this chapter references the repertoire of folk dance culture including dance, music, and costumes derived from Bayanihan Dance Company, which is derived from Francisca Reyes Aquino's work.

8. In 2010, at University of California–Los Angeles, I co-facilitated with American Studies scholar Anna Alves the course Asian American Studies 97: "History, Theory and Practice of Pilipino Cultural Night: SPCN Committee Winter Course & Workshop." As part of the course, we invited Rani de Leon to speak on a panel entitled: "UCLA SPCN Process and Production Discussion: Alternative Aesthetics and Meanings." In this panel, de Leon recounted the unnamed opposition in the form of emails from community members during the production process. In many ways, the longstanding PCN tradition informed the refusal of many community veterans to promote and participate in *Home* (2000) and some individual attempts to persuade the organizers to revert to more standard multiculturalist PCN practices.

9. Garrick Macatangay, interview with author, digital recording, Culver City, CA, August 10, 2012.

10. Gonzalves, *When the Lights Go Down*, 178.

11. Victor Bascara, *Model-Minority Imperialism* (Minneapolis: University of Minnesota Press, 2006), xxxvi.

12. Margaret Rhee, "In Search of My Robot: Race, Technology, and the Asian American Body," *Scholar and Feminist Online* 13, no. 3 (2016): 1–2. Rhee, drawing on Stephen Sohn, Greta Niu, and Wendy Chun, writes how in the U.S. imagination, Asian Americans and robots are co-constituted as tropes for "second-class citizens."

13. Michael Omi and Howard Winant, *Racial Formation in the United States: From the 1960s to the 1980s* (New York: Routledge, 1986/1989). U.S. racial formation, a theoretical framework first introduced by Michael Omi and Howard Winant, presents a concept of race that is fluid and contingent, contested and constructed. Racial formation, as a means of challenging the *a priori* concept of race, is shaped by the specific contexts and conditions with which it coexists.

14. Patricia J. Williams, *The Alchemy of Race and Rights: Diary of a Law Professor* (Cambridge, MA: Harvard University Press, 1991); Kimberlé Crenshaw, *Critical Race Theory: The Key Writings that Formed the Movement* (New York: New Press, 1995); Mari J. Matsuda, *Where Is Your Body? And Other Essays on Race, Gender and The Law* (Boston: Beacon Press, 1997); Richard Delgado and Jean Stefancic, *Critical Race Theory: An Introduction* (New York: New York University Press, 2017).

15. Angelo N. Ancheta, "Pilipino Americans, Foreigner Discrimination, and the Lines of Racial Sovereignty," in *Positively No Filipinos Allowed: Building Communities and Discourse*, eds. Antonio Tiongson Jr. et al. (Philadelphia: Temple University Press, 2006), 90–110. Angelo N. Ancheta, for instance, demonstrates the ways that anti-Filipino racism has differed from anti-Black racism. While Black and Filipino peoples are often figured similarly as racial others subordinate to whites, Filipinos may also undergo a "foreigner within" racialization despite actual documentation, birth origin, language skills, or immigrant status. For example, employers have committed workplace discrimination by restricting folks from speaking Filipino language in the workplace, despite the allowance of European foreign languages. Other legislation that directly affected Pilipinos includes Alien Land Laws, the Tydings-McDuffie Act, anti-miscegenation laws, and the Immigration and Nationality Act of 1965.

16. Charles R. Lawrence and Mari Matsuda, *We Won't Go Back: Making the Case for Affirmative Action* (Boston: Houghton Mifflin, 1997); Citadelle Priagula, "Comment: Examining Race-Conscious Remediation Through the Pilipino/a American Experience," *UCLA Asian Pacific American Law Journal* 15, no. 1 (2010): 135–159; Antonio T. Tiongson Jr. et al., eds., *Positively No Filipinos Allowed: Building Communities and Discourse* (Philadelphia: Temple University Press, 2006); "US Equal Employment Opportunity Commission Home Page," US Equal Employment Opportunity Commission, Eeoc.gov, accessed December 15, 2011, http://www.eeoc.gov/eeoc /history/35th/thelaw/eo-10925.html.

17. Scholars such as these have theorized an exceptional liminality as characteristic of Filipino racialization: Antonio Tiongson Jr. (between Filipino and Asian American formation), S. Lily Mendoza (between Philippine and Western intellectual production), and Tracy Buenavista (between people of color and colonial subject status). See Antonio T. Tiongson Jr., "Introduction," in *Positively No Filipinos Allowed*; S. Lily Mendoza, *Between the Homeland and the Diaspora* (Manila: University of Santo Tomas Publishing House, 2006); Tracy Lachica Buenavista, *Movement from the Middle: Pilipina/o 1.5-Generation College Student Access, Retention, and Resistance* (PhD diss., Department of Education, UCLA, 2007).

18. Tracy Lachica Buenavista, Uma M. Jayakumar, and Kimberly Misa-Escalante, "Contextualizing Asian American Education Through Critical Race Theory: An Example of U.S. Pilipino College Student Experiences," *New Directions for Institutional Research*, no. 142 (Summer 2009): 75.

19. I am grateful to Ellen Wu for encouragement about this dynamic.

20. J. Okamura and A. Agbayani, "Pamantasan: Pilipino American Higher Education," in *Pilipino Americans: Transformation and Identity*, ed. Maria P. Root (Thousand Oaks, CA: Sage Publications 1997), 191. Proposition 209 is formally known as The

California Civil Rights Initiative and informally known as "Prop 209." In addition to education, the policy also aimed at public employment and contracting.

21. Buenavista, *Movement from the Middle*. This group of states includes Texas, California, Washington, and Florida.

22. Ibid.; Delgado, *The Rodrigo Chronicles: Conversations About America and Race* (New York: New York University, 1995); Mendoza, *Between the Homeland and the Diaspora*. Richard Delgado's character, Rodrigo, evaluates the construction of "merit" as "basically white people's affirmative action," and astutely identifies how standardized tests produce a culture of testocracy rather than meritocracy. Mendoza is also clear in identifying the productive qualities, such as the emergence of multiple definitions of "Filipino," of the interstitial location between homeland and diaspora.

23. Beth H. Parker, "Proposition 209 ~ A Decade Later: The Impacts of Prop 209 on Public Education, Employment and Contracting," *Equal Rights Advocates*, June 1998, accessed September 23, 2011, http://www.equalrights.org/publications/reports/affirm/full209.asp. Link is no longer available per May 6, 2020.

24. Buenavista, *Movement from the Middle*, 32; Karabel, "Freshman Admissions at Berkeley," 41–42.

25. The definition of over-representation in this case refers to differences between the percentage of Asian Americans within the institution versus within the state's general population.

26. Ellen D. Wu, *The Color of Success: Asian Americans and the Origins of the Model Minority* (Princeton, NJ: Princeton University Press, 2013).

27. Ibid. Madeline Y. Hsu, *The Good Immigrants: How the Yellow Peril Became the Model Minority* (Princeton, NJ: Princeton University Press, 2015); Nicholas Daniel Hartlep and Brad J. Porfilio, eds., *Killing the Model Minority Stereotype: Asian American Counterstories and Complicity* (Charlotte, NC: Information Age Publishing, 2015).

28. Hartlep and Porfilio, eds., *Killing the Model Minority Stereotype*.

29. Priagula, "Comment," 156; OiYan Poon et al., "A Critical Review of the Model Minority Myth in Selected Literature on Asian Americans and Pacific Islanders in Higher Education," *Review of Educational Research* 86, no. 2 (2016): 469–502.

30. See also Jonathan Y. Okamura, "Filipino American Access to Public Higher Education in California and Hawai'i," in *The "Other" Students: Filipino Americans, Education, and Power*, eds. Dina C. Maramba and Rick Bonus (Charlotte, NC: Information Age Publishing, 2013), 213–235.

31. Priagula, "Comment," 156–157.

32. Ibid. Legal scholars like Priagula suspect institutional representatives use stereotypes against Asian Americans during admissions to preserve a majority white population.

33. Buenavista, *Movement from the Middle*, 73.

34. Ibid., 157. Priagula cites Thomas J. Espenshade and Chang Y. Chung, "The Opportunity Cost of Admission Preferences at Elite Universities," *Social Science Quarterly* 86 (2005): 293, 298.

35. Buenavista, *Movement from the Middle*, 75; the 2000 Chinese undergraduate enrollment (20%) differs from that of Filipinos (3%) despite similar state census populations.

36. Ibid., 75–76; Okamura and Agbayani, "Pamantasan: Pilipino American Higher Education," 191. For another look at Asian American and Filipino American divergences, see E. J. R. David, *Brown Skin, White Minds: Filipino-/American Postcolonial Psychology* (Charlotte, NC: Information Age Publishing, Inc., 2013), xix; Anthony Ocampo, "Am I Really Asian?: Educational Experiences and Panethnic Identification among Second-Generation Filipino Americans," *Journal of Asian American Studies* 16, no. 3 (2013): 295–324.

37. Okamura, "Filipino American Access to Public Higher Education," 221. Okamura notes that for the period 1997 to 2009, African Americans at U.C. Berkeley experienced a 27 percent decreased undergraduate population (1,300 to 900), and Latinos experienced an increase (2,800 to 3000) but continue to display enrollment disproportionate to their public high school graduates.

38. See Oiyan A. Poon, "Haunted by Negative Action: Asian Americans, Admissions, and Race in the 'Color-Blind Era,'" *Asian American Policy Review* 18 (2009): 81–90; Antonio Tiongson Jr., "Reflections on the Trajectory of Filipina/o American Studies: An Interview with Rick Bonus," in *Positively No Filipinos Allowed: Building Communities and Discourse*, eds. Antonio T. Tiongson Jr. et al. (Philadelphia: Temple University Press, 2006), 162–171.

39. Priagula, "Comment," 139.

40. Ibid., 156.

41. See Vijay Prashad, *The Karma of Brown Folk* (Minneapolis: University of Minnesota Press, 2000); Buenavista, *Movement from the Middle*, 78.

42. Prashad, *The Karma of Brown Folk*, 7;

43. Jared Sexton, *Amalgamation Schemes: Antiblackness and the Critique of Multiracialism* (Minneapolis: University of Minnesota Press, 2008). I thank an anonymous reviewer for bringing this to my attention.

44. Hortense J. Spillers, "Mama's Baby, Papa's Maybe: An American Grammar Book," *Diacritics* 17, no. 2 (1987): 65–81.

45. The issues of missing rehearsals or lateness prompt organizers to do reminder and wake-up phone calls ("call-outs") or require tardy participants to do push-ups.

46. Reme A. Grefalda et al. *Towards a Cultural Community: Identity, Education and Stewardship in Filipino American Performing Arts*, a National Federation of Filipino American Association (NaFFAA) cultural project with support from the Ford Foundation) (First Fruits, 2003). At the same time, PCN might be seen as one of many Culture Night traditions for ethnically identified groups of Asian American students. In 2011, I observed that Chinese, Hong Kong, Indian, Indonesian, Japanese American, Korean, Khmer (Cambodian), Taiwanese, and Vietnamese groups at UCLA produced their own individual culture nights.

47. This includes variants like Pilipino American Culture Night, Pilipino Culture Show, Pilipino Cultural Celebration, and Barrio Fiesta.

48. The inaugural PCN for each University of California campus occurred as follows: Berkeley (1976–1977), Davis (1986–1987), Irvine (1978–1979), Los Angeles (1978–1979), Merced (2007–2008), San Diego (1991–1992), Santa Barbara (1990–1991), and Santa Cruz (1991–1992).

49. U.S. Census Bureau, Census 2000.

50. Gonzalves introduces the term "PCN genre" to discuss the phenomenon in *When the Lights Go Down*; E. San Juan Jr. undertakes a brief, yet critical, exploration of the PCN phenomena in *From Exile to Diaspora: Versions of the Pilipino Experience in the United States* (Boulder, CO: Westview Press, 1998).

51. Gonzalves, "The Day the Dancers Stayed," 163–182.

52. In 1996, "Regional Dances" included Lumagen (Kalinga festival dance), Takiling (Kalinga successful headhunting dance), Binaylon (Higaonon mimetic dance featuring mother hen and chick dance), and Banog (Higaonon tribal dance with hunters and a hawk). In 1998, the "Regional Suite" was renamed the "Mountain Suite." The Mountain dances included Banga, Salidsid (Kalinga wedding ceremony), and Elilay (post-wedding dance). The year 1998 introduced the "Tribal Suite," whose dances included those from highlands and mountain-dwelling agrarian, pagan tribes of Mindanao, like Bagobos, known for escaping Muslim and Christian influence, like Soten, Dumadel, and Sugod Uno (toil-like land preparation). In 1999, the Tribal Suite included binaylan/banog and pandamggo (a coming-of-age dance for women), the Mountain Suite included ragragsakan (Kalinga women peace pact) and lumagen.

53. For an excellent description of the suites common to Philippine folk dance, see Kanami Namiki, "Hybridity and National Identity: Different Perspectives of Two National Folk Dance Companies in the Philippines," *Special Issue: Asian Studies* 47 (2011): 65–66; Alves, "In Search of 'Meaning,' " 12.

54. "Bayanihan—The Philippine National folk Dance Company," Bayanihannational-danceco.ph (website), last modified 2003, accessed April 10, 2013, http://www.bayanihannationaldanceco.ph/milestones1959_1958.html. Link no longer available per May 6, 2020.

55. Francisca Reyes-Tolentino, *Philippine National Dances* (New York: Silver Burdett Co., 1946); Francisca Reyes Aquino, *Fundamental Dance Steps and Music* (Manila, 1957); Francisca Reyes Aquino, *Philippine Folk Dances: Volumes 1–6* (Manila, 1957–1966).

56. Gonzalves, *The Day the Dancers Stayed*, 29–61.

57. J. Lorenzo Perillo, "Embodying Modernism: A Postcolonial Intervention across Filipino Dance," *Amerasia Journal* 43, no. 2 (2017): 122–140.

58. Gonzalves, *The Day the Dancers Stayed*.

59. Ibid.; Alves, "In Search of 'Meaning' "; Bautista, "Philippine Cultural Nights," 157; San Juan Jr., *From Exile to Diaspora*, 12; Gaerlan, "In the Court of the Sultan."

60. Reyes-Tolentino, *Philippine National Dances*.

61. Jacqueline Shea Murphy, *The People Never Stopped Dancing: Native American Modern Dance Histories* (Minneapolis: University of Minnesota Press, 2007).

62. Lisa Lowe, "Foreword," in *Positively No Filipinos Allowed: Building Communities and Discourse*, ed. Antonio T. Tiongson Jr. et al. (Philadelphia: Temple University Press, 2006), vii–ix.

63. In modern dance, this turn emerged with a response to contemporary practices of ballet and vaudeville, specifically their traits of gender and class devaluement for white, middle-class women.

64. The Modern Suite cannot be found in the Bayanihan's roster of dances or any other Philippine folk dance troupe's ouevre, and for this reason rarely incurs critiques of authenticity as Filipino diasporic dance pieces do.

65. Elizabeth Almario Casasola and Lorraine Rodrigo Marasigan, *Pakinggan Mo Ako (Program)*, Pilipino American Alliance, University of California–Berkeley, 1996, 7.

66. Ibid.

67. J. Lorenzo Perillo, "Embodying Modernism: A Postcolonial Intervention across Filipino Dance," *Amerasia Journal* 43, no. 2 (2017): 122–140.

68. The renaming could also read as provincializing American dance culture as relative to the other ethno-cultural dance suites.

69. Evelyn Ibatan Rodriguez, *Celebrating Debutantes and Quinceañeras: Coming of Age in American Ethnic Communities* (Philadelphia: Temple University Press, 2013).

70. Frank Lozier, *Tagasalaysay/Storyteller: A Story of Culture (Program)*, Pilipino American Alliance, University of California–Berkeley, 1998.

71. Sharlene Aquiler and Kelly Dumlao, *Re: Collections Culture (Program)*, Pilipino American Alliance, University of California–Berkeley, 1999.

72. Benito M. Vergara Jr., *Displaying Filipinos: Photography and Colonialism in Early 20th Century Philippines* (Quezon City: University of the Philippines Press, 1995).

73. Robert Farris Thompson, "Dance and Culture, an Aesthetic of the Cool: West African Dance," *African Forum* 2, no. 2 (Fall 1966): 88; Thomas F. DeFrantz, "The Black Beat Made Visible: Hip Hop Dance and Body Power," in *Of the Presence of the Body: Essays on Dance and Performance Theory*, ed. Andres Lepecki (Middletown, CT: Wesleyan University Press, 2004), 64–81; Halifu Osumare, *The Africanist Aesthetic in Global Hip-Hop: Power Moves* (New York: Palgrave Macmillan, 2007).

74. Matwiran De Leon, *Home (Program)*, Pilipino American Alliance, University of California–Berkeley, April 2000, 9.

75. Gonzalves, *The Day the Dancers Stayed*; Gaerlan, *In the Court of the Sultan*; San Juan Jr., *From Exile to Diaspora*. The denaturalization of "Pilipino" stands as a common thread running through the critiques of scholars like Gaerlan, Gonzalves, and San Juan.

76. Marta Savigliano, *Tango and the Political Economy of Passion* (Boulder, CO: Westview Press, 1995). Savigliano uses this term to describe Tango as a means of adjusting to and confronting (neo)colonialism exotic wherein exoticized representations become symbols of national identity.

77. DeFrantz, *The Black Beat Made Visible*, 71.

78. Sarita See, "'An Open Wound': Colonial Melancholia and Contemporary Pilipino/ American Texts," in *Vestiges of War: The Philippine-American War and the Aftermath of an Imperial Dream, 1899–1999*, eds. A. Shaw and L. Francia (New York: New York University Press, 2002), 376–400.

79. Ibid. Sarita Echavez See, *The Decolonized Eye: Filipino American Art and Performance* (Minneapolis: University of Minnesota Press, 2009).

80. José García Villa, *Volume Two* (New York: New Directions, 1949). Each fragmented sequence of movement in their blend of popping and folk aesthetics also conjures Jose Garcia Villa's "comma poems." In the preface of *Volume Two*, Villa wrote: "The

commas are an integral and essential part of the medium: regulating the poem's verbal density and time movement: enabling each word to attain a fuller tonal value, and the line movement to become more measured."

81. Jorge Pabon, "Physical Graffiti: The History of Hip Hop Dance," in *Total Chaos: The Art and Aesthetics of Hip Hop*, ed. Jeff Chang (New York: Basic Books, 2006), 18–26.

82. Ibid. In largely different contexts, White modern dancers at the time were also turning to the quotidian as a move against formalism or high aesthetics.

83. Hitmaster Fish, personal communication with author.

84. Ibid.

85. The latter two phrasings reference Sacramento and San Francisco originating movement styles respectively and further localize "Assembly Line" within Bay Area street dance culture.

86. Macatangay, interview with the author.

87. Williams, *The Alchemy of Race and Rights*, 116.

88. Ibid.

89. See Alice Jade A. Alburo, "Box Populi: A Socio-Cultural Study of the Filipino American Balikbayan Box" (master's thesis, Memorial University of Newfoundland, 2001).

90. S. Lily Mendoza, "A Different Breed of Pilipino Balikbayans: The Ambiguities of (Re-) Turning," in *Positively No Filipinos Allowed: Building Communities and Discourse*, eds. Antonio T. Tiongson Jr. et al. (Philadelphia: Temple University Press, 2006), 199–214.

91. Barbara M. Posadas, *The Filipino Americans* (Westport, CT: Greenwood Press, 1999).

92. Anthony C. Ocampo, "Gifts that Go the Distance: The Social Organization of Philippine In-Kind Remittances," paper presented at the Association of Asian American Studies Annual Meeting, Honolulu, HI, April 2009.

93. Ibid.

94. Ibid.

95. Ibid.

Chapter 4

In 2011, I judged competitions in Quezon City, Marikina, and Los Angeles. For Hip-Hop International (HHI) 2013, I judged for Varsity and MegaCrew preliminary and semifinal rounds. I conducted in-depth interviews with sixteen judges and competitors at HHI from 2012 to 2014. Between competition rounds in the venue hallways, rehearsal spaces, and private homes, I met judges for periods of 60 to 180 minutes to discuss their ideas about performance criteria, race, gender, sexuality, nationality, and hip-hop. Some names have been omitted or changed to protect the privacy of the individuals.

1. Ariel, Hip Hop International Rules and Regulations Workshop, August 6, 2013.

2. Vincent, interview with the author, digital recording, Las Vegas, NV, August 7, 2013.

3. Madison Mainwaring, "The Death of the American Dance Critic," *Atlantic*, August 6, 2015, accessed November 7, 2015, http://www.theatlantic.com/entertainment/archive/2015/08/american-dance-critic/399908/.

4. Ibid.

5. Ibid.

6. Ibid.

7. Ibid.

8. Ibid.

9. Ibid.

10. Jonathan S. Marion, *Ballroom: Culture and Costume in Competitive Dance* (New York: Bloomsbury Academic, 2008), 81. Marion sees these three issues as evidence for considering dance as sport and athletics.

11. Halifu Osumare, *The Africanist Aesthetic in Global Hip-Hop: Power Moves* (New York: Palgrave Macmillan, 2007); Thomas F. DeFrantz, "The Black Beat Made Visible: Hip Hop Dance and Body Power," in *Of the Presence of the Body: Essays on Dance and Performance Theory*, ed. Andres Lepecki (Middletown, CT: Wesleyan University Press, 2004), 64–81. In dance studies, hip-hop is typically defined as a tight-bodied, improvisational and freestyle dance form, unlike staged ballet or folk dance, and in relationship to other elements of Africanist aesthetic like "polyrhythmic isolations," "narrative gesture," and "signifying." Osumare contends this aesthetic "facilitates the movement-by-movement mix of local and global embodiments" (58).

12. In the context of HHI, traditional dancing and folklore is encouraged to promote individuality and refers to non-hip-hop forms like Maori haka, Bollywood dance, and capoeira.

13. Ju Yon Kim, *The Racial Mundane: Asian American Performance and the Embodied Everyday* (New York: New York University Press, 2015); Shilpa S. Dave, *Indian Accents: Brown Voice and Racial Performance in American Television and Film* (Springfield: University of Illinois Press, 2013).

14. Michael Omi and Howard Winant, *Racial Formation in the United States: From the 1960s to the 1990s* (1986; repr., New York: Routledge, 2015), 56.

15. Christine Bacareza Balance, *Tropical Renditions: Making Musical Scenes in Filipino America* (Durham, NC: Duke University Press, 2016), 26.

16. Thomas F. DeFrantz, "Hip-Hop Habitus v.2.0," in *Black Performance Theory*, eds. Thomas F. DeFrantz and Anita Gonzalez (Durham, NC: Duke University Press, 2014), 234–237.

17. See Anna Sarao's "Boba Talk" podcast for many of these histories: Anna Sarao, "Boba Talk," accessed May 8, 2020, https://www.youtube.com/user/nassarao/videos

   In the Filipino diaspora, many dance crew/company founders and directors self-identify as Filipino, including but not limited to: Anna Sarao (Bodyrock/Culture Shock San Diego/U.S.), Arnel Calvario (Kaba Modern/Cultural Shock Los Angeles/U.S.), Randy Bernal, Ron Laserna, Cliff Cabute (Mindtricks/U.S.), Danny Batimana (Team Millenia/The Bridge Dance Competition/U.S.), Leslie Patacsil, Jon Jon Asperin, and Brian Blancaflor (Pilipino American Coalition Modern/U.S.), Emerson Aquino (Funkanometry SF/U.S.), Shaun Evaristo (Gen2/Movement Lifestyle/U.S.), Eddie Macaranas, and Emmet Agapay (Choreo Cookies/U.S.), Chris Martin (Choreo Cookies/U.S.), Erik Saradpon (Formality/U.S.), Mary Elizabeth Ebo-Reyes (Praise TEAM/Canada), Carlo Atienza (24/7 Company/The Faculty/Canada), Matt Pumanes (Puzzle League/U.S.), Clara Bajado (In Da House/Juste Debout/U.K.), and Mark "Swarf" Calape (Animaneax/A Team/U.K.), and Jeffrey Jimenez (Team Recycled/Germany).

18. There are many influential worldwide breakers who self-identify as Filipino including but not limited to: Abigail "AB-Girl" Herrara (Domestic Apes Crew/U.S.), Alfredo "Bboy Free" Vergara, Jr. (Circle of Fire/U.S.), Anthony "Lil Bob" Cabaero (Killafornia/U.S.), Ariston "Bboy Remind" Ripoyla (Style Elements Crew), Bailey "Bboy BailRok" Munoz (Rock Steady Crew/U.S.), Bea "Bgirl Bea" Lesaca (Funk Roots Crew/Philippines), Belle Abuyo (Culture Shock SD/U.S.), Daniel "Cloud" Campos (Skill Methodz/U.S.), Ereson "Bboy Mouse" Catipon (Funkstylers UK/United Kingdom), Ingel Catindig (Outer Circle Crew/U.S.), Ives "Bboy Ives" Viray (Rock Force Crew), Ivy "Bgirl Eyevee" Lobrin (in memoriam) (The Crew/Philippines), Jay "Bboy J Masta" Cambay (Battle Crew/Philippines), Jesse "Bboy Reflex" Gotangco (Soulstice/Philippines), Bgirl JessFX (Vivid Vixens/U.S.), Jerome "Jeromeskee" Aparis (Massive Monkees, Rocksteady Crew/U.S.), Jhong "Bboy Gatorade" Mesina (Philippine Allstars/Philippines), Kevin "Bboy Kevo (Main Ingredients/U.S.), Kyxz "Flying Kyxz" Mendiola (Philippine Allstars/Philippines), Leon "Bboy Vietnam" Carswell (Rock Force Crew), Logan "Logistx" Adra (Red Bull BC One All Stars/U.S.), Lowe, Richard, and Don Napalan (Street Kulture Breakers/Australia), Maya Carandang (Philippine Allstars/Philippines), Michelle "Bgirl Tzy" Salazar Mesina (Philippine Allstars), Paul "Paulskeee" Ruma (Rock Force Crew/U.S.), Rayan "Bboy Reveal" Casicas (Rock Force Crew/U.S.), Rene "Bboy NayTron" Abalos (Head Hunters/U.S.), Rèo Canonoy Matugas (DYO/Norway), Ron "Bboy Profo Won" Creer (Floor Gangz/U.S.), Ronnie "Bboy Ronnie" Abaldonado (Red Bull BC One All Stars/U.S.), Rynan "Kid Rainen" Paguio (Jabbawockeez/U.S.), and Bboy Wicket (Renegade Rockers/U.S.).

19. "About vibe," vibedance.com (website), accessed July 22, 2017, http://vibedancecomp.com/about/.

20. Anna Sarao, interview with author, digital recording, San Diego, California, December 10, 2014.

21. The debate between "urban dance" and "hip-hop dance" is important, but beyond the scope of this chapter. See " 'Why You Shouldn't Call Urban Dance 'Hip Hop'," *steezy blog*, accessed May 15, 2020, https://www.steezy.co/posts/urban-dance-and-hip-hop.

22. PacificRimVideoPress, "In Depth Interview with Howard Schwartz of Hip Hop International," YouTube (online video), July 11, 2011, accessed May 29, 2014, Part 1: https://www.youtube.com/watch?v=yahheYze_-A.

I danced and occasionally choreographed as a member of Culture Shock Dance Troupe in Oakland, California in the late 1990s and early 2000s.

23. "About Us << Hip Hop International," Hip Hop International (2012) (website), accessed September 1, 2013, http://hiphopinternational.com/about-us/.

24. PacificRimVideoPress, "In Depth Interview with Howard Schwartz, Part 1: https://www.youtube.com/watch?v=yahheYze_-A; and Part 2: https://www.youtube.com/watch?v=o6sBDArhhgg.

The official twitter account is also OfficialHHI. Howard Schwartz explains what catalyzed HHI, "In our travels worldwide, we just saw so many people around the world dancing on the streets, dancing in front of store windows . . . street dancing.

We felt that there wasn't enough opportunity for them really to be seen worldwide, and for it to be broad. . . . And we really felt that if we could take this movement that we saw regenerating itself after all these years and be able to get it onto television and develop it into a worldwide event with rules and respectability, then maybe we could help in that area."

25. "Scores and Results," Hip Hop International (website), accessed September 1, 2013, http://hiphopinternational.com/scores-results/ Link is no longer available per May 7, 2020. Past scores are available, per May 7, 2020, at http://www.hiphopinternational.com/medalists/past/. In regard to winnings, interestingly, although U.S. crews like Knucklehead Zoo and solo battlers like Tiffany Bong have won in the World Battles, since 2003 U.S. crews have actually never won in the World HHI Championships Adult category, usually the main event of the competition. The Adult crew winners have represented Canada (2003, 2004), Philippines (2006, 2008, 2012), Trinidad and Tobago (2007), France (2009), New Zealand (2010), United Kingdom (2011) (Note: 2005 results were not available). Crews from countries lacking Hip-Hop International organization are allowed to submit individual entries/petitions for inclusion.

26. "World Hip Hop Dance Championship," *Hip Hop International* (2012) (website), accessed September 1, 2013, http://hiphopinternational.com/world-hip-hop-dance-championship/.

27. Other such crews include Boogie Bots (Season 2), Team Millenia (Season 3), Boxcuttuhz (Season 3), Massive Monkees (Season 3), Mos Wanted Crew (Season 7), and Kinjaz (Season 8). Howard Schwartz is also co-creator and executive producer/writer of *America's Best Dance Crew*.

28. Mina Yang, "Yellow Skin, White Masks," *Daedalus* 142, no. 4 (2013): 24–37. HHI is also responsible for popularizing Parris Goebel and ReQuest Crew, who hold the record for the fastest video to reach two billion views on YouTube with Justin Bieber's "Sorry."

29. Antonio T. Tiongson Jr., *Filipinos Represent: DJs, Racial Authenticity, and the Hip-Hop Nation* (Minneapolis: University of Minnesota Press, 2013). The latter event served as subject of the documentary film *Planet B-Boy* (2007).

30. The first three categories feature crews of five to eight members; since 2011, Mega crews have competed featuring fifteen to forty members.

31. Tovin Lapan, "Olympic Spirit Permeates Las Vegas in World Hip-Hop Dance Championship," *Las Vegas Sun News*, August 2, 2012, accessed December 23, 2013, https://lasvegassun.com/news/2012/aug/02/olympic-spirit-permeates-las-vegas-world-hip-hop-d/; Peterson Gonzaga, "Nine Dance Crews from PHL to Join 'Olympics' of Hip-Hop Competitions in US," *GMA News Online*, July 13, 2012, accessed December 23, 2013, http://www.gmanetwork.com/news/story/265345/pinoyabroad/ofwguide/nine-dance-crews-from-phl-to-join-olympics-of-hip-hop-competitions-in-us.

32. *Official Rules and Regulations of Hip Hop International Crews of 5–8 Crewmembers—Amended for 2013*, Hip Hop International 2013, 5.

33. Hip Hop International Rules and Regulations Workshop, August 6, 2013.
    For more on Tony "Go-Go" Lewis Foster's work in Asia, see Karen Lim, "58 and Still 'Locking,'" posted June 21, 2013, AsiaOne.com, accessed December 29, 2013, http://

www.asiaone.com/print/News/Latest%2BNews/Sports/Story/A1Story20130621-431205.html.

34. Ariel, Hip Hop International Rules and Regulations Workshop, August 6, 2013.

35. Participant ages ranged from late teens to forties.

36. Among the different types of judges are the skills, performance, technical, and head judges.

37. Julie Malnig, "'But How Do I Write about Dance?': Thoughts on Teaching Criticism," *Dance Research Journal* 41, no. 2 (2009): 91–95.

38. *Official Rules and Regulations of Hip Hop International Crews of 5–8 Crewmembers—Amended for 2013*, Hip Hop International 2013, 1–12. This figure excludes the technical director as his role is less related to the dance. The deductions vary between 0.05 points (0.5%) for a minor fall and 0.25 points (2.5%) for use of props (8).

39. Ibid., 10. For the international competition there is a minimum of four performance judges, four skills judges, one head judge, and one technical director.

40. Ariel, Hip Hop International Rules and Regulations Workshop. Ariel states his reason for not having judges recuse themselves from judging their own crew at HHI: "No, because we believe in the credibility of the judges. And so too should the directors, head judges, technical directors, and so on. It doesn't matter. At Worlds we encourage countries to send judges from their country. Especially if they have crews coming, we want them to be on the panel."

41. If a judge scoring his or her own crew is suspected of bias, the head judge is responsible for providing evidence and may possibly remove that judge. While HHI promotes judging one's own crew at the international level, the practice varies at the national level. I will discuss this in the section on cultural specificity later in the chapter.

42. Should the performance and skills judges see something to be evaluated for possible deduction or disqualification, they may write a note in the comments section of score sheets to alert the head judge.

43. The evolution of variety points will be discussed in detail in the "Standardization" section.

44. *Official Rules and Regulations of Hip Hop International Crews of 5–8 Crewmembers—Amended for 2013*, 8. These styles are: BBoying/BGirling (breaking), Hip-Hop Dance/Choreography, House Dance, Krumping, Locking, Party Dances or Club Dances (popular or trendy dances), Popping, Stepping/Gumboots, Vogueing, Whacking/Punking, Dancehall.

45. Joel Gallarde, interview with the author, digital recording, Los Angeles, California, August 13, 2012. Interestingly, Gallarde observes that American HHI competitors appear more "brainwashed," in their interviews and audience behavior, to claim a pride that is tied to the United States, whereas New Zealanders attach that pride to themselves as individuals and crews.

46. Ibid.

47. Ibid.

48. For more on migration issues related to dancers, see Chapter 3.

49. Another example: For instance, with World of Dance, a touring competition that recently took place in Chicago (2015), only one of four judges currently lived in

Chicagoland and the rest resided in Southern California. One local competitor told me that the lack of local representation could be problematic. He disagreed with the high ranking of one group that incorporated a dance that was in his opinion familiar and "played out" to locals but might have appeared new and original to non-local judges.

50. Arnel Calvario, interview with the author, Las Vegas, August 6, 2014.

51. *Official Rules and Regulations of Hip Hop International Crews of 5–8 Crewmembers—Amended for 2013*, 12.

52. Competitions are not the only modes of hip-hop that implement or imply standards by way of evaluative mechanisms. Hip-hop dance classes have rubrics. Dance concerts have traditional critics.

53. *Official Rules and Regulations of Hip Hop International Crews of 5–8 Crewmembers*, 8.

54. Ibid.

55. *Official Rules and Regulations of Hip Hop International Crews of 5–8 Crewmembers—Amended for 2013*, 12. Judges discourage crews from composing a routine with a large portion of the dance to be traditional and/or cultural dance. The 2020 version of the rules similar encourage traditional, folkloric, and cultural dance elements (excluding costumes, clothing, and masks), but include penalizations of 0.5 points for excessive amounts.

56. Allen Pineda Lindo (professionally known as Apl.de.Ap) is mixed race African American and Filipino and Black Amerasian, or the son of an African American military father and Filipina mother.

57. *Official Rules and Regulations of Hip Hop International Crews of 5–8 Crewmembers—Amended for 2013*, 4. For junior crews this segment is twenty seconds, for Varsity and Adult crews it is thirty seconds.

58. Ibid., 12.

59. Tricia Rose, *Black Noise: Rap Music and Black Culture in Contemporary America* (Hanover, NH: University Press of New England, 1994).

60. André Lepecki, *Exhausting Dance: Performance and the Politics of Movement* (New York: Routledge, 2006), 1.

61. Head judge, Hip Hop International Rules and Regulations Workshop, August 6, 2013.

62. *Official Rules and Regulations of Hip Hop International Crews of 5–8 Crewmembers—Amended for 2013*, 12.

63. Ariel, Hip Hop International Rules and Regulations Workshop. Ariel explains the idea behind the category of controlled mobility: "Static control is easy. You could just stand and do the moves, boom-boom-boom, because most of the time, the dance concept is hands only. And the rest of the body well they're just hanging out at the beach. So the whole body needs to be involved. It's a dance! Not just arms or not just legs. Needs to be whole body. So when you're doing that that is now what we're starting to call the groove that is missing. Being able to just do movement with just the legs or the arms, where the body is not involved, hitting that movement the way that it needs to be hit, then, it must affect your score, in terms of the quality of that move—it must affect it. Because there must be that groove element in all of these styles. And it's specific. It's specific."

64. See Sally R. Sommer, "C'mon to My House: Underground-House Dancing," *Dance Research Journal* 33, no. 2 (2001): 72–86; Thomas F. DeFrantz, "Bone-Breaking, Black Social Dance, and Queer Corporeal Orature," *Black Scholar* 46, no. 1 (2016): 66–74.

65. Jasmine, interview with the author, digital recording, Las Vegas, NV, August 10, 2013. When asked about the effects of standardizing hip-hop, Jasmine explained: "It's complicated because it should be an art form that evolves. Unfortunately, I think a lot of contests have kind of stopped that growth. Because a lot of dancers, because of these standardizations, think or choreograph, thinking about what other people want them to do, rather than actually being completely original. I think it's kind of slowing the process of evolution of hip-hop dance, but it's also reasoned to be."

66. Vincent, interview with the author. And yet, at times, there are dancers that find ways to transcend the system of rules. Vincent mentioned a team in New Zealand that enters competitions, but not to win. Rather, they enter to express themselves artistically and gain exposure, thus subverting the system.

67. Hip-hop and R&B songs often fall between 80 and 115 beats per minute whereas House music averages around 120 to 130 beats per minute.

68. Nicole R. Fleetwood, *Troubling Vision: Performance, Visuality, and Blackness* (Chicago: University of Chicago Press, 2011), 157.

69. There is at least one example of competitive choreography that engages the Movement for Black Lives: Chicago-based Puzzle League and their winning choreography at World of Dance Chicago (2016). Official World of Dance, "The Puzzle League | Winners Circle | World of Dance Chicago 2016 | #WODCHI16," *YouTube*, accessed May 12, 2020, https://www.youtube.com/watch?v=76ljGuEEU0w.

70. "Poverty to Glory: Philippine Allstars Empowering Youth Through Hip Hop," *Kalatas Media*, February 14, 2012, accessed April 29, 2019, http://kalatas.com.au/2012/02/15/poverty-to-glory-philippine-allstars-empowering-youth-through-hip-hop/.

71. Allen, "Black Filipino Amerasian Identity."

72. In a similar fashion, formerly, the judges used to factor in age, but they have since abandoned this practice because the younger dancers would often out-dance the adults.

73. The product is not "one love" as it promotes because it does not judge equitably or provide the resources for those that need it the most to succeed and close the achievement gap. Particularly those from groups without the resources to hire sought-after choreographers, book valuable spaces, and connect with U.S.-based pioneers. Judges adopt regulations in attempts to ensure the "playing field is more level" by providing counter-bias devices, transparent criteria and regulations, and space for feedback.

74. Vincent, interview with the author.

75. *Official Rules and Regulations of Hip Hop International Crews of 5–8 Crewmembers—Amended for 2013*, 11. It is important to note that this is a separate issue than the process for discrepancies in the rules, their interpretation or translation, or competition procedures.

76. "The Palace Dance Studio," *thepalacedancestudio* (website), accessed November 22, 2013, http://www.thepalacedancestudio.co.nz/. The Royal Family is a dance group

that is made up of five different crews—ReQuest, Misfits, Sorority, Inlaws, and Bubblegum—that represents New Zealand at HHI.

77. OfficialHHI, "Brotherhood—Canada (Gold Medalist/Varsity) @HHI's 2013 World Hip Hop Dance Championship Finals," posted August 13, 2013, YouTube (online video), accessed January 7, 2013, http://www.youtube.com/watch?v=FFOvj kHORmw&list=PL00W8JtTRbyCKeWjp9qsyjQjFIGlOlzl; OfficialHHI, "Royal Family—New Zealand (Gold Medalist/MegaCrew) @ HHI's 2013 World Hip Hop Championship Finals," posted August 13, 2013, YouTube (online video), accessed January 7, 2013, http://www.youtube.com/watch?v=YofTe-mhB24&list=PL00W-8JtTRbyCKeWjp9qsyjQjFIGlOlzl; OfficialHHI, "EleColdXHot - Malaysia (Bronze Medalist /Adult) @ HHI's 2013 World Hip Hop Dance Championship Finals," posted August 13, 2013, YouTube (online video), accessed January 7, 2013, http://www.youtube.com/watch?v=lS9sE3fjkyw&feature=c4-overview-vl&list=PL00W-8JtTRbyCKeWjp9qsyjQjFIGlOlzl.

78. "Hip Hop International Partners with Paywall and iStreamPlanet to Bring the World Hip Hop Dance Championship to a Global Audience," August 8, 2013, *prweb*, accessed December 24, 2013, http://www.prweb.com/releases/hhi/2013/prweb11008940.htm.

79. In 2017, the company live-streamed the events free of charge.

80. During the 2013 HHI Championship semi-finals, Cirque du Soleil held auditions at the competition venue.

81. In 2011, the Philippine Allstars, for example, worked with folks at the University of Nevada, Las Vegas, to produce a dance concert. In 2012, The Crew and Quest Learning Center in Artesia, California held a Filipino language and cultural workshop that included choreography workshops. In 2013, ReQuest Crew produced a sold-out "Skulls and Crowns" at the Movement Lifestyle studio in Los Angeles, California.

82. Andrew Ross, *Nice Work If You Can Get It: Life and Labor in Precarious Times* (New York: New York University Press, 2009).

83. James F. English, *Economy of Prestige: Prizes, Awards, and the Circulation of Cultural Value* (Cambridge, MA: Harvard University Press, 2005), 9–11.

84. Xernan Alfonso was the first judge to represent the Philippines (2013) although there were Asian American and Pacific Islander judges before then.

85. Nesh Janiola, interview with the author, digital recording, Las Vegas, NV, August 8, 2014.

86. Ibid.

87. Ibid.

88. Ibid.

89. HHI Philippines, "Ian Levia Talks About HHI Philippines," YouTube (online video), posted October 11, 2013, accessed November 2, 2013, https://www.youtube.com/watch?v=4v75TTA7Pzc Link is no longer available per May 7, 2020.

Emphasizing the determination of Filipino dancers to seek knowledge about hip-hop, the HHI technical director stated, "Having completed this workshop in the Philippines, I was extremely pleased and extremely satisfied with several things. One of them had to do with the fact that we were under a typhoon warning, a typhoon watch. And in spite of all the rain, all of the flooding, and all of the potential hazards that could have prevented an individual from attending this workshop, every single person came out."

90. HHI Philippines, "Ian Levia Talks About HHI Philippines," YouTube (online video), posted October 11, 2013, accessed November 2, 2013, https://www.youtube.com/ watch?v=4v75TTA7Pzc Link is no longer available per May 7, 2020.

91. "Competitiveness Rankings," *World Economic Forum*, accessed June 1, 2016, http:// reports.weforum.org/global-competitiveness-report-2015-2016/competitiveness-rankings/.

92. Philip "Adrum" Pamintuan, interview with the author, digital recording, Quezon City, Philippines, August 15, 2011.

93. Christina Zanfagna, "The Multiringed Cosmos of Krumping/Hip-Hop Dance at the Intersections of Battle, Media, and Spirit," in *Ballroom, Boogie, Shimmy Sham, Shake: A Social and Popular Dance Reader*, ed. Julie Malnig (Urbana: University of Illinois Press, 2009), 337–353.

94. Ibid.

95. Tiongson, *Filipinos Represent*, 50–51.

96. Ibid., 51–52.

Chapter 5

1. SM stands for ShoeMart and EDSA is short for Epifanio de los Santos Avenue.

2. Jason Cruz, interview with the author, digital recording, Manila, Philippines, April 27, 2011. Krump is understood to have begun in the early 1990s in South Los Angeles by Tommy the Clown. The krumper in "Pinays Rise" is an unknown member of KrumPinoy. The hip-hop dancer and bgirl are Madelle Paltu-ob and Bgirl Beatch, respectively.

3. Bgirl Beatch, interview with the author, digital recording, Manila, Philippines, May 25, 2011.

4. Anna "Lollipop" Sanchez, interview with the author, digital recording, Banning, California, February 12, 2013. As noted earlier, Wacking and Punking are known as feminine dance forms that emerged in the early 1970s amidst the Los Angeles clubs and practiced by gay, Black, and Latino communities.

5. See Mina Roces, "Gender, Nation and the Politics of Dress in Twentieth-Century Philippines," in *The Politics of Dress in Asia and the Americas*, eds. Mina Roces and Louise Edwards (Portland, OR: Sussex Academic Press, 2007), 19–41.

6. An undercut is an asymmetrical haircut where one side of the head is shaved and the other side is left long.

7. Chelo A., email message to author, April 24, 2019.

8. Monteras also directed *Respeto* (2017), a rap and poetry drama that won six awards at Cinemalaya Philippine Independent Film Festival, including Best Film.

9. Soledad S. Reyes, "From Darna to ZsaZsa Zaturnnah: Desire and Fantasy," in *From Darna to ZsaZsa Zaturnnah: Desire and Fantasy: Essays on Literature and Popular Culture*, ed. Soledad S. Reyes (Pasig City, Philippines: Anvil Publishing, 2009), 2–34.

10. Ibid.

11. Ibid., 18.

12. Ibid., 16–17. Reyes's reading is productive here: "Darna probably became a symbol of empowerment, an objective real-life women suffragettes were fighting for as early as the 1930s in Philippine society. With her death-defying feats, her awesome ability to soar into the sky searching for her enemies, her tremendous strength always deployed for the good of the helpless victims, her compassion and love for her family, Darna spelled freedom and power in the dark days of the 1950s. She was just so different from a long line of weeping and persecuted heroines in numerous novels who, in the face of injustice and violence, found recourse only in tears. With Darna, the landscape became brighter, and the possibility of effecting changes in the body politic became a reality."

13. bell hooks, "Eating the Other: Desire and Resistance," in *Media and Cultural Studies: Keywords*, eds. Meenakshi Gigi Durham and Douglas M. Kellner (Maldwell, MA: Wiley-Blackwell Publishing, 2006).

14. hooks, "Eating the Other," 376.

15. R.Z. Ordoñez, "Mail-Order Brides: An Emerging Community," in *Filipino Americans: Transformation and Identity*, ed. Maria P. Root (Thousand Oaks, CA: Sage, 1997), 121–142; Lucy Mae San Pablo Burns, "Your Terno's Draggin': Fashioning Filipino American Performance," *Women & Performance: A Journal of Feminist Theory* 21, no. 2 (2011): 199–217.

16. Commission on Filipinos Overseas, "Public Advisory: Mail Order Spouse Scheme in China," June 25, 2018, accessed April 5, 2019, https://cfo.gov.ph/public-advisory-mail-order-spouse-scheme-in-china/.

17. Jonathan M. Hicap, "Filipina Mail Order Brides Vulnerable to Abuse," *Korea Times*, October 11, 2009, accessed April 5, 2019, https://www.koreatimes.co.kr/www/news/nation/2009/10/211_53320.html.

18. Commission on Filipinos Overseas, "Primer on Republic Act 10906 or The Anti-Mail Order Spouse Act of 2016," accessed April 5, 2019, https://www.cfo.gov.ph/images/pdf/2017/Primer-on-R.A.-10906.pdf.

19. Negrito is also a term used in regard to Blackface bufo theater in Cuba. See Jill Lane, *Blackface Cuba, 1840–1895* (Philadelphia: University of Pennsylvania Press, 2005). I thank Elizabeth Schwall for leading me to this connection.

20. Hortense J. Spillers, "Mama's Baby, Papa's Maybe: An American Grammar Book," *Diacritics* 17, no. 2 (1987): 65–81; Roderick A. Ferguson, *Aberrations in Black: Toward a Queer of Color Critique* (Minneapolis: University of Minnesota Press, 2004).

21. Spillers, "Mama's Baby," 67.

22. Ta-Nehisi Coates, "In Defense of a Loaded Word," *New York Times*, nytimes.com, November 23, 2013, accessed April 28, 2018, https://www.nytimes.com/2013/11/24/opinion/sunday/coates-in-defense-of-a-loaded-word.html.

23. Raymond Bonner, *Waltzing with a Dictator: The Marcoses and the Making of American Policy* (New York: Times Books, 1987).

24. Diaz, interview.

25. To kendeng one also places their arms straight out in front of their torso.

26. See Nikko Dizon, "Villar bet frowns on NP's scantily-clad 'Kembot Girls'—INQUIRER.net, Philippine News for Filipinos," *Inquirer.net*, February 24, 2010, accessed March 13, 2013, http://newsinfo.inquirer.net /breakingnews/nation/view/20100224-255176/Villar-bet-frowns-on-NPs-scantily-clad-Kembot-Girls . Shembot (2010) is a song that was popularized by the female girl group, Sexbomb girls on *Eat Bulaga*, also built around shaking one's hips left and right in various phrases with fists up by one's chest. Kembot (2007) dance popularized on *ASAP* that is more co-ed, but still focuses on jumping, switching, and swaying one's hips.

27. Gottschild, *The Black Dancing Body*, 2003.

28. Diaz, interview.

29. Ibid. Diaz said this phrase when talking about promo girls gyrating.

30. Chelo A., email message to author, April 24, 2019. See "Philippines Blasts 'Filipina' Entry in Greek Dictionary," *Kyodo News*, August 10, 1998, accessed April 26, 2019, https://www.thefreelibrary.com/Philippines+blasts+%27Filipina%27+entry+in+Greek+dictionary.-a053000395.

31. Chelo A., "Pinays Rise," Love, Life, and D'Light, 2011, compact disc, 3:35.

32. In our conversation, Chelo revealed to me that she once witnessed a dancing traffic cop in Makati who inspired her to include this figure in her song. The lyric, "We ruling nations," refers to the Philippines' then-president Gloria Macapagal Arroyo.

33. Catherine Ceniza Choy, *Empire of Care: Nursing and Migration in Filipino American History* (Durham, NC: Duke University Press, 2003).

34. Martin V. Manalansan, IV, "Queer Intersections: Sexuality and Gender in Migration Studies," *International Migration Review* 40, no. 1 (2006): 224–249. Manalansan writes on the ways particular literature on globalization and migration tends to reproduce narratives of normative sexuality.

35. PAEF provides invaluable direction and assistance to the Philippine and U.S. Fulbright scholarship program, by which my project was supported. PAEF is also known as the Fulbright Commission for the Philippines.

36. Ambassador Thomas commented upon my project and acknowledged that he was no stranger to hip-hop. I was slightly startled when he gave me and my project a shout out in his opening remarks, openly implicating my work within the arms of U.S. diplomacy.

37. For more discussion around hip-hop and the Obama administration see Travis L. Gosa, "Not Another Remix: How Obama Became the First Hip-Hop President," *Journal of Popular Music Studies* 22, no. 4 (2010): 389–415; Christopher K. Jackson, *"Let's Move": Examining First Lady Michelle Obama's Childhood Obesity Campaign in the News Media* (PhD diss., Howard University, 2012).

38. Secretary of State Hillary Clinton, "Opening Remarks on the President's FY 2009 War Supplemental Request," Testimony before the Senate Appropriations Committee, Washington, DC, April 30, 2009, accessed December 4, 2012, http://www.state.gov/secretary/rm/2009a/04/122463.htm.

39. Nafees Asya Syed, "The 3 D's of Foreign Affairs," *Harvard Political Review*, September 17, 2010, accessed December 4, 2012, http://hpronline.org/arusa/the-3ds-of-foreign-affairs/.

40. Secretary of State Clinton, "Opening Remarks on the President's FY 2009 War Supplemental Request."

41. "Ex-Military Leaders Bemoan Trump's Proposed Cuts to Diplomacy," *National Public Radio Morning Edition*, March 12, 2019, accessed April 6 2019, https://www.npr.org/2019/03/12/702464526/ex-military-leaders-bemoan-trumps-proposed-cuts-to-diplomacy.

42. Joseph S. Nye, *Soft Power: The Means to Success in World Politics* (New York: Public Affairs, 2004); Captain Nathan Finney, "A Culture of Inclusion: Defense, Diplomacy, and Development as a Modern American Foreign Policy," *Small Wars Journal*, accessed December 4, 2012, http://smallwarsjournal.com/jrnl/art/a-culture-of-inclusion. Soft power is the use of appeal and attraction through culture, values, and policy, rather than coercion or hard power.

43. The events were not limited to the Block but also took place in other parts of the SM North EDSA complex. There was a weekend-long job fair in the Annex.

44. The clinic took place from 10:30 am until 4:30 pm and the age groups were 6–9 years old, 10–12 years old, and 13–16 years old.

45. Obama Administration, "National Security Strategy," Whitehouse.gov, accessed December 4, 2012, http://www.whitehouse.gov/sites/default/files/rss_viewer/national_security_strategy.pdf.

46. Rebecca Cowell, "Representin' the Dirty North: The Indigenisation of Rap Music and Hip-Hop Culture in Beijing," 2010, accessed May 8, 2013, http://www.rockinchina.com/wiki/images/Representin_%28online_version%29.pdf; Angela Diane Steele, "Zai Beijing: A Cultural Study of Hip Hop," Stanford University, 2006, accessed May 8, 2013, http://www.rockinchina.com/w/Category:Research.

47. Lenny Lipton, *Foundations of the Stereoscopic Cinema: A Study in Depth* (New York: Van Nostrand Reinhold Publishing, 1982), 54–59. Pyschological cues include aerial/horizontal perspective, retinal image size, interposition, light and shade, textual gradient, motion parallax. Physiological cues include accommodation, convergence, and disparity.

48. Ray Zone, *3-D Revolution: The History of Modern Stereoscopic Cinema* (Lexington: University Press of Kentucky, 2012), 387–390. More recently, in the second half of the aughts, 3D film received another resurgence as movies like James Cameron's *Avatar*, a Native/white colonizer battle, earned record-breaking box office success. *Avatar* received praise by prominent film critics like Roger Ebert and Kenneth Turan and became a cultural phenomenon. Zone writes of papal denunciation, media programs that mock the film, people depressed about the inability to visit Pandora, and activists in Gaza dressing as the film's native Na'vi characters to parallel the Palestinian claims to land and livelihood.

49. Dana Stevens, "The Great 3-D Debate," Slate.com, August 26, 2010, accessed December 4, 2012, http://www.slate.com/articles/news_and_politics/dialogues/features/2010/the_great_3d_debate/if_3ds_just_a_fad_will_we_miss_it_when_its_gone.html.

50. Sam Biddle, "Lucasfilm Kills 3D Star Wars Re-Releases After Realizing It's Horrible and Everyone Hates It," *Gizmodo.com*, January 28, 2013, accessed May 3, 2013, http://gizmodo.com/5979671/lucasfilm-kills-3d-star-wars-prequels-after-realizing-its-horrible-and-everyone-hates-it.

51. Dan Engber, "The Great 3-D Debate: The Best Was Still To Come—Slate Magazine," Slate.com, August 27, 2010, accessed December 4, 2012, http://www.slate.com/ articles/news_and_politics/dialogues/features/2010/the   _great_3d_debate/the_ bestwas_still_to_come.html.

52. See Ray Zone, *Stereoscopic Cinema and the Origins of 3-D Film, 1838–1952* (Lexington: University Press of Kentucky, 2007); Lipton, *Foundations of the Stereoscopic Cinema*, 61. The technological breakthrough of 3D, according to Ray Zone's comprehensive historical treatment, finds its roots in 1838 with Sir Charles Wheatstone's stereoscopic film, which later found new life in the first color 3D feature film, Arch Oboler's *Bwana Devil* (1952), a tale of white male heroism in Africa. According to 3D expert Lenny Lipton, "The mind transforms two essentially planar retinal images into a single view of the world with stereoscopic or three-dimensional depth. In whatever way this happens, slight horizontal shifts of left and right image elements on the retinas are turned into the useful and pleasurable sensation, stereopsis."

53. Engber, "The Great 3-D Debate"; Dan Engber, "3-D Movies Like Monsters vs. Aliens Hurt Your Eyes. They Always Have, and They Always Will," Slate.com, April 2, 2009, accessed December 4, 2012, https://slate.com/technology/2009/04/3-d-movies-like-monsters-vs-aliens-hurt-your-eyes-they-always-have-and-they-always-will.html; Samantha Rollins, "Why Is the Hobbit Making Some Moviegoers Sick?" *The Week*, December 12, 2012, accessed December 4, 2012, http://theweek.com/article/index/ 237247/why-isnbspthe-hobbit-making-some-moviegoers-sick.

Despite its economic successes, however, cinematic 3D has also received criticism. In April 2009, Engber argued that the fundamental technology behind the 3D revival hasn't changed one bit since the early 1950s and the reason that it failed to successfully take over 2-D cinema was that 3D hurts our eyes: "We're still using polarized light to send offset images to each eye, and that means we're still subjecting filmgoers to a stimulus that has been shown in the laboratory to cause headache, nausea, and eyestrain." In general, 3D has been shot down by film critics as gimmicky, cheesy, excessive, and flatly applied.

54. There were, however, military aspects to the cultural performances in the form of the Navy Band.

55. Armand Galang, Jeannette I. Andrade, and Tonette Orejas, "Police Caught Napping While Vandals Attack US Embassy," *Global Nation Inquirer*, April 17, 2012, accessed December 4, 2012, http://globalnation.inquirer.net/33481 / police-caught-napping-while-vandals-attack-us-embassy.

56. Chelo Aestrid and Michelle Salazar, "The Road to the 2008 World Hip Hop Dance Championships," 4. This derision seems to have lessened from 2009 to 2019.

57. "Poverty Incidence Unchanged, as of First Semester 2012 NSCB," Philippine Statistics Authority, April 23, 2013, accessed April 11, 2019, https://psa.gov.ph/poverty-press-releases/pr/2012%201st%20Sem%20Poverty%20Incidence.

58. Joseph G. Schloss, *Foundation: B-Boys, B-Girls, and Hip-Hop Culture in New York* (New York: Oxford University Press, 2009).

59. Perlita M. Frago, Sharon M. Quinsaat, and Verna Dinah Viajar, eds., *Philippine Civil Society and the Globalization Discourse* (Quezon City, Philippines: Third World Studies Center, 2004).

60. In addition to the Philippine Allstars, who won gold medals in 2006 and 2008, the Philippine winners' circle includes The Crew (2012), A-Team (2015), and UPeepz (2016, 2017). These last three groups all have ties to the University of the Philippines.

61. M. G. Piety, "Wait Until White People Need Affirmative Action! The Rhetoric of Entitlement," Counterpunch.org, March 27, 2013, accessed March 28, 2013, http://www.counterpunch.org/2013/03/27/the-rhetoric-of-entitlement/.

62. Engber, "The Great 3-D Debate."

Glossary

These definitions are meant to assist readers. Please note that definitions are partial and their accuracy depends on community and context.

Astig: A playful slang expression used to described a subject, dance, or performance that is cool and hard. The word derives from "tigas" [hard] with "as" and "tig" transposed.

Bakla: An effeminate Filipino who desires a masculine man. In dance, bakla refers to softness of execution or female orientated dance styles that males choose to dance.

Battle: An event where individuals and crews of dancers compete for social capital.

Breaking/Bboying/Bgirling: An expressive dance culture that is associated with origins in 1970s Bronx gang culture, Africanist aesthetic, break beats, and the cypher. Elements include toprocking, buns, floorwork, the get down, power moves, and freezes. In the Philippines, breaking began in the 1980s out of exchanges between local Filipino people and the children of Americans stationed in U.S. military bases.

Budots: The social dance form popularized in Southern Philippines that blends indigenous dance, "loitering" culture, and techno music.

Burns: Physical insults in competitive modes of breaking.

Choreo dance: A term used to describe the culture of dance that grew in the 1990s out of California dance crews, garage sessions, cotillions and debuts, Air Band competitions, high school dance teams, afterschool programs, nightclub promotions, import car shows, dance studios, and dance competitions and showcases like Bodyrock. Choreo dance is inclusive of—but does not necessarily center—hip-hop dance forms and cultures.

Competition: A mode of hip-hop dance in which events organized by community leaders address weaknesses in the community.

Crew: A group of people with whom one trains, competes, and dances. Depending on contexts, one's crew might include family members, friends, classmates, and may involve recruitment, initiation rituals (i.e., getting "battled in"), or auditions. In Philippines contexts, crews often adopt educational and physical education lingo and categorize generations as "batches" and leaders as "coaches."

Cypher: A term that refers to the circular social space of breaking with parallels in African dance, religious rituals, and martial arts. The space is defined by improvisation, authenticity, and other dance forms.

Dance Challenges: Social dances that involve a contest or competitive element in the process of their circulation and popularization.

Dance Crazes: Dances like the Dougie, Gangnam Style, and Ocho-ocho that experience a discrete period of heightened popularization usually tied to a specific artist's single.

Dance Drain: Human capital flight shaped by Philippine state labor brokerage, discursive construction of heroic migrant, and exodus of the Philippine dance community members for family- and employment-based purposes.

Dancehall: The genre and dance culture associated with Jamaican social dances. Sometimes includes Carnival dance from Trinidad, Barbados, and other Caribbean cultures. This term is different from that used in reference to 1920s and 1930s U.S. taxi dancehalls, involving dances like Lindy Hop and the Charleston.

Flavor: A term that refers to a dancer's style and originality as demonstrated by their dancing, clothing, character portrayed on the dance floor, and identity off the floor.

Floorwork: A component of breaking that usually takes place after the get down and incorporates movements close to the ground like footwork, slides, and sweeps, and which the arms, back, shoulders, and head may be supporting the dancer's body weight.

Foundation: A term that refers to the set of basic principles and ideas surrounding a dance form like breaking. These might include basic movements, the history of the form, and the teaching philosophies and cultural conventions around the dance.

Freeze: In breaking, freezes are static, finale, and signature moves that counter toprocking and floorwork and demonstrate core and arm strength, balance, and control over one's momentum. Typically named after the shape or floor–body contact—chair freeze, L-kick, hollowback, and head bridge—freezes in crew competitions serve as individual highlights juxtaposed against uniform group choreography.

Get Down: In breaking, get downs are transitional moves between high and upright dancing and low, floor dancing. Sometimes called "go downs" or "drops", get downs can add drama like diving worms and coin drops or quickness like thigh hooks and knee drops. In crew competitions, get downs add to the choreography's performance value by the criterion of Staging and subcategory of Level Changes.

Hip-Hop Dance: General term used to refer to a set of separate yet overlapping dance cultures including but not limited to locking, popping, breaking, party dances, dance crazes, and music video choreography.

HHI: Hip-Hop International, the largest international competition of hip-hop dance.

House Dance: The genre and culture of dance associated with the house music scene with origins in Chicago and New York clubs in the 1970s and involving fast-paced upright footwork, loose posturing, connecting spiritually with the music, and body grooving. Movements include jacking, lofting, and various continuous combinations of skates, shuffles, and steps. In the Filipino context, "padyak" [stomp] refers to House dance culture movement.

Kembot: A co-ed type of Filipino social dance, or novelty dance, involving cute hip-swaying side-to-side movement. The kembot was popularized on noontime television program, *ASAP*, in 2007 and focuses on jumping, switching, and swaying one's hips.

Kendeng-kendeng: A feminine type of Filipino social dance consisting of hips moving side-to-side, bouncing, or shaking, and one also places their arms straight out in front of their torso. Popularized on noontime television programs by spokesmodels and William Revillame on *Will Time Big Time* (2011).

Krump: A dance culture with origins in South Los Angeles by Tommy the Clown in the 1990s. Krump grew in popularity in Manila in the 2000s with groups like KrumPinoy. The dance movement involves hard, masculine aggression and jabs, punches, balance points, bounce, stomps, and spirituality.

Locking: A dance culture that involves creative improvisation with movements like locks, jumps, and points, popularized in the Philippines through television shows like *Penthouse 7* in the 1970s. In the U.S., locking is recognized as part of the bold, colorful West Coast funk culture grounded in the Civil Rights Era struggles of minoritarian communities for equality in voting, employment, housing, and education, as well as the shift toward increased visibility of racial minorities in television programming like Don Cornelius's *Soul Train*.

New Jack (swing): The genre of dance associated with the 1980s and early 1990s, upright high energy, large gestures, upright bounce, loose and bright colored clothing, and discrete party dances often named after popular culture like the Roger Rabbit, Robocop, Cabbage Patch, and Kid-n-Play. This style of Black social dance crossed over to mainstream by musicians, television, and films that defined and showcased New Jack Swing music like Janet Jackson, Bobby Brown, *House Party, Fresh Prince of Bel Air*, and *In Living Color*. Attributed to Teddy Riley and Guy, New Jack Swing music, blended hip-hop beats, pop medleys, contemporary R&B vocal styles, and samplings.

Nosebleed: A performative euphemism that expresses the subject's psycho-social discomfort toward an English speaker based on the subject's level of English fluency. The act subverts social hierarchies along racial, sexual, and class borders, and was popularized by Ruffa Mae Quinto and Ethel Booba in Philippine entertainment industry in the late 1990s and early 2000s.

Overseas Filipino Workers (OFWs) Overseas Filipino Workers are migrant workers who emigrate temporarily from the Philippines to labor abroad, often separate from family members in the Philippines, and send remittances back. The Philippine government brokers OFW labor (10% of the country's population) and markets them as modern national heroes. They range in type of employment spanning domestic workers, hospitality, entertainment, healthcare, seafarers, construction, and engineers.

Petisyonado: A type of migrant Filipino that leaves through family preference visas, or family sponsorship or petition, to reunite with relatives who have already emigrated through employment to the United States; also known as "chain migration."

Pilipino Culture Night (PCN): An annual theatrical show in Filipino student communities that reaffirms diasporic identity through performance of traditional folk dances, music, songs, attire, and drama.

Popping: An improvisational upright dance culture whose movements involve rapid muscle contractions of the chest, forearms, and legs—called pops—and take inspiration from popular culture and cartoon animations. The dance typically involves clear linear aesthetics, segmented rotations at joints, and lack of emotion. In the Philippines, popping was first popularized by Filipinos and Filipino Americans in the early 1980s in the television competition *Dance10* and in Northern California with Boogaloo Sam, who created Boogalooing and Popping in the 1970s.

Power Moves: In breaking, power moves like windmills, crickets, halos, flares, and headspins, display flexibility, endurance, and one's ability to build and control momentum and command space.

Sayaw: The Filipino word for dance following the nationalization movement.

Shembot: A 2010 dance that involves shaking one's hips left and right in various phrases with fists up by one's chest. It is also a song that was popularized by the female girl group, Sexbomb girls on *Eat Bulaga*.

Stepping: A form of dance with origins in Black Greek Letter Organizations, or African American fraternities and sororities. It is sometimes associated with Strolling and Saluting.

Street Dance: A term that refers to social dances inclusive of hip-hop dances and other dances sometimes appearing at hip-hop dance events like Krump, L.A. Style, Ladies' Hip-Hop, Waackin', Vogueing, general Hip-Hop, Swag, House, Dancehall, Tutting, and Jazz funk. In the Philippines, street dance abounds in universities, noon-time television shows, and local barangay gatherings and competitions and is not to be confused with processional festival folk dances also known as street dance.

Swag: A style of hip-hop choreography marked by low-effort, high-attitude, loose, hip-centric, and smooth movements. Swag is normativized as heterosexual and masculine.

Toprocking: In breaking, the upright, groovy, improvisational dancing that introduces the dancer's character and style. Toprocking draws from a variety of sources including but not limited to Brooklyn uprocking, James Brown, salsa, African and Native American dance, martial arts films, and sets the tone for their dance.

Traditional Dance: A term used by PCN and HHI organizers that changes depending on contexts but often refers to folkloric, "national", and "cultural" dances like Tinikling, Haka, Irish dance, capoeira, Bollywood, and salsa.

Tricking: Gymnastic, acrobatic martial arts flips, kicks, and spins.

Tutting: A style of dance typically upright that emphasizes hand, finger, and forearm angles, shapes, and boxes, often associated with popping, boogaloo, and Boogaloo Tut (Mark Benson).

Urban Dance: A term that refers to a wide range of street dances and hip-hop dances, but often in studio, educational, collegiate dance teams, and industrial communities rather than hip-hop cultural contexts.

Vogueing (Ballroom): The culture and form of dance that draws from fashion house culture and emphasizes realness, dips, catwalk, duckwalk, hands, floorwork, and spins. Originated in Harlem ballrooms by queer communities of color as resistance to social exclusion, and increased in popularity in Manila with choreographers like Xyza Ragunjun (House of Mizrahi) in the 2010s.

Waacking: The form of dance that emphasizes wrist rolls, arm extensions, facial framing and dramatics. In the 1970s, queer communities of color in Los Angeles clubs originated dances as resistance to social exclusion drawing from Hollywood film glamour, cartoons, Bruce Lee, and live action TV shows like Batman. Early artists include Viktor Manoel, Tinker Toy, Archie Burnett, and Tyrone Proctor. Waacking resurged in popularity due to Brian Green in New York City in the 2000s and in Manila by choreographers like Eldin Christian Lao (Afrodite) in the 2010s.

Bibliography

"About." Ballet Philippines. Accessed March 27, 2013. https://ballet.ph/about/

"About Us << Hip Hop International." Hip Hop International. Accessed September 1, 2013. http://www.hiphopinternational.com/about-us/

"About Vibe." vibedance.com. Accessed July 22, 2017. https://www.vibedancecomp.com/about-vibe/

Aestrid, Chelo. "Pinays Rise." Track 1 on *Love, Life & D'Light*. Muse-ic Productions & Homeworkz, 2011, compact disc.

Aestrid, Chelo, and Michelle Salazar. "The Road to the 2008 World Hip Hop Dance Championships." 1–50.

Agoncillo, Teodoro A., and Oscar M. Alfonso. *A Short History of the Filipino People*. Manila: University of the Philippines, 1960.

Aidi, Hishaam. "The Grand (Hip-Hop) Chessboard: Race, Rap and Raison D'État." *Middle East Report*, no. 260 (2011): 25–39.

Alburo, Alice Jade A. "Box Populi: A Socio-Cultural Study of the Filipino American Balikbayan Box." Master's thesis, Memorial University of Newfoundland, 2002.

Alcedo, Patrick. "Sacred Camp: Transgendering Faith in a Philippine Festival." *Journal of Southeast Asian Studies* 38, no. 1 (2007): 107–132. doi:10.1017/S0022463406000956. https://www-cambridge-org.proxy.cc.uic.edu/core/article/sacred-camp-transgendering-faith-in-a-philippine-festival/521DB2110D94D4993EB35EA9A6CE9137.

Alejandro, Reynaldo, and Amanda Abad Santos-Gana. *Sayaw: Philippine Dance*. Edited by Ramon Obusan. Manila and Pasig City: National Book Store and Anvil Publishing, 2002. http://philippineperformance-repository.upd.edu.ph.proxy.cc.uic.edu/370/.

Alim, H. S., A. Ibrahim, and A. Pennycook, eds. (2008). *Global Linguistic Flows: Hip Hop Cultures, Youth Identities, and the Politics of Language*. New York: Routledge.

Alves, Anna Maria. "In Search of 'Meaning': Collective Memory and Identity in Pilipino Cultural Night at UCLA." Master's thesis, University of California–Los Angeles, 1999.

Ancheta, Angelo N. "Pilipino Americans, Foreigner Discrimination, and the Lines of Racial Sovereignty." In *Positively No Filipinos Allowed: Building Communities and Discourse*, edited by Antonio Tiongson Jr., Edgardo V. Gutierrez, and Ricardo V. Gutierrez, 90–110. Philadelphia: Temple University Press, 2006.

Appadurai, Arjun. "Disjuncture and Difference in the Global Cultural Economy." *Theory, Culture & Society* 7, no. 2–3 (June 1, 1990): 295–310. doi:10.1177/026327690007002017. https://doi-org.proxy.cc.uic.edu/10.1177/026327690007002017.

Aquiler, Sharlene, and Kelly Dumlao. *Re: Collections Culture*. University of California–Berkeley, 1999.

Aquino, Francisca Reyes. *Fundamental Dance Steps and Music*. Manila, 1957.

Aquino, Francisca Reyes. *Philippine Folk Dances: Volumes 1–6*. Manila, 1966.

Arnaldo, Constancio R. *Embodying Scales of Filipina/o American Sporting Life: Transnational Sporting Cultures and Practices in the Filipina/o Diaspora*. University of Illinois, Urbana-Champaign, 2015.

Arnold, Eric K. "From Azeeem to Zion-I: The Evolution of Global Consciousness in Bay Area Hip-Hop." In *The Vinyl Ain't Final: Hip Hop and the Globalization of Black Popular Culture*, edited by Dipannita Basu and Sidney J. Lemelle, 71–84. Ann Arbor, MI: Pluto Press, 2006.

Asian Americans Break Stereotypes through Urban Dance. Directed by Elizabeth Lee, 2013.

Associated Press. "Filipino Inmates' Video is a 'Thriller' on the Web." *NPR*. August 9, 2007a. https://www.npr.org/templates/story/story.php?storyId=12643181.

Associated Press. "Smooth Criminals? Inmates Dance on YouTube: Millions Watched Filipino Prisoners' Version of Michael Jackson's 'Thriller.'" Accessed April 28, 2008. http://www.nbcnews.com/id/20203606/ns/world_news-asia_pacific/t/smooth-criminals-inmates-dance-youtube/.

Austin, J. L. *How to Do Things with Words*. Cambridge, MA: Harvard University Press, 1962.

Balance, Christine Bacareza. *Tropical Renditions: Making Musical Scenes in Filipino America*. Durham, NC: Duke University Press Books, 2016. http://proxy.cc.uic.edu/login?url=http://search.ebscohost.com.proxy.cc.uic.edu/login.aspx?direct=true&db=nlebk&AN=1221339.

Balce, Nerissa S. "Filipino Bodies, Lynching, and the Language of Empire." In *Positively No Filipinos Allowed: Building Communities and Discourse*, edited by Antonio T. Tiongson, Edgardo V. Gutierrez, and Ricardo Valencia Gutierrez, 43–60. Philadelphia: Temple University Press, 2006.

Baldoz, Rick. *The Third Asiatic Invasion: Migration and Empire in Filipino America, 1898–1946*. New York: New York University Press, 2011.

Baldwin, Brooke. "The Cakewalk: A Study in Stereotype and Reality." *Journal of Social History* 15, no. 2 (1981): 205–218. http://www.jstor.org.proxy.cc.uic.edu/stable/3787107.

Balfour, M., ed. *Theatre in Prison*. Bristol: Intellect Books Ltd., 2004a.

Baluyut, Pearlie Rose S. *Institutions and Icons of Patronage: Arts and Culture in the Philippines during the Marcos Years, 1965–1986*. Manila: University of Santo Tomas Publishing House, 2012.

Bascara, Victor. *Model-Minority Imperialism*. Minneapolis: University of Minnesota Press, 2006.

Basu, Dipannita, and Sidney J. Lemelle. "Introduction." In *The Vinyl Ain't Final: Hip Hop and the Globalization of Black Popular Culture*, edited by Dipannita Basu and Sidney J. Lemelle, 1–15. Ann Arbor, MI: Pluto Press, 2006.

Bautista, Mark Angelo Delacruz. "Through the Mic: Stories of Filipino American Emcee Crews in the Margins." Master's thesis, San Francisco State University, 2005.

Bautista, Michelle. "Philippine Cultural Nights." In *Fil-Am: The Filipino American Experience*, edited by Alfred A. Yuson. Makati City: Publico, Inc., 1999.

"Bayanihan—The Philippine National Folk Dance Company." 2003. Bayanihannational danceco.ph. Accessed April 10, 2013. http://bayanihannationaldanceco.ph/milestones1959_1958.html.

Bhabha, Homi. *The Location of Culture*. London: Routledge, 1994.

Bhabha, Homi. "Of Mimicry and Man: The Ambivalence of Colonial Discourse." *October* 28 (Spring 1984): 125–133. doi:10.2307/778467. http://www.jstor.org.proxy.cc.uic.edu/stable/778467.

Biddle, Sam. "Lucasfilm Kills 3D Star Wars Re-Releases After Realizing it's Horrible and Everyone Hates It." Accessed May 3, 2013. https://gizmodo.com/lucasfilm-kills-3d-star-wars-re-releases-after-realizin-5979671.

Bischoff, Stephen Alan. "Filipino Americans and Polyculturalism in Seattle, WA, through Hip Hop and Spoken Word." Master's thesis, Washington State University, 2008.

Black-ish. "Pilot." Season 1, Episode 1, performed by Anthony Anderson. Disney-ABC domestic television, 2014.

Bonner, Raymond. *Waltzing with a Dictator: The Marcoses and the Making of American Policy.* New York: Times Books, 1987.

Bowen, Deirdre. *Race in Colorblind Spaces.* 2009.

Bowen, William G., and Derek Curtis Bok. *The Shape of the River: Long-Term Consequences of Considering Race in College and University Admissions.* Princeton: Princeton University Press, 1998.

Brooks, Siobhan, and Thomas Conroy. "Hip-Hop Culture in a Global Context: Interdisciplinary and Cross-Categorical Investigation." *American Behavioral Scientist* 55, no. 1 (2011): 3–8. doi:10.1177/0002764210381723. https://doi-org.proxy. cc.uic.edu/10.1177/0002764210381723.

Buenavista, Tracy Lachica. *Movement from the Middle: Pilipina/o 1.5-Generation College Student Access, Retention, and Resistance.* PhD diss., University of California–Los Angeles, 2007.

Buenavista, Tracy Lachica, Uma M. Jayakumar, and Kimberly Misa-Escalante. "Contextualizing Asian American Education through Critical Race Theory: An Example of U.S. Pilipino College Student Experiences." *New Directions for Institutional Research* no. 142 (2009): 69–81. doi:10.1002/ir.297. http://proxy.cc.uic.edu/ login?url=http://search.ebscohost.com.proxy.cc.uic.edu/login.aspx?direct=true&db= ehh&AN=41136722.

Bureau of Public Affairs Office of the Spokesman. "U.S. Department of State and the John F. Kennedy Center for the Performing Arts to Present Hip-Hop Artists from Argentina, Lebanon, the Palestinian Territories, the Philippines, and Vietnam on the Millennium Stage." Accessed May 4, 2019. 2009–2017. state.gov/r/pa/prs/ps/2009/july/126510. htm.

Burns, Lucy Mae San Pablo. *Puro Arte: Filipinos on the Stages of Empire.* New York: NYU Press, 2012.

Burns, Lucy Mae San Pablo. "Your Terno's Draggin'": Fashioning Filipino American Performance." *Women & Performance: A Journal of Feminist Theory* 21, no. 2 (2011): 199–217.

Butler, Judith. *Gender Trouble.* Routledge, 2002.

Candelario, Rosemary. *Flowers Cracking Concrete: Eiko and Koma's Asian/American Choreographies.* Middletown, CT: Wesleyan University Press, 2016.

Cannell, Fenella. *Power and Intimacy in the Christian Philippines.* New York: Cambridge University Press, 1999.

Casasola, Elizabeth Almario, and Lorraine Rodrigo Marasigan. *Pakinggan Mo Ako (Program).* University of California–Berkeley, 2000.

"Cast—Prison Dancer." Accessed December 6, 2017. www.prisondancer.com/live/cast.

Castro, Christi-Anne. *Musical Renderings of the Philippine Nation.* New York: Oxford University Press, 2011.

"Cebu Dancing Inmates in 'This Is It' DVD Launch." Accessed January 21, 2017. https:// news.abs-cbn.com/entertainment/01/19/10/cebu-dancing-inmates-it-dvd-launch.

Cebu Provincial Detention and Rehabilitation Center Inmates, *Thriller* (Original Upload). Directed by Byron Garcia. 2007.

Census 2000. US Census Bureau.

Certeau, Michel De. *The Practice of Everyday Life*. Translated by Steven Rendall. Berkeley: University of California Press, 1984.

Chang, Jeff. *Can't Stop, Won't Stop: A History of the Hip-Hop Generation*. 1st ed. New York: St. Martin's Press, 2005.

Chang, Jeff. "It's a Hip-Hop World." *Foreign Policy*, no. 163 (2007): 58–65. http://www.jstor.org.proxy.cc.uic.edu/stable/25462232.

Charry, Eric. "A Capsule History of African Rap." In *Hip-Hop Africa: New African Music in a Globalizing World*, edited by Eric Charry, 1–26. Bloomington: Indiana University Press, 2012.

Chin, Christina B., Meera E. Deo, Faustina M. DuCrocs, Jenny J. Lee, Noriko Milman, and Nancy W. Yuen. "Tokens on the Small Screen: Asian Americans and Pacific Islanders in Prime Time and Streaming Television." Accessed October 12, 2017. www.aapisontv.com/uploads/3/8/1/3/38136681/aapisontv.2017.pdf.

Choy, Catherine Ceniza. *Empire of Care: Nursing and Migration in Filipino American History*. Durham, NC: Duke University Press, 2003.

Chu, Daniel, and Barbara Rowes. "Michael Peters Is the Hot New Choreographer Who Makes Dancers Out of Video's Rock Stars." Accessed December 6, 2017. https://people.com/archive/michael-peters-is-the-hot-new-choreographer-who-makes-dancers-out-of-videos-rock-stars-vol-21-no-25/.

Clinton, Hillary. Secretary of State. "Opening Remarks on the President's FY 2009 War Supplemental Request." Washington, DC, 2009. //2009–2017.state.gov/secretary/20092013clinton/rm/2009a/04/122463.htm.

Coates, Ta-Nehisi. "In Defense of a Loaded Word." *New York Times*. November 23, 2013. https://www.nytimes.com/2013/11/24/opinion/sunday/coates-in-defense-of-a-loaded-word.html.

Commission on Filipino Overseas. "Primer on Republic Act 10906 Or the Anti-Mail Order Spouse Act of 2016." Accessed April 5, 2019. https://www.cfo.gov.ph/images/pdf/2017/Primer-on-R.A.-10906.pdf.

Commission on Filipinos Overseas. "Public Advisory: Mail Order Spouse Scheme in China." Accessed April 5, 2019. http://www.cfo.gov.ph/images/CFO_NEWS/2018/advisory_-china_mob-rev2.png.

"Competitiveness Rankings." Accessed June 1, 2016. www.reports.weforum.org/global-competitveness-report-2015–2016/competitiveness-rankings/.

Condry, Ian. *Hip-Hop Japan: Rap and the Paths of Cultural Globalization*. Durham, NC: Duke University Press, 2006.

Constantino, Renato. *The Philippines: A Past Revisited*. Vol. 1. Quezon City, Philippines: Tala Pub. Services, 1975.

Coonan, Clifford. "YouTube's Dancing Prisoners Denied New License to Thrill." Accessed January 9, 2011.

Corpus, Rina Angela P. *Defiant Daughters Dancing: Three Independent Women Dance*. Quezon City: University of the Philippines Press, 2007.

Cowell, Rebecca. "Representin' the Dirty North: The Indigenisation of Rap Music and Hip-Hop Culture in Beijing." Accessed May 8, 2013. http://www.rockinchina.com/wiki/images/Representin_%28online_version%29.pdf.

Crenshaw, Kimberlé. *Critical Race Theory: The Key Writings that Formed the Movement*, edited by Cornel West, Kimberlé Crenshaw, Neil Gotanda, Gary Peller, and Kendall Thomas. New York: New Press, 1995.

Croft, Clare. "Dance Returns to American Cultural Diplomacy: The U.S. State Department's 2003 Dance Residency Program and its After Effects." *Dance Research Journal* 45, no. 1 (2013): 23–39. http://www.jstor.org.proxy.cc.uic.edu/stable/23524724.

Croft, Clare. *Dancers as Diplomats: American Choreography in Cultural Exchange*. New York: Oxford University Press, 2015.

Curaming, Rommel A. "Filipinos as Malay: Historicising an Identity." *Melayu: Politics, Poetics and Paradoxes of Race* (2011): 241–274.

Dave, Shilpa S. *Indian Accents: Brown Voice and Racial Performance in American Television and Film*. Urbana: University of Illinois Press, 2013. http://ebookcentral.proquest.com. proxy.cc.uic.edu/lib/uic/detail.action?docID=3414229.

David, Eric John Ramos. *Brown Skin, White Minds: Filipino/American Postcolonial Psychology*. Information Age Publishing Inc., 2013.

Davis, Angela Y. "Foreword: A World Unto itself: Multiple Invisibilities of Imprisonment." In *Behind the Razor Wire: Portrait of a Contemporary American Prison System*, edited by Michael Jacobson-Hardy. New York: New York University Press, 1999.

Davis, Angela Yvonne, and David Barsamian. *The Prison Industrial Complex*. San Francisco: AK Press, 1999.

de Dios, Aurora. "Japayuki-San: Filipinas at Risk." In *Filipino Women Overseas Contract Workers ... at What Cost?*, edited by Mary R. Palma-Beltran and Aurora Javate de Dios, 39–58. Manila: Goodwill Trading Co., 1992.

De Leon, Matwiran. *Home (Program)*. University of California–Berkeley, 2000.

de Leon, Sunshine L. "'Amerasians' in the Philippines Fight for Recognition." Accessed January 8, 2018. https://www.cnn.com/2012/03/03/world/asia/philippines-forgotten-children/index.html.

DeFrantz, Thomas J. "The Black Beat made Visible: Hip Hop Dance and Body Power." In *Of the Presence of the Body: Essays on Dance and Performance Theory*, edited by Andres Lepecki, 64–81. Middletown, CT: Wesleyan University Press, 2004.

DeFrantz, Thomas F. "Bone-Breaking, Black Social Dance, and Queer Corporeal Orature." *Black Scholar* 46, no. 1 (2016): 66–74. doi:10.1080/00064246.2015.1119624. http:// proxy.cc.uic.edu/login?url=http://search.ebscohost.com.proxy.cc.uic.edu/login.aspx? direct=true&db=ehh&AN=113275733.

DeFrantz, Thomas F. *Dancing Revelations: Alvin Ailey's Embodiment of African American Culture*. Oxford: Oxford University Press, Inc., 2004.

DeFrantz, Thomas F. "Hip-Hop V.2.0." In *Black Performance Theory*, edited by Thomas J. DeFrantz and Anita Gonzalez, 233–242. Durham, NC: Duke University Press, 2014.

DeFrantz, Thomas F. "Unchecked Popularity: Neoliberal Circulation of Lack Social Dance." In *Neoliberalism and Global Theatres: Performance Permutations*, edited by Lara D. Nielsen and Patricia Ybarra, 128–140. New York: Palgrave Macmillian, 2012.

Delgado, Richard. *The Rodrigo Chronicles: Conversations about America and Race*. New York: New York University Press, 1995.

Delgado, Richard, and Jean Stefancic. *Critical Race Theory: An Introduction*, edited by Jean Stefancic and Angela P. Harris. 3rd ed. New York: New York University Press, 2017.

Devitt, Rachel. "Lost in Translation: Filipino Diaspora(s), Postcolonial Hip Hop, and the Problems of Keeping It Real for the 'Contentless' Black Eyed Peas." *Asian Music* 39, no. 1 (2008): 108–134. http://www.jstor.org.proxy.cc.uic.edu/stable/25501577.

Dolan, Jill. "Geographies of Learning: Theatre Studies, Performance, and the 'Performative.'" *Theatre Journal* 45, no. 4 (1993): 417–441. doi:10.2307/3209014. http:// www.jstor.org.proxy.cc.uic.edu/stable/3209014.

Dolan, Jill. "Performance, Utopia, and the 'Utopian Performative.'" *Theatre Journal* 53, no. 3 (2001): 455–479. https://search-proquest-com.proxy.cc.uic.edu/docview/2063572.

Dougherty, Jill. "International Hip-Hop Artists Find their Roots in U.S." Accessed June 4, 2014. https://www.cnn.com/2009/SHOWBIZ/07/30/international.hip.hop/index.html?eref=rss_us.

Dungca, Enrico. "The Forgotten Amerasians." Accessed January 8, 2018. https://opencitymag.aaww.org/the-forgotten-amerasians/.

Durham, Aisha S. *Home with Hip Hop Feminism: Performances in Communication and Culture.* New York: Peter Lang Publishing, Inc., 2010.

Encinas-Franco, Jean. "Overseas Filipino Workers (OFWs) as Heroes: Discursive Origins of the 'Bagong Bayani' in the Era of Labor Export." *Humanities Diliman* 12, no. 2 (2015): 56–78.

Engber, Daniel. "The Best was Still to Come." Accessed December 4, 2012. https://slate.com/news-and-politics/2010/08/the-best-was-still-to-come.html.

Engber, Daniel. "The Problem with 3-D: It Hurts Your Eyes. Always Has, Always Will." Accessed December 4, 2012. https://slate.com/technology/2009/04/3-d-movies-like-monsters-vs-aliens-hurt-your-eyes-they-always-have-and-they-always-will.html.

English, James F. *The Economy of Prestige: Prizes, Awards, and the Circulation of Cultural Value.* Cambridge, MA: Harvard University Press, 2005.

Enriquez, Elizabeth L. *Appropriation of Colonial Broadcasting: A History of Early Radio in the Philippines, 1922–1946.* Quezon City: University of the Philippines Press, 2008.

Espenshade, Thomas J., and Chang Y. Chung. "The Opportunity Cost of Admission Preferences at Elite Universities." *Social Science Quarterly* 86, no. 2 (2005): 293–305. doi:10.1111/j.0038–4941.2005.00303.x. https://doi-org.proxy.cc.uic.edu/10.1111/j.0038–4941.2005.00303.x.

"Ex-Military Leaders Bemoan Trump's Proposed Cuts to Diplomacy." Accessed April 6, 2019. https://www.npr.org/2019/03/12/702464526/ex-military-leaders-bemoan-trumps-proposed-cuts-to-diplomacy.

"Expansion Before and After." *Boston Sunday Globe*, 1899, reprinted in Ignacio et al., *The Forbidden Book*, 80.

Fajardo, Kale Bantigue. *Filipino Crosscurrents: Oceanographies of Seafaring, Masculinities, and Globalization.* Minneapolis: University of Minnesota Press, 2011.

Ferguson, Roderick A. *Aberrations in Black: Toward a Queer of Color Critique.* Minneapolis: University of Minnesota Press, 2004.

Fernandes, Sujatha. *Close to the Edge: In Search of the Global Hip Hop Generation.* New York: Verso Books, 2011.

Ferran, Lee. "Boogie Behind Bars: Inmates Dance Days Away." Accessed January 9, 2011. https://abcnews.go.com/icaught/story?id=3415920.

"Filipino Pride in Hong Kong Disneyland." *Manila Times.* 2015. Accessed April 4, 2019. www.manilatimes.net/filipino-pride-in-hong-kong-disneyland/166282/.

The Filipino Prisoners Who Dance to Thriller. Directed by Journeyman Pictures. 2007.

Finney, Captain N. "A Culture of Inclusion: Defense, Diplomacy, and Development as a Modern American Foreign Policy." Accessed December 4, 2012. https://smallwarsjournal.com/jrnl/art/a-culture-of-inclusion.

Fleetwood, Nicole R. *Troubling Vision: Performance, Visuality, and Blackness.* Chicago: University of Chicago Press, 2011. http://ebookcentral.proquest.com.proxy.cc.uic.edu/lib/uic/detail.action?docID=713793.

Foreman, P. Gabrielle, et al. *Writing about Slavery/Teaching about Slavery: This Might Help.*

Foster, Susan Leigh. "Choreographies of Gender." *Signs: Journal of Women in Culture and Society* 24, no. 1 (1998): 1–33.

Foster, Susan L. "Choreographies of Writing." Accessed April 29, 2019. http://danceworkbook.pcah.us/susan-foster/choreographies-of-writing.html.

Foster, Susan Leigh. "Introduction." In *Corporealities: Dancing Knowledge, Culture and Power*, edited by Susan Leigh Foster, 1995.

Foster, Susan Leigh. *Reading Dancing: Bodies and Subjects in Contemporary American Dance*. Berkeley: University of California Press, 1986.

Foucault, Michel. *Discipline and Punish: The Birth of the Prison*. Translated by Sheridan, Alan. New York: Pantheon, 1977.

Frago, Perlita M., Sharon M. Quinsaat, and Verna Dinah Q. Viajar. *Philippine Civil Society and the Globalization Discourse*. Quezon City, Philippines: Third World Studies Center, 2004.

Francia, Luis H. *History of the Philippines: From Indios Bravos to Filipinos*. New York: Abrams, 2010.

Gaerlan, Barbara S. "In the Court of the Sultan: Orientalism, Nationalism, and Modernity in Philippine and Filipino American Dance." *Journal of Asian American Studies* 2, no. 3 (1999): 251–287. doi:10.1353/jaas.1999.0022. https://muse-jhu-edu.proxy.cc.uic.edu/article/14559.

Galang, Armand, Jeannette I. Andrade, and Tonette Orejas. "Police Caught Napping While Vandals Attack US Embassy." Accessed December 4, 2012. https://globalnation.inquirer.net/33481/police-caught-napping-while-vandals-attack-us-embassy.

Garcia, Ana "Rokafella." "Herstory." In *We B*Girls*, edited by Martha Cooper and Nika Kramer, 58–59. New York: powerHouse Books, 2005.

Garcia, J. Neil C. *Philippine Gay Culture: Binabae to Bakla, Silahis to MSM*. 2nd ed. Quezon City: University of the Philippines Press, 2008.

Gatewood Jr., Willard B. *Black Americans and the White Man's Burden, 1898–1903*. Urbana: University of Illinois Press, 1975.

George, Nelson. *Hip Hop America*. London: Penguin, 1998.

Gilmore, Ruth Wilson. *Golden Gulag: Prisons, Surplus, Crisis, and Opposition in Globalizing California*. Vol. 21. Berkeley: University of California Press, 2007.

Glissant, Edouard. *Caribbean Discourse: Selected Essays*. Charlottesville: University of Virginia Press, 1989.

Gonzaga, Peterson. "Nine Dance Crews from PHL to Join 'Olympics' of Hip-Hop Competitions in US." Accessed December 23, 2013. https://www.gmanetwork.com/news/story/265345/news/pinoyabroad/nine-dance-crews-from-phl-to-join-olympics-of-hip-hop-competitions-in-us/.

Gonzalves, Theodore S. *The Day the Dancers Stayed: Performing in the Filipino/American Diaspora*. Philadelphia: Temple University Press, 2009.

Gonzalves, Theodore S. "The Day the Dancers Stayed: On Pilipino Culture Nights." In *Filipino Americans: Transformation and Identity*, edited by Maria P. P. Root, 173–176. Thousand Oaks, CA: Sage Publications, 1997.

Gonzalves, Theodore S. *When the Lights Go Down: Performing in the Filipina/o Diaspora, 1934–1998*. PhD diss., University of California–Irvine, 2001.

Gosa, Travis L. "Not Another Remix: How Obama Became the First Hip-Hop President." *Journal of Popular Music Studies* 22, no. 4 (2010): 389–415. doi:10.1111/j.1533–1598.2010.01252.x. https://doi-org.proxy.cc.uic.edu/10.1111/j.1533–1598.2010.01252.x.

Gottschild, Brenda Dixon. *The Black Dancing Body: A Geography from Coon to Cool*. 1st ed. New York: Palgrave Macmillan, 2003.

Gottschild, Brenda Dixon. *Digging the Africanist Presence in American Performance: Dance and Other Contexts*. Westport, CT: Greenwood Press, 1996.

Grefalda, Remé A., Lucy M. Burns, Theodore S. Gonzalves, and Anna M. Alves. *Towards a Cultural Community: Identity, Education, and Stewardship in Filipino American Performing Art*. First Fruits, 2003.

Guevarra, Anna Romina. *Marketing Dreams, Manufacturing Heroes: The Transnational Labor Brokering of Filipino Workers*. New Brunswick, NJ: Rutgers University Press, 2009.

Harrison, Anthony Kwame. "Post-Colonial Consciousness, Knowledge Production, and Identity Inscription within Filipino-American Hip-Hop Music." *Perfect Beat* 13, no. 1 (2012): 29–48.

Hartlep, N. D., and B. J. Porfilio, eds. *Killing The Model Minority Stereotype: Asian American Counterstories and Complicity*, 395. Charlotte, NC: Information Age Publishing, Inc., 2015.

Harvey, David. *A Brief History of Neoliberalism*. New York: Oxford University Press, 2005.

Headland, Janet, Thomas N. Headland, and Ray T. Uehara. "Agta Demographic Database: Chronicle of a Hunter-Gatherer Community in Transition." Accessed November 11, 2017. http://web.archive.org/web/20120112055716/http://www.sil.org/silepubs/abstract.asp?id=49227.

Hess, Mickey. "Introduction: 'It's Only Right to Represent Where I'm from': Local and Regional Hip Hop Scenes in the United States." In *Hip Hop in America: A Regional Guide*, edited by Mickey Hess, 7–29. Santa Barbara, CA: Greenwood Press, 2009.

Hicap, Jonathan M. "Filipina Mail-Order Brides Vulnerable to Abuse." Accessed April 5, 2019. http://www.koreatimes.co.kr/www/nation/2019/10/211_53320.html.

Higgins, James R., Tony Gogo, and Peekaboo Frenke. "Editorial: The Terms Or Dances Locking, Roboting and 'PopLocking' Valid." Accessed March 27, 2013. https://www.lockerlegends.net/?page_id=359.

"Hip Hop International Partners with Paywall and iStreamPlanet to Bring the World Hip Hop Dance Championship to a Global Audience." *PRWeb*. 2013. Accessed December 24, 2013. https://www.prweb.com/releases/hhi/2013/prweb11008940.htm.

"Hip Hop International Rules and Regulations Workshop." 2013b.

Hong, Grace Kyungwon, and Roderick A. Ferguson. "Introduction." In *Strange Affinities: The Gender and Sexual Politics of Comparative Racialization*, edited by Grace Kyungwon Hong and Roderick A. Ferguson, 1–24. Durham, NC: Duke University Press, 2011.

hooks, bell. "Eating the Other: Desire and Resistance." In *Black Looks: Race and Representation*, 21–40. Boston: South End Press, 1992.

hooks, bell. "Eating the Other: Desire and Resistance." In *Media and Cultural Studies: Keywords*, edited by Meenakshi Gigi Durham and Douglas M. Kellner, 366–380. Wiley-Maldwell, MA: Blackwell Publishing, 2006.

Horton, Akesha. "Hip-Hop as a Global Passport: Examining Global Citizenship and Digital Literacies through Hip-Hop Culture." In *Hip-Hop(e): The Cultural Practice and Critical Pedagogy of International Hip-Hop*, edited by Brad J. Porfilio and Michael J. Viola, 249–269. New York: Peter Lang Publishing, 2012.

"How Philippines Can Reverse 'Brain Drain.'" *ABS-CBN News*. 2015. Accessed October 30, 2017. https://news.abs-cbn.com/business/03/11/15/how-philippines-can-reverse-brain-drain.

Hsu, Madeline Yuan-Yin. *The Good Immigrants: How the Yellow Peril Became the Model Minority*. Princeton, NJ: Princeton University Press, 2015.

Hunte, Tracie. "Prisoners' Dance: Celebration Or Human Rights Violation? Viral Video of Inmates Performing 'Thriller' Video Generates Concerns, Along with Clicks." Accessed January 16, 2011. www.abcnews.go.com/icaught/story?id=3478161&page=1.

"Ian Levia Talks about HHI Philippines." Directed by HHI Philippines. 2013.

Ignacio, Abe, Enrique de la Cruz, Jorge Emmanuel, and Helen Toribio. *The Forbidden Book: The Philippine-American War in Political Cartoons*. 1st ed. San Francisco: T'Boli, 2004.

Ileto, Reynaldo Clemeña. *Pasyon and Revolution: Popular Movements in the Philippines, 1840–1910*. Quezon City, Philippines: Ateneo de Manila University Press, 1979.

Isaac, Allan Punzalan. *American Tropics: Articulating Filipino America*. Minneapolis: University of Minnesota Press, 2006.

Israel, Dale G. "Gwen Wants Donations to CPDRC Inmates Accounted For." Accessed January 9, 2011. https://globalnation.inquirer.net/cebudailynews/news/view/20100213-252934/Gwen-wantsdonations-to-CPDRC-inmates-accounted-for.

Ito, Mizuko. "Technologies of the Childhood Imagination: Yugioh, Media Mixes, and Everyday Cultural Production." In *Network Netplay: Structures of Participation in Digital Culture*, edited by Joe Karaganis and Natalie Jeremijenko, 88–111. Durham, NC: Duke University Press, 2005.

Iwabuchi, Koichi. *Recentering Globalization: Popular Culture and Japanese Transnationalism*. Durham, NC: Duke University Press, 2002.

Iyer, Pico. *Video Night in Kathmandu and Other Reports from the Not-so-Far East*. New York: Knopf Doubleday Publishing Group, 1988.

Jackson, Christopher K. *'Let's Move': Examining First Lady Michelle Obama's Childhood Obesity Campaign in the News Media*. Howard University, 2012.

Jeffries, Michael P. *Thug Life: Race, Gender, and the Meaning of Hip-Hop*. Chicago: University of Chicago Press, 2011.

Jenkins, Henry. *Convergence Culture: Where Old and New Media Collide*. New York: New York University Press, 2006.

Johnson, Henry Theodore. "The Black's Man Burden," *Voice of Missions*.

Johnson, Mark. *Beauty and Power: Transgendering and Cultural Transformation in the Southern Philippines*. Bloomsbury Academic, 1997.

Johnson, Mark. "Diasporic Dreams, Middle-Class Moralities and Migrant Domestic Workers among Muslim Filipinos in Saudi Arabia." *Asia Pacific Journal of Anthropology* 11, no. 3–4 (2010): 428–448.

Joyce, Richard E., and Chester L. Hunt. "Philippine Nurses and the Brain Drain." *Social Science & Medicine* 16, no. 12 (1982): 1223–1233.

Julie Malnig. "'But How Do I Write about Dance?': Thoughts on Teaching Criticism." *Dance Research Journal* 41, no. 2 (Winter 2009): 91–95. https://muse-jhu-edu.proxy.cc.uic.edu/article/364655.

Karabel, Jerome. "Freshman Admissions at Berkeley: A Policy for the 1990s and Beyond. A Report of the Committee on Admissions and Enrollment, Berkeley Division, Academic Senate." University of California–Berkeley, 1989.

Karapatan: Alliance for the Advancement of People's Rights. "The 2007 Year-End Report on the Human Rights Situation in the Philippines." Accessed August 31, 2011. https://www.karapatan.org/2007-HR-report.

Kato, M. T. *From Kung Fu to Hip Hop: Globalization, Revolution, and Popular Culture*. Albany: State University of New York Press, 2007.

Kelley, Robin D. G. "Foreword." In *The Vinyl Ain't Final: Hip Hop and the Globalization of Black Popular Culture*, edited by Dipannita Basu and Sidney J. Lemelle, 11–17. Ann Arbor, MI: Pluto Press, 2006.

Kim, Ju Yon. *The Racial Mundane: Asian American Performance and the Embodied Everyday*. New York: New York University Press, 2015.

Kim, Suk-Young. *Illusive Utopia: Theater, Film, and Everyday Performance in North Korea*. Ann Arbor: University of Michigan Press, 2010.

Kowal, Rebekah J. *How to Do Things with Dance: Performing Change in Postwar America*. Middletown, CT: Wesleyan University Press, 2010. http://ebookcentral.proquest.com.proxy.cc.uic.edu/lib/uic/detail.action?docID=805032.

Kramer, Paul A. *The Blood of Government: Race, Empire, the United States, and the Philippines*. Chapel Hill, NC: University of North Carolina Press, 2006.

Kwan, SanSan. *Kinesthetic City: Dance and Movement in Chinese Urban Spaces*. New York: Oxford University Press, 2012.

Lane, Jill. *Blackface Cuba, 1840–1895*. Philadelphia: University of Pennsylvania Press, 2005.

Lapan, Tovin. "Olympic Spirit Permeates Las Vegas in World Hip-Hop Dance Championship." Accessed December 23, 2013. https://lasvegassun.com/news/2012/aug/02/olympic-spirit-permeates-las-vegas-world-hip-hop-d/.

Larasti, Rachimi Diyah. *The Dance That Makes You Vanish: Cultural Reconstruction in Post-Genocide Indonesia*. Minneapolis: University of Minnesota Press, 2013.

Lawrence, Charles, and Mari J. Matsuda. *We Won't Go Back: Making the Case for Affirmative Action*. Boston: Houghton Mifflin, 1997.

Lepecki, André. *Exhausting Dance: Performance and the Politics of Movement*. New York: Routledge, 2006.

Lim, Eng-Beng. *Brown Boys and Rice Queens: Spellbinding Performance in the Asias*. New York: New York University Press, 2014.

Lim, Kim. "58 and Still 'Locking.'" Accessed December 29, 2013. https://www.asiaone.com/print/News/Latest%2BNews/Sports/Story/A1Story20130621-431205.html.

Lipton, Lenny. *Foundations of the Stereoscopic Cinema: A Study in Depth*. Van Nostrand Reinhold, 1982.

Liu, John M., Paul M. Ong, and Carolyn Rosenstein. "Dual Chain Migration: Post-1965 Filipino Immigration to the United States." *International Migration Review* 25, no. 3 (1991): 487–513.

Lowe, Lisa. "Foreword." In *Positively No Filipinos Allowed: Building Communities and Discourse*, edited by Antonio Tiongson Jr., Edgardo V. Gutierrez, and Ricardo V. Gutierrez, 7–9. Philadelphia: Temple University Press, 2006.

Lozier, Frank. *Tagasalaysay/Storyteller: A Story of Culture (Program)*. University of California–Berkeley, 1998.

MacDonald, Michael B. "Hip-Hop Citizens: Local Hip-Hop and the Production of Democratic Grassroots Change in Alberta." In *Hip-Hop(e): The Cultural Practice and Critical Pedagogy of International Hip-Hop*, edited by Brad J. Portilio and Michael J. Viola, 95–109. New York: Peter Lang Publishing, 2012.

Maceda, Teresita Gimenez. "Problematizing the Popular: The Dynamics of Pinoy Pop(ular) Music and Popular Protest Music." *Inter-Asia Cultural Studies* 8, no. 3 (2007): 390–413. doi:10.1080/14649370701393766. http://proxy.cc.uic.edu/login?url=http://search.ebscohost.com.proxy.cc.uic.edu/login.aspx?direct=true&db=a9h&AN=26419394.

Macharia, Keguro. "Queer Genealogies (Provisional Notes)." *Bully Bloggers* (2013): 150.

Madden, Mary. "The Audience for Online Video." Accessed April 12, 2019. https://www.pewresearch.org/internet/2007/07/25/the-audience-for-online-video/.

Rafael Magaña, Maurice. *Cartographies of Youth Resistance: Hip-Hop, Punk, and Urban Autonomy in Mexico.* Oakland, CA: University of California Press, 2020.

Magno, Alexander R. *Kasaysayan: The Story of the Filipino People.* Hong Kong: Asia Publishing Company Limited, 1998.

Mainwaring, Madison. "The Death of the American Dance Critic." Accessed November 7, 2015. https://www-theatlantic-com.proxy.cc.uic.edu/entertainment/archive/2015/08/american-dance-critic/399908/.

Maira, Sunaina. "Henna and Hip Hop: The Politics of Cultural Production and the Work of Cultural Studies." *Journal of Asian American Studies* 3, no. 3 (2000): 329–369. doi:10.1353/jaas.2000.0038. https://muse-jhu-edu.proxy.cc.uic.edu/article/14606.

Maira, Sunaina Marr. *Desis in the House; Indian American Youth Culture in New York City.* Philadelphia: Temple University Press, 2002.

Manalansan IV, Martin F. *Global Divas: Filipino Gay Men in the Diaspora.* Durham, NC: Duke University Press, 2003.

Manalansan IV, Martin F. "Queer Intersections: Sexuality and Gender in Migration Studies." *International Migration Review* 40, no. 1 (2006): 224–249. http://www.jstor.org.proxy.cc.uic.edu/stable/27645585.

Manlansan, Martin F. "Speaking of AIDS: Language and the Filipino 'Gay' Experience in America." In *Discrepant Histories: Translocal Essays on Filipino Cultures*, edited by Vicente L. Rafael, 193–223. Philadelphia: Temple University Press, 1995.

Manalansan IV, M. F., and A. F. Espiritu, eds. *Filipino Studies: Palimpsests of Nation and Diaspora*, 419. New York: New York University Press, 2016.

Marasigan, Cynthia L. *"Between the Devil and the Deep Sea": Ambivalence, Violence, and African American Soldiers in the Philippine-American War and Its Aftermath.* Ann Arbor: University of Michigan, 2010.

Marcelo, Sam L. "Start Small but Start Well: Alice Reyes and Ballet Philippines." Accessed March 27, 2013. http://www.bworldonline.com/content.php?section=Arts&Leisure&title=start-small-but-start-well-alice-reyes-and-ballet-philippines&id=89717.

Marcus, George E. "Ethnography in/of the World System: The Emergence of Multi-Sited Ethnography." *Annual Review of Anthropology* 24, no. 1 (1995): 95–117. http://www.jstor.org.proxy.cc.uic.edu/stable/2155931.

Marion, Jonathan S. *Ballroom: Culture and Costume in Competitive Dance.* London: Bloomsbury Publishing Plc, 2008.

Martin, Randy. "Overreading 'The Promised Land': Towards a Narrative of Context in Dance." In *Corporealities, Dancing Knowledge, Culture and Power*, edited by Susan Leigh Foster, 177–198. New York: Routledge, 1996.

Matsuda, Mari J. *Where Is Your Body? And Other Essays on Race, Gender, and the Law.* Boston: Beacon Press, 1996.

Mayol, Ador V. "No Commercial Deal for Inmates." Accessed January 9, 2011. https://globalnation.inquirer.net/cebudailynews/news/view/20100202-250835/No-commercial-deal-for-inmates.

McAlister, Elizabeth. "Slaves, Cannibals, and Infected Hyper-Whites: The Race and Religion of Zombies." *Anthropological Quarterly* 85, no. 2 (2012): 457–486. http://www.jstor.org.proxy.cc.uic.edu/stable/41857250.

McCall, Amanda, and Albertina Rizzo. *Hold My Gold: A White Girl's Guide to the Hip-Hop World*. New York: Simon and Schuster, 2005.

McCoy, Alfred W., and Francisco Antonio Scarano. *Colonial Crucible: Empire in the Making of the Modern American State*. Madison: University of Wisconsin Press, 2009.

McKay, Deirdre. *Global Filipinos: Migrants' Lives in the Virtual Village*. Bloomington: Indiana University Press, 2012.

McKay, Steven C. "Filipino Sea Men: Constructing Masculinities in an Ethnic Labour Niche." *Journal of Ethnic & Migration Studies* 33, no. 4 (May 2007): 617–633. doi:10.1080/13691830701265461. http://proxy.cc.uic.edu/login?url=http://search.ebscohost.com.proxy.cc.uic.edu/login.aspx?direct=true&db=a9h&AN=24504985.

Mendoza, S. Lily. *Between the Homeland and the Diaspora: The Politics of Theorizing Filipino and Filipino American Identities*. Manila: University of Santo Tomas Publishing House, 2006a.

Mendoza, S. Lily. "A Different Breed of Filipino Balikbayans: The Ambiguities of (Re-) Turning." In *Positively No Filipinos Allowed: Building Communities and Discourse*, edited by Antonio Tiongson Jr., Edgardo V. Gutierrez, and Ricardo V. Gutierrez, 199–214. Philadelphia: Temple University Press, 2006b.

Mendoza, Victor Román. *Metroimperial Intimacies: Fantasy, Racial-Sexual Governance, and the Philippines in U.S. Imperialism, 1899–1913*. Durham, NC: Duke University Press, 2015.

Mitchell, Gail. "Exclusive: How Michael Jackson's 'Thriller' Changed the Music Business." Accessed January 7, 2011. https://www-billboard-com.proxy.cc.uic.edu/articles/news/268212/exclusive-how-michael-jacksons-thriller-changed-the-music-business.

Mitchell, Michele. "'The Black Man's Burden': African Americans, Imperialism, and Notions of Racial Manhood 1890–1910." *International Review of Social History* 44, no. S7 (1999): 77–99. doi:10.1017/S0020859000115202. https://www-cambridge-org.proxy.cc.uic.edu/core/article/black-mans-burden-african-americans-imperialism-and-notions-of-racial-manhood-18901910/5379876505209B1354A0E94307933567.

Mitchell, Michele. *Righteous Propagation: African Americans and the Politics of Racial Destiny After Reconstruction*. Chapel Hill, NC: University of North Carolina Press, 2004.

Mitchell, Tony, ed. *Global Noise: Rap and Hip-Hop Outside the USA*. Music/Culture, 336. Middletown, CT: Wesleyan University Press, 2001a.

Mitchell, Tony, ed. "*Introduction: Another Root—Hip-Hop outside the USA*." In *Global Noise: Rap and Hip-Hop Outside the USA*, edited by T. Mitchell, 1–38. Middletown, CT: Wesleyan University Press, 2001b.

Montañez, Jannis T., Paulynn P. Sicam, and Carmelita G. Nuqui. *Pains and Gains: A Study of Overseas Performing Artists in Japan: From Pre-Departure to Reintegration*. Manila: Development Action for Women Network, 2003.

Morgan, Marcyliena. *The Hip-Hop Archive and the Globalization of Hip-Hop Language* 2012.

Mulder, Niels. "The Legitimacy of the Public Sphere and Culture of the New Urban Middle Class in the Philippines." In *Social Change in Southeast Asia*, edited by Johannes Dragsbaek Schmidt, Jacques Hersh, and Niels Fold, 98–113. New York: Addison Wesley Longman Limited, 1997.

Mullen, Bill. *Afro-Orientalism*. Minneapolis: University of Minnesota Press, 2004.

Muñoz, José Esteban. *Disidentifications: Queers of Color and the Performance of Politics*. Minneapolis: University of Minnesota Press, 1999.

Murphy, Jacqueline Shea. *People Have Never Stopped Dancing: Native American Modern Dance Histories*. Minneapolis: University of Minnesota Press, 2007. http://ebookcentral. proquest.com.proxy.cc.uic.edu/lib/uic/detail.action?docID=328377.

Naff, Katherine C. *Diversity in Education*: Center for California Studies, 1998.

Nagai, Tyrone. "An Interview with Joe Bataan: Torrance, California, February 14, 2013." *Kalfou: A Journal of Comparative and Relational Ethnic Studies* I, no. 2 (2014): 191–202. doi:10.15367/kf.v1i2.40. https://search-proquest-com.proxy.cc.uic.edu/docview/2017355489.

Nair, Ajay, and Murali Balaji. *Desi Rap: Hip-Hop and South Asian America*. Lanham, MD: Lexington Books, 2008.

Namiki, Kanami. "Hybridity and National Identity: Different Perspectives of Two National Folk Dance Companies in the Philippines." *Special Issue: Asian Studies* 47 (2011): 63–86.

Napallacan, Jhunnex. "Cebu's Dancing Inmates Hit It Big Again." Accessed January 15, 2011. https://newsinfo.inquirer.net/inquirerheadlines/nation/view/20100127–249691/Cebus-dancing-inmates-hit-it-big-again.

Napallacan, Jhunnex. "Inmates Do the 'Drill'—another YouTube Hit." Accessed January 15, 2011. https://globalnation.inquirer.net/cebudailynews/news/view/20100127–249702/Inmates-do-the-Drillanother-YouTube-hit.

Neate, Patrick. *Where You're At: Notes from the Frontline of a Hip-Hop Planet*. 1st ed. New York: Riverhead Books, 2004.

Ness, Sally A. "When Seeing Is Believing: The Changing Role of Visuality in a Philippine Dance." *Anthropological Quarterly* 68, no. 1 (1995): 1–13. doi:10.2307/3317460. http://www.jstor.org.proxy.cc.uic.edu/stable/3317460.

Ng, Stephanie. "Performing the 'Filipino' at the Crossroads: Filipino Bands in Five-Star Hotels Throughout Asia." *Modern Drama* 48, no. 2 (2005): 272–296. doi:10.3138/md.48.2.272. http://gateway.proquest.com.proxy.cc.uic.edu/openurl?ctx_ver=Z39.88–2003&xri:pqil:res_ver=0.2&res_id=xri:ilcs-us&rft_id=xri:ilcs:rec:abell:R03802176.

Novack, Cynthia Jean. *Sharing the Dance: Contact Improvisation and American Culture*. Madison: University of Wisconsin Press, 1990.

Nye, Joseph S. *Soft Power: The Means to Success in World Politics*. 1st ed. New York: Public Affairs, 2004.

Obama Administration. "National Security Strategy." Accessed December 4, 2012. www.whitehouse.gov/sites/default/files/rss_viewer/national_security_strategy.pdf.

Ocampo, Anthony C. "'Am I Really Asian?': Educational Experiences and Panethnic Identification among Second–Generation Filipino Americans." *Journal of Asian American Studies* 16, no. 3 (2013): 295–324.

Ocampo, Anthony C. "Gifts that Go the Distance: The Social Organization of Philippine in-Kind Remittances." 2009.

Ocampo, Anthony Christian. *The Latinos of Asia: How Filipino Americans Break the Rules of Race*. Palo Alto, CA: Stanford University Press, 2016.

OfficialHHI. *Brotherhood - Canada (Gold Medalist/Varsity) @HHI's 2013 World Hip Hop Dance Championship Finals*. 2013a.

OfficialHHI. *EleColdXHot - Malaysia (Bronze Medalist/Adult) Z2 HHI's 2013 World Hip Hop Dance Championship Finals*.

OfficialHHI. *Royal Family - New Zealand (GOld Medalist/MegaCrew) @ HHI's 2013 World Hip Hop Championship Finals*. 2013b.

Official Rules and Regulations of Hip Hop International Crews of 5–8 Crewmembers—Amended for 2013. Hip Hop International 2013.

OFW Statistics. Philippine Overseas Employment Agency (POEA).

Okamura, Jonathan Y. "Filipino American Access to Public Higher Education in California and Hawai'i." In *The "Other" Students: Filipino Americans, Education, and Power*, edited by Dina C. Maramba and Rick Bonus, 213–235. Charlotte, NC: Information Age Publishing, 2013.

Okamura, J. Y., and A. R. Agbayani. "Pamantasan: Filipino America NHigher Education." In *Filipino Americans: Transformation and Identity*, edited by Maria P. P. Root, 183–197. Thousand Oaks, CA: Sage Publications, 1997.

Omi, Michael, and Howard Winant. *Racial Formation in the United States: From the 1960s to the 1990s*, edited by Howard Winant. 2nd ed. New York: Routledge, 1994.

Ordoñez, R. Z. "Mail-Order Brides: An Emerging Community." In *Filipino Americans: Transformation and Identity*, edited by Maria P. P. Root, 121–142. Thousand Oaks, CA: Sage Publishing, 1997.

Osborne, Dana. "'Ay, Nosebleed!': Negotiating the Place of English in Contemporary Philippine Linguistic Life." *Language & Communication* 58 (2018): 118–133. doi:https://doi-org.proxy.cc.uic.edu/10.1016/j.langcom.2017.08.001. http://www.sciencedirect.com.proxy.cc.uic.edu/science/article/pii/S0271530917300125.

Osumare, Halifu. *The Africanist Aesthetic in Global Hip-Hop: Power Moves*. 1st ed. New York: Palgrave Macmillan, 2007.

Pabon, Jorge. "Physical Graffiti: The History of Hip Hop Dance." In *Total Chaos: The Art and Aesthetics of Hip Hop*, edited by Jeff Chang, 18–26. New York: Basic Books, 2006.

PacificRimVideoPress. *In-Depth Interview with Howard Schwartz of Hip Hop International*. 2011a.

PacificRimVideoPress. *In-Depth Interview with Howard Schwartz of Hip Hop International Part 2*. 2011b.

"The Palace Dance Studio." The Palace Dance Studio. Accessed November 22, 2013. www.thepalacedancestudio.co.nz.

Parker, Beth H. "Proposition 209 ~ A Decade Later: The Impacts of Prop 209 on Public Education, Employment and Contracting." Accessed September 23, 2011. https://www.equalrights.org/publications/reports/affirm/full209.asp.

Parrenas, Rhacel Salazar. "Trafficked—Filipino Hostesses in Tokyo's Nightlife Industry Symposium: Sex for Sale." *Yale Journal of Law and Feminism* 18, no. 1 (2006): 145–180. https://heinonline-org.proxy.cc.uic.edu/HOL/P?h=hein.journals/yjfem18&i=149 https://heinonline-org.proxy.cc.uic.edu/HOL/PrintRequest?handle=hein.journals/yjfem18&collection=0&div=9&id=149&print=section&sction=9.

Patajo-Legasto, Priscelina. "Introduction." In *Philippine Studies: Have We Gone Beyond St. Louis?*, edited by Priscelina Patajo-Legasto. Diliman: University of Philippine Press, 2008.

"Performing Artists Cultural Visitors Program." Explore the Arts. *The Kennedy Center*. 2009. Accessed June 4, 2014.

Perillo, J. Lorenzo. "Embodying Modernism: A Postcolonial Intervention Across Filipino Dance." *Amerasia Journal* 43, no. 2 (2017): 122–140. doi:10.17953/aj.43.2.122–140. https://doi-org.proxy.cc.uic.edu/10.17953/aj.43.2.122–140.

Perillo, J. Lorenzo. *Hip-Hop, Streetdance, and the Remaking of the Global Filipino*. University of California–Los Angeles, 2013a.

Perillo, J. Lorenzo. "Theorising Hip-Hop Dance in the Philippines: Blurring the Lines of Genre, Mode and Dimension." *International Journal of Asia-Pacific Studies* 9, no. 1 (2013b): 93–94.

Perkins, William Eric. "Youth's Global Village: An Epilogue." In *Droppin' Science: Critical Essays on Rap Music and Hip Hop Culture*, edited by William Eric Perkins, 258–274. Philadelphia: Temple University Press, 1996.

Philippine Allstars. "Beyond Hip Hop—Penthouse 7: The Grand Reunion." Accessed February 26, 2011. allstars2005.multiply.com/reviews/item/5.

The Philippine Exposition Souvenir Booklet. 1904. Accessed April 9, 2019. http://humanzoos.net/?page_id=175.

"Philippine Jailhouse Rocks to Thriller." BBC News. 2007. Accessed August 31, 2011. http://news.bbc.co.uk/2/hi/asia-pacific/6917318.stm.

Philippine Prisoners: Performing to Reform. Directed by Ortigas, Margo. 2007.

"Philippines Blasts 'Filipina' Entry in Greek Dictionary." Accessed April 26, 2019. https://www.thefreelibrary.com/Philippines+blasts+%27Filipina%27+entry+in+Greek+dictionary.-a053000395.

Picart, Caroline Joan S. *Critical Race Theory and Copyright in American Dance: Whiteness as Status Property*. New York: Palgrave Macmillan, 2013.

Piety, M. G. "The Rhetoric of Entitlement." Accessed March 28, 2013. https://www.counterpunch.org/2013/03/27/the-rhetoric-of-entitlement/.

Piquero-Ballescas, Maria Rosario. *Filipino Entertainers in Japan: An Introduction*. Quezon City, Philippines: Foundation for Nationalist Studies, 1992.

Ponce, Martin Joseph. *Beyond the Nation: Diasporic Filipino Literature and Queer Reading*. New York: New York University Press, 2012.

Poon, Oiyan A. "Haunted by Negative Action: Asian Americans, Admissions, and Race in the 'Color-Blind Era.'" *Asian American Policy Review* 18 (2009): 81–90. http://proxy.cc.uic.edu/login?url=http://search.ebscohost.com.proxy.cc.uic.edu/login.aspx?direct=true&db=a9h&AN=44571508.

Poon, OiYan, Dian Squire, Corinne Kodama, Ajani Byrd, Jason Chan, Lester Manzano, Sara Furr, and Devita Bishundat. "A Critical Review of the Model Minority Myth in Selected Literature on Asian Americans and Pacific Islanders in Higher Education." *Review of Educational Research* 86, no. 2 (2016): 469–502. doi:10.3102/0034654315612205. https://doi-org.proxy.cc.uic.edu/10.3102/0034654315612205.

Porfilio, Brad J., and Shannon M. Porfilio. "Hip-Hop Pedagogues: Youth as a Site of Critique, Resistance, and Transformation in France and in the Neoliberal Social World." In *Hip-Hop(e): The Cultural Practice and Critical Pedagogy of International Hip-Hop*, edited by Brad J. Porfilio and Michael J. Viola, 110–131. New York: Peter Land Publishing, 2012.

Porfilio, B. J., and M. J. Viola, *Hip-Hop(e): The Cultural Practice and Critical Pedagogy of International Hip-Hop*, 329. New York: Peter Lang Publishing, Inc., 2012.

Posadas, Barbara Mercedes. *The Filipino Americans*. Westport, CT: Greenwood Publishing Group, 1999.

"Poverty Incidence Unchanged, as of First Semester 2012 NSCB." Philippine Statistics Authority. 2013. Accessed April 11, 2019. https://psa.gov.ph/poverty-press-releases/pr/2012%201st%20Sem%20Poverty%20Incidence.

"Poverty to Glory: Philippine Allstars Empowering Youth Through Hip Hop." Ang Kalatas. 2012. Accessed April 29, 2019. http://kalatas.com.au.proxy.cc.uic.edu/2012/02/15/poverty-to-glory-philippine-allstars-empowering-youth-through-hip-hop/.

Prashad, Vijay. *Everybody Was Kung Fu Fighting: Afro-Asian Connections and the Myth of Cultural Purity.* Boston: Beacon Press, 2001.

Prashad, Vijay. *The Karma of Brown Folk.* Minneapolis: University of Minnesota Press, 2000.

Priagula, Citadelle B. "Examining Race-Conscious Remediation through the Filipino/a American Experience." *Asian Pac.Am.LJ* 15 (2009): 135.

"Prison Dancer." www.prisondancer.com.

prisondancer. "Prison Dancer Episode 1: Finally Free," YouTube video, 5:25. Posted March 6, 2013. Accessed June 27, 2017. https://www.youtube.com/watch?v=N-BRNI94LQQ

prisondancer. "Episode 1: Choice Point: Lola" YouTube video, 1:11. Posted March 6, 2012. Accessed June 27, 2017. http://www.youtube/watch?annotation_id=annotation_838234&feature=iv&src_vid=RQIG4IokRTI&v=uwGayqiMwH0

prisondancer. "Episode 1: Choice Point: Shakespeare," YouTube video, 1:20. Posted March 6, 2012. Accessed June 27, 2017. https://www.youtube.com/watch?annotation_id=annotation_330632&feature=iv&src_vid=KX8bMDzclA&v=RQIG4IokRTI

Pulgo, Izobelle T. "Warden: No Monthly Dances by Inmates." Accessed February 28, 2018. https://cebudailynews.inquirer.net/119816/warden-no-monthly-dances-inmates.

Rae, Issa. *The Misadventures of Awkward Black Girl.* Simon and Schuster, 2016.

Rafael, Vicente L. "Parricides, Bastards, and Counterrevolution: Reflections on the Philippine Centennial." In *Vestiges of War: The Philippine-American War and the Aftermath of an Imperial Dream, 1899–1999,* edited by Luis Francia and Angel Shaw, 361–375. New York: New York University Press, 2002.

Rafael, Vicente L. *White Love and Other Events in Filipino History.* Durham, NC: Duke University Press, 2000.

Raphael-Hernandez, H., and S. Steen, eds. *AfroAsian Encounters: Culture, History, Politics,* 342. New York: New York University Press, 2006.

Rajakumar, Mohanalakshmi. *Hip Hop Dance.* Santa Barbara, CA: Greenwood, 2012.

Reyes, José Edmundo Ocampo. "Fungibility, Dead Souls, and Filipino OCWs." *Kritika Kultura* no. 8 (May 7, 2008): 111–126. doi:10.3860/kk.v0i8.54. https://journals.ateneo.edu/ojs/index.php/kk/article/view/1529.

Reyes, Soledad S. "From Darna to ZsaZsa Zaturnnah: Desire and Fantasy." In *From Darna and ZsaZsa Zaturnnah: Desire and Fantasy: Essays on Literature and Popular Culture,* edited by Soledad S. Reyes, 2–34. Pasig City, Philippines: Anvil Publishing, 2009.

Rhee, Margaret. "In Search of My Robot: Race, Technology, and the Asian American Body." *Scholar & Feminist Online* 13, no. 3 (2016).

Rivera, Raquel Z. *New York Ricans from the Hip Hop Zone.* 1st ed. New York: Palgrave Macmillan, 2003.

Robertson, Roland. "Glocalization: Time-Space and Homogeneity-Heterogeneity." In *Global Modernities,* edited by Mike Featherstone, Scott Lash, and Roland Robertson, 25–44. Thousand Oaks, CA: Sage Publications, 1995.

Roces, Mina. "Gender, Nation and the Politics of Dress in Twentieth-Century Philippines." In *The Politics of Dress in Asia and the Americas,* edited by Mina Roces and Louise Edwards, 19–41. Portland: Sussex Academic Press, 2007.

Rodriguez, Dylan. "The Meaning of 'Disaster' Under the Dominance of White Life." In *What Lies Beneath: Katrina, Race, and the State of the Nation,* edited by the South End Press Collective, 133–156. Cambridge, MA: South End, 2007.

Rodriguez, Evelyn Ibatan. *Celebrating Debutantes and Quinceañeras: Coming of Age in American Ethnic Communities*. Philadelphia: Temple University Press, 2013.

Rodriguez, Robyn M. "Migrant Heroes: Nationalism, Citizenship and the Politics of Filipino Migrant Labor." *Citizenship Studies* 6, no. 3 (2002): 341–356.

Rodriguez, Robyn Magalit. *Migrants for Export: How the Philippine State Brokers Labor to the World*. Minneapolis: University of Minnesota Press, 2010. http://ebookcentral. proquest.com.proxy.cc.uic.edu/lib/uic/detail.action?docID=548071.

Rollins, Samantha. "Why Is the Hobbit Making some Moviegoers Sick?" Accessed December 12, 2012. https://theweek.com/articles/469863/why-isthe-hobbit-making-some-moviegoers-sick.

Root, M. P. P., ed. *Filipino Americans: Transformation and Identity*. Thousand Oaks, CA: Sage Publications, 1997.

Rosa, Jonathan. *Looking Like a Language, Sounding Like a Race: Raciolinguistic Ideologies and the Learning of Latinidad*. New York: Oxford University Press, 2018.

Ross, Andrew. *Nice Work if You Can Get It: Life and Labor in Precarious Times*. New York: New York University Press, 2009. http://ebookcentral.proquest.com.proxy. cc.uic.edu/lib/uic/detail.action?docID=865907.

Salazar, Michelle. "After 10 Days of being Uprooted." *And I Wander* (blog). 2011.

Salazar, Michelle. "If Life Throws You Apples . . . It Means I Didn't Eat It." *And I Wander* (blog). 2010.

Salman, Michael. "Nothing without Labor: Penology, Discipline, and Independence in the Philippines Under United States Rule." In *Discrepant Histories: Translocal Essays on Filipino Cultures*, edited by Vicente L. Rafael, 113–129. Philadelphia: Temple University Press, 1995.

Salva-Alueta, Suzzane. "Dancing Prisoners, Bonuses Mark Cebu's 438th Birthday." Accessed January 9, 2011. globalnation.inquirer.net/cebudailynews/news/view/ 20070807–81088/Dancing_prisoners,_bonuses_mark_Cebu%27s_438th_ birthday.

San Juan, Carolina de Leon. *From Vaudeville to Bodabil: Vaudeville in the Philippines*. PhD diss., University of California–Los Angeles, 2010.

San Juan Jr., E. "The 'Field' of Language: Articulating Class, Ethnicity, Race." In *From Globalization to National Liberation: Essays of Three Decades*, 56–79. Diliman: University of the Philippines Press, 2008.

San Juan Jr., E. *From Exile to Diaspora: Versions of the Filipino Experience in the United States*. Boulder, CO: Westview Press, 1998.

San Pablo Burns, Lucy Mae. "'Splendid Dancing': Filipino 'Exceptionalism' in Taxi Dancehalls." *Dance Research Journal* 40, no. 2 (2008): 23–40. http://www.jstor.org. proxy.cc.uic.edu/stable/20527607.

Santa Cruz Sentinel and Donna Jones. "Riots in 1930 Revealed Watsonville Racism: California Apologizes to Filipino Americans." Accessed April 19, 2019. http://www.santacruzsentinel.com/general-news/20110903/riots-in-1930-revealed-watsonville-racism-california-apologizes-to-filipino-americans.

Savigliano, Marta. *Tango and the Political Economy of Passion*. Boulder, CO: Westview Press, 1995.

Schloss, Joseph G. *Foundation: B-Boys, B-Girls and Hip-Hop Culture in New York*. New York: Oxford University Press, 2009.

Schlund-Vials, Cathy J. *War, Genocide, and Justice: Cambodian American Memory Work*. Minneapolis: University of Minnesota Press, 2012. http://ebookcentral.proquest.com. proxy.cc.uic.edu/lib/uic/detail.action?docID=1204678.

Scolieri, Paul. "Global/Mobile: Re-Orienting Dance and Migration Studies." Chap. 2 in *Choreographies of Migration: New Orientations for Dance and Migration Studies*, Vol. 40, edited by Paul Scolieri. 5–20, 2008.

"Scores and Results." Hip Hop International. Retrieved September 1, 2013, from <hiphopinternational.com/scores-results>

See, Sarita. "'An Open Wound': Colonial Melancholia and Contemporary Filipino/American Texts." In *Vestiges of War: The Philippine-American War and the Aftermath of an Imperial Dream, 1899–1999*, edited by Angel Shaw and Luis Francia, 376–400. New York: New York University Press, 2002.

See, Sarita Echavez. *The Decolonized Eye: Filipino American Art and Performance*. Minneapolis: University of Minnesota Press, 2009.

Sexton, Jared. *Amalgamation Schemes: Antiblackness and the Critique of Multiracialism*. Minneapolis: University of Minnesota Press, 2008. http://ebookcentral.proquest.com. proxy.cc.uic.edu/lib/uic/detail.action?docID=433204.

Sharma, Nitasha Tamar. *Hip Hop Desis: South Asian Americans, Blackness, and a Global Race Consciousness*. Durham, NC: Duke University Press, 2010.

Shott, Brian. "Forty Acres and a Carabao: T. Thomas Fortune, Newspapers, and the Pacific's Unstable Color Lines, 1902–03." *Journal of the Gilded Age and Progressive Era* 17, no. 1 (2018): 98–120. doi:10.1017/S1537781416000372. https://www-cambridge-org.proxy.cc.uic.edu/core/article/forty-acres-and-a-carabao-t-thomas-fortune-newspapers-and-the-pacifics-unstable-color-lines-190203/EF9FEB319DDC9D958F5 1A253BC50EE8A.

Sklar, Deidre. "Five Premises for a Culturally Sensitive Approach to Dance." In *Moving History Dancing Cultures: A Dance History Reader*, edited by Ann Dils and Ann Cooper Albright, 30–32. Middletown, CT: Wesleyan University Press, 2001.

Smith, Linda Tuhiwai. *Decolonizing Methodologies: Research and Indigenous Peoples*. New York: Zed Books Ltd., 1999.

Sommer, Sally R. "'C'Mon to My House': Underground-House Dancing." *Dance Research Journal* 33, no. 2 (2001): 72–86. doi:10.2307/1477805. http://www.jstor.org.proxy. cc.uic.edu/stable/1477805.

Spillers, Hortense J. "Mama's Baby, Papa's Maybe: An American Grammar Book." *Diacritics* 17, no. 2 (1987): 65–81.

Srinivasan, Priya. *Sweating Saris: Indian Dance as Transnational Labor*. Philadelphia: Temple University Press, 2011. http://ebookcentral.proquest.com.proxy.cc.uic.edu/lib/ uic/detail.action?docID=798021.

Stanley Niaah, Sonjah. *DanceHall: From Slave Ship to Ghetto*. Ottawa, Canada: University of Ottawa Press, 2010.

Steele, Angela D. "Zai Beijing: A Cultural Study of Hip Hop." Accessed May 8, 2013. www. rockinchina.com/w/Category:Research.

Steinbock-Pratt, Sarah. *Educating the Empire: American Teachers and Contested Colonization in the Philippines*. Cambridge, UK: Cambridge University Press, 2019.

Stevens, Dana. "If 3-D's Just a Fad, Will We Miss It When It's Gone?" Accessed December 4, 2012. https://slate.com/news-and-politics/2010/08/if-3-d-s-just-a-fad-will-we-miss-it-when-it-s-gone.html.

Suarez, Theresa C. "Militarized Filipino Masculinity and the Language of Citizenship in San Diego." In *Militarized Currents: Toward a Decolonized Future in Asia and the Pacific*, edited by Setsu Shigematsu and Keith L. Camacho, 181–201. Minneapolis: University of Minnesota Press, 2010.

Sudbury, Julia. *Global Lockdown: Race, Gender, and the Prison-Industrial Complex*. New York: Routledge, 2014.

Suzuki, Nobue. "'Japayuki,' Or, Spectacles for the Transnational Middle Class." *Positions: East Asia Cultures Critique* 19, no. 2 (2011): 439–462. https://muse-jhu-edu. proxy.cc.uic.edu/article/453334.

Syed, Nafees A. "The 3 D's of Foreign Affairs | Harvard Political Review." Accessed December 4, 2012. http://harvardpolitics.com/arusa/the-3ds-of-foreign-affairs/.

"Table V (Part 1). Immigrant Visas Issued and Adjustments of Status Subject to Numerical Limitations Fiscal Year 2009." 2009. U.S. Visas. *Department of State*. Bureau of Consular Affairs. <https://travel.state.gov/content/dam/visas/Statistics/ FY09AnnualReport_TableV_1.pdf>

Tadiar, Neferti Xina M. *Fantasy Production: Sexual Economies and Other Philippine Consequences for the New World Order*. Vol. 1. Hong Kong: Hong Kong University Press, 2004.

Tadiar, Neferti Xina M. *Things Fall Away: Philippine Historical Experience and the Makings of Globalization*. Durham, NC: Duke University Press, 2009.

Taylor, Diana. *The Archive and the Repertoire: Performing Cultural Memory in the Americas*. Durham, NC: Duke University Press, 2003.

Technical Education and Skills Development Authority. "Training Regulations." Accessed December 17, 2017. http://www.tesda.gov.ph/download/training_regulations?Search TItle=performing+arts&Searchcat=Training+Regulations.

Thompson, Robert Farris. "Dance and Culture, an Aesthetic of the Cool: West African Dance." *African Forum* 2, no. 2 (1966): 85–102.

Tiongson Jr., Antonio. "Reflections on the Trajectory of Filipina/o American Studies: An Interview with Rick Bonus." In *Positively No Filipinos Allowed: Building Communities and Discourse*, edited by Antonio Tiongson Jr., Edgardo V. Gutierrez, and Ricardo V. Guiterrez, 162–171. Philadelphia: Temple University Press, 2006.

Tiongson Jr., Antonio T. *Filipinos Represent: DJs, Racial Authenticity, and the Hip-Hop Nation*. Minneapolis: University of Minnesota Press, 2013. http://ebookcentral. proquest.com.proxy.cc.uic.edu/lib/uic/detail.action?docID=1362020.

Tiongson Jr., Antonio T. "Introduction." In *Positively No Filipinos Allowed: Building Communities and Discourse*, edited by Antonio Tiongson Jr., Edgardo V. Gutierrez, and Ricardo V. Gutierrez, 1–15. Philadelphia: Temple University Press, 2006.

Tiongson, A. T., Gutierrez, E. V., and R. V. Gutierrez, eds. *Positively No Filipinos Allowed: Building Communities and Discourse*. Philadelphia: Temple University Press, 2006.

Tolentino, Francisca Reyes. *Philippine National Dances*. New York: Silver Burdett Company, 1946.

Tolentino, Roland B. *Sa Loob at Labas Ng Mall Kong Sawi Kaliluha'y Siyang Nangyayaring Hari: Ang Pagkatuto at Pagtatanghal Ng Kulturang Popular*. Diliman: University of the Philippines Press, 2001.

Trimillos, Ricardo. "Introduction." In *Stage Presence: Conversations with Filipino American Performing Artists*, edited by Theodore S. Gonzalves. San Francisco: Meritage Press, 2007.

"Trump Wants End to 'Chain Migration.'" ABS-CBN News. Accessed February 21, 2018. https://news.abs-cbn.com/overseas/01/31/18/trump-wants-end-to-chain-migration.

Tyner, James A. *The Philippines: Mobilities, Identities, Globalization*. New York: Routledge, 2008.

"US Equal Employment Opportunity Commission Home Page." U.S. Equal Employment Opportunity Commission. Accessed December 15, 2011. https://www.eeoc.gov/eeoc/history/35th/thelaw/eo-10925.html.

Vergara, Benito Manalo. *Displaying Filipinos: Photography and Colonialism in Early 20th Century Philippines*. Quezon City: University of the Philippines Press, 1995.

Villa, José Garcia. *Volume Two*. New York: New Directions, 1949.

Villaruz, Basilio Esteban S. *Sayaw: An Essay on the American Colonial and Contemporary Traditions and Philippine Dance*. Manila: Sentrong Pangkultura ng Pilipinas, Cultural Center of the Philippines, 1994.

Villaruz, Basilio Esteban S. "Tapping Thoughts on Black and Brown Dances in the Americas." In *Saysay Himig: A Sourcebook on Philippine Music History, 1880–1941*, edited by Arwin Q. Tan, 339–346. Diliman: University of the Philippines Press, 2018.

Villaruz, Basilio Esteban S. *Treading Through: 45 Years of Philippine Dance*. Quezon City: University of the Philippines Press, 2006.

Villaruz, Basilio Esteban, and Ramon A. Obusan. *Sayaw: An Essay on Philippine Ethnic Dance*. Manila: Sentrong pangkultura ng Pilipinas, 1992.

Villegas, M. R., Kuttin, K., and Labrador, R. N., eds. *Empire of Funk: Hip Hop and Representation in Filipina/o America*, 321. San Diego, CA: Cognella Academic Publishing, 2014.

Viola, Michael. "Hip-Hop and Critical Revolutionary Pedagogy: Blue Scholarship to Challenge 'the Miseducation of the Filipino.'" *Journal for Critical Education Policy Studies* 4, no. 2 (2006): 171–194.

Wang, Oliver. *Legions of Boom: Filipino American Mobile DJ Crews of the San Francisco Bay Area*. Durham, NC: Duke University Press, 2015.

Wang, Oliver S. "Rapping and Repping Asian: Race, Authenticity, and the Asian American MC." In *Alien Encounters: Popular Culture and Asian America*, edited by Mimi Thi Nguyen and Thuy Linh Nguyen, 35–68. Durham, NC: Duke University Press, 2007.

Weheliye, Alexander G. "'Feenin': Posthuman Voices in Contemporary Black Popular Music." *Social Text* 20, no. 2 (2002): 21–47.

Weheliye, Alexander G. "Pornotropes." *Journal of Visual Culture* 7, no. 1 (2008): 65–81.

Williams, Janice. "Issa Rae's Book Calls Filipinos 'the Blacks of Asians.'" *Newsweek*. May 1, 2018. https://www.newsweek.com/issa-rae-book-asian-dating-906886.

Williams, Patricia J. *The Alchemy of Race and Rights*. Cambridge, MA: Harvard University Press, 1991.

Winant, Howard. "Race in Colorblind Spaces." *Workshop on Terrorist Rehabilitation Implementation (WTRI)*. Posted November 25–30, 2009. Accessed January 9, 2011. www.pvtr.org/pdf/Report/RSIS_WTRI_Report.pdf.

"World Hip Hop Dance Championship." Hip Hop International. 2012. Accessed September 1, 2013. hiphopinternational.com/world-hip-hop-dance-championship.

Wong, Yutian. *Choreographing Asian America*. Middletown, CT: Wesleyan University Press, 2010. http://ebookcentral.proquest.com.proxy.cc.uic.edu/lib/uic/detail.action?docID=776777.

Wu, Ellen D. *The Color of Success: Asian Americans and the Origins of the Model Minority*. Princeton, NJ: Princeton University Press, 2013. http://ebookcentral.proquest.com.proxy.cc.uic.edu/lib/uic/detail.action?docID=1458381.

Yang, Mina. "Yellow Skin, White Masks." *Daedalus* 142, no. 4 (2013): 24–37. http://www.jstor.org.proxy.cc.uic.edu/stable/43297995.

Zanfagna, Christina. "The Multiringed Cosmos of Krumping/Hip-Hop Dance at the Intersections of Battle, Media, and Spirit." In *Ballroom, Boogie, Shimmy Sham, Shake: A Social and Popular Dance Reader*, edited by Julie Malnig, 337–353. Urbana: University of Illinois Press, 2009.

Zimbardo, Philip, Craig Haney, and Curtis Banks. "A Study of Prisoners and Guards in a Stimulated Prison." In *Theatre in Prison: Theory and Practice*, edited by Michael Balfour, 19–34. Portland, OR: Intellect Books, 2004.

Zone, Ray. *3-D Revolution: The History of Modern Stereoscopic Cinema*. Lexington: University Press of Kentucky, 2012.

Zone, Ray. *Stereoscopic Cinema and the Origins of 3-D Film, 1838–1952*. Lexington: University Press of Kentucky, 2007.

Index

Tables and figures are indicated by *t* and *f* following the page number

For the benefit of digital users, indexed terms that span two pages (e.g., 52–53) may, on occasion, appear on only one of those pages.